Hard Cases

True Stories of Irish Crime

Hard Cases

True Stories of Irish Crime

GENE KERRIGAN

Gill & Macmillan

Published in Ireland by
Gill & Macmillan Ltd
Hume Avenue, Park West, Dublin 12
with associated companies throughout the world

© Gene Kerrigan 1996, 2005
ISBN-13: 978 07171 3862 3
ISBN-10: 0 7171 3862 3
First published 1996
Print origination by Graham Thew Design
Printed in Malaysia

The paper used in this book comes from the wood pulp of managed forests. For every tree felled, at least one tree is planted, thereby renewing natural resources.

A CIP catalogue record for this book is available from the British Library.

3 5 7 6 4

For Julie Lordan

Contents

Preface

Most of these stories are concerned with cases that came before the courts, from the Coroner's Court to the Supreme Court. Some of the cases involved the civil courts, most of them are criminal. In some, there were arrests but no court appearances. If there is a theme, it is the arbitrary nature of justice.

When I came across these cases one by one I found each individually interesting in itself. I believe that together they show us, from unusual angles, something of how modern Ireland is constructed. We are reasonably well geared-up to deal with shop-lifting, but the law is endlessly tolerant of what we might term questionable behaviour in the business world. We lay claim to democracy, but it can be suspended by a signature. We place the family at the centre of our constitution, but for some there is no more dangerous place than the home. We have our habitual criminals, but our system of justice can be as mindlessly oppressive as any thug.

In covering some of these cases I worked for *Magill* magazine. I covered others for the *Sunday Independent* and the *Sunday Tribune*. The book format allows greater length and depth and most of the stories included here are distant relations to the stories as originally written. To all my editors down through the years, for their generous indulgence and only occasional impatience, thank you.

Thanks to Derek Speirs, as always, for the photographs. And to Willie Kealy and the *Sunday Independent* for the use of their pictures. Thanks to Vincent Browne, who introduced me to Karl Crawley and Finbar Lynagh and who gave me his notes of interviews with associates of Michael and Jim Lynagh. Thanks to the staff of Dublin Corporation's invaluable newspaper library in Pearse Street. Thanks also to Riona McNamara, to Jacob Ecclestone of the National Union of Journalists, to solicitor Ruth Gladwin and to Michael O'Doherty.

Gene Kerrigan

❶ Dessie O'Hare's Last Stand

When the case came to court it was not the criminal who attracted the attention but the victim. The criminal was a small-time knocker-off named James Conlon, aged forty-one, who had thirty-four previous convictions, none of them for stealing the crown jewels. He was caught preparing to cart off a flat-ful of furniture in September 1993. He got into what he claimed to believe was a derelict flat and locked the door behind him and went to work. He was sorting out what he was going to steal, with a van parked outside to take the stuff, when someone tried the locked door and couldn't get it to open. Whoever was trying to get in wasn't going away. There was a knock on the door. Conlon had a story ready when he answered the knock. He didn't live here, he would say. No, it wasn't that he lived here, because the flat was derelict now, what he was doing here, you see, was he was collecting his grandmother's furniture from the flat. Which is why he was here, sorting through the furniture. OK?

It might have worked, had the guy who knocked on the door not been the one who owned the flat. And it wasn't Conlon's granny who lived here, it was this guy's aunt. Conlon was rumbled, the cops were called, and he was on his way to his thirty-fifth conviction. By the time the matter came to court, in June 1994, Conlon had already been sentenced to twelve months for his thirty-fourth conviction.

When the name of the owner of the flat was revealed some expressed surprise that he was in any position to set the cops on anyone else. The owner of the flat was Gerry Wright. And if it was the Gerry Wright who got involved with Dessie O'Hare, wasn't he supposed to be in jail? Didn't he get, what was it, seven or eight years, at least? Did he have a hand in shooting the cop, or wasn't he just there when the cop was shot? How far back was that? It was perhaps 1986 or 1987, and if Wright got seven or eight years he'd maybe be about due for release by now, so it was probably the same guy. The address of Wright's flat was 41 Parkgate Street, and that clinched it. It was Conlon's lawyer, Luigi Rea, who first openly mentioned the significance of the flat. Some might have found it amusing, Gerry Wright ending up on the right side of the law, after his little adventure.

· · · · ·

In the beginning was the IRA. In 1969 the pressure of events, as the North fell apart, tore the organisation in two. The Officials claimed to be developing a left-wing strain of republican politics. The Provisionals held to the traditional republican line. There was more to it than that, of course. There were divisions between activists North and South, and about the role of parliamentary politics and the gun. Official Sinn Féin was heading down a road which would see its name change from Sinn Féin to Sinn Féin the Workers' Party, and then simply the Workers' Party, before it in turn split in two. A significant portion of the Workers' Party departed in the early 1990s and set up Democratic Left.

For most of this time, through the 1970s and 1980s, the Officials, under whatever name, were linked to a secret army, the Official IRA. The Official IRA supposedly went out of business in 1972, but it continued to exist, as a strong-arm backup for fundraising and protection from other armed groups.

In September 1973 the Official IRA carried out an armed robbery at Heuston railway station in Dublin. They got £17,000. The police rounded up the usual suspects and grilled them. One suspect outside the usual network was Billy Wright, a hairdresser with a shop on the

Cabra Road. Wright had done a make-up job to disguise the robbers. Under interrogation he cracked and made a statement.

Wright knew that in cooperating with the police he was going to upset people. 'I'm a dead man,' he told friends.

One of those involved in the robbery, who now had to flee abroad to escape the police, was bitterly angry at Wright's failure to keep his mouth shut. He promised himself revenge against Billy Wright.

In 1974, a section of the Officials became restless. Led by Seamus Costello, a veteran of the IRA campaign of the 1950s, the faction espoused a left-wing theory of sorts that was supposedly more radical than the Officials' mixture of Stalinism and what would become social democracy. It was also unhappy that the Officials had called a ceasefire in the armed fight against the British and the Northern state. The Official leadership skilfully and ruthlessly out-manoeuvred Costello, isolating him and his faction. The inevitable split followed, and in December 1974 Costello's Irish Republican Socialist Party was born. It held a founding conference at the Spa Hotel, in Lucan, and at the end of the morning session Costello spoke words laden with nods and winks: 'For those who are interested, there's an afternoon meeting. Other avenues will be explored.'

The 'other avenues' consisted, of course, of setting up an armed wing of the IRSP. It initially used the front name of the People's Liberation Army, then the National Liberation Army, and it was some months before it was admitted that the Irish National Liberation Army (INLA) existed. The IRSP would stumble through several years of activity on the periphery of radical politics before expiring in the mid-1980s due to lack of interest. The armed wing, however, the INLA, would spawn a horrific succession of atrocities over the following two decades.

From the start, the INLA dominated its political wing. Some political policies were adopted, some were in a sense bought in, taken wholesale from non-violent socialist groups and given an own-brand IRSP label so that they could be brandished when needed. But there was little commitment to, or even understanding of, such policies.

Almost immediately, the INLA and the Official IRA began a feud. There were beatings and knee cappings and, inevitably, killings. Old comrades shot each other dead. Up-and-coming gunmen, teenagers, made their names by killing veterans. One man who wasn't involved in the feud was the Official IRA gunman who had to flee the country after Billy Wright cracked under police questioning about the Heuston railway station robbery. He had bided his time. Now, in October 1975, two years after the robbery, he returned to Dublin. He went to Billy Wright's barber shop on the Cabra Road and shot the barber dead. The gunman then fled abroad again, satisfied that he'd got the bee out of his bonnet.

The hairdresser's brother, Gerry Wright, who would one day knock on the door of his aunt's flat and find a small-time thief inside, nicking her furniture, wasn't a gunman. He was a barber with an interest in boxing, who ran a boxing club over his barber's shop. People with Official IRA connections (at least one of whom later became a fervent John Bruton supporter) had some years earlier used the boxing club as a meeting place from time to time, but Wright was not known as an activist. In his heart of hearts, though, he knew that if he ever got a chance to get back at the man who killed his brother, whose name was well known to the police and in republican circles, he would take it.

· · · · ·

Seamus Costello set up the INLA but he never fully controlled it. The feud between the INLA and the Official IRA immediately put the organisation on a war footing and local leaders with smoking guns began flexing their muscles. Within months Costello's leadership was being challenged. Northern gunmen criticised his failure to provide enough weapons. Money was in short supply. Fundraising robberies were cocked up. Over three dozen members of the INLA ended up behind bars and the organisation was supposed to financially support their dependants.

In October 1977 an Official IRA gunman shot Costello dead in Dublin, a consequence of the killing of a leading Official IRA leader, Billy McMillan, in the feud. (Almost five years later the man believed to have killed Costello was himself shot dead just around the corner from where Costello died.) After Costello's death the INLA drifted. It achieved a moment of glory among its peers in March 1979, when it managed to penetrate security at the House of Commons and explode a bomb under a car being driven by Airey Neave MP, a close political and personal friend of Margaret Thatcher. On the whole, the INLA was losing ground. The Provisionals had credibility as an efficient guerrilla army with a strong political base in the North. The Officials, as the Workers' Party, were achieving some electoral success in the South. The IRSP was the feeble political wing of an INLA with little sense of direction.

After a while, any hard man with a gun could join the INLA and many did. Some had genuine if naive political motives; others had a raw nationalist instinct that if enough of the right people were shot there would be a revolutionary breakthrough. Criminals joined up, pulling off robberies that sometimes benefited the INLA, sometimes benefited themselves, sometimes a bit of both. Inevitably, informers were recruited by the RUC and the organisation was thrown into chaos. Factions emerged, each more paranoid than the last. Quarrels were settled with guns. Some killed for Ireland, some killed for power within the INLA, some killed for fear that if they didn't strike first they would be struck down by their erstwhile comrades. The mid-1980s feud took a dozen lives.

One gunman or another became briefly prominent within the group — Dominic McGlinchey, Gerard Steenson, John O'Reilly — before being jailed or shot dead. From the mid-1980s the factions became somewhat complicated, with various tendencies within the INLA aligning themselves with either the INLA GHQ group or the IPLO/Army Council group (the IPLO was the Irish People's Liberation Organisation). Some of the killings had nothing to do with the feuds; they resulted from old scores being settled. Dominic McGlinchey's wife, Mary, had at one point set up the murder of two men from south Armagh. Three years later, in 1986, their friends broke into her house as she was bathing her children and shot her dead.

The public knew little of the details of all this feuding and man-oeuvring, beyond the occasional news that another body had turned up. From time to time the likes of Dominic McGlinchey, nicknamed 'Mad Dog', would make a media impact, but only in a cartoon fashion, as a bogyman. The dogfight which the INLA had become remained an obscure matter. The main impact the INLA had on the public was to make republicanism seem a savage, fear-laden, brutish sect that was better avoided.

Few paid any attention when an INLA gunman named Dessie O'Hare emerged from Portlaoise prison in October 1986, having served seven years for possession of a rifle. O'Hare, then aged twenty-seven, was from farming country near Keady, in south Armagh. He joined the Provos in the mid-1970s, when he was a teenager. The RUC claimed to want to interview him in connection with twenty-seven killings. Such allegations should not be taken at face value, but O'Hare was undoubtedly a hardened and ruthless gunman who had killed a number of people while still in his teens. By the time he was caught in the South in possession of an Armalite, in 1979, he was already drifting away from the Provisionals, regarding them as too tame. In Portlaoise prison he joined up with the INLA. In 1980 he was married in the prison, to a woman named Clare Doyle, also from Keady. Their daughter, Julieanne, was born some months later.

He lived through some hairy events in which others were not so lucky. He and two other gunmen hijacked a car near Keady RUC station in 1979 and in a shoot-out one of his companions, twenty-three-year-old Peadar McIlvenna, was shot dead. Later that year Dessie O'Hare and his companion Anthony McClelland were in a car chased by gardaí in Monaghan. There was an Armalite rifle in the car. McClelland was killed when the car crashed into another car, seriously injuring the two occupants. O'Hare was charged with possession of the rifle and went to Portlaoise prison for the first half of the 1980s. McClelland was the second companion to die while travelling in a car with Dessie O'Hare. There would be a third. O'Hare was not the man to choose if you wanted a lucky travelling partner.

After his release from prison in November 1986 he went at first to live with his wife and daughter in Castleblayney. In December 1986 he was arrested for questioning by gardaí in Dundalk. The gardaí who questioned him were impressed with his intelligence and fluency. He talked freely about 1916 and Irish history in general but he wouldn't cooperate when asked questions relevant to INLA activities. He assured the gardaí that he had renounced violence. Shortly afterwards he moved away from home and sided with the INLA GHQ faction in the feud, but within a short time he had broken from them and formed a minuscule group which he (and hardly anyone else) called the Irish Revolutionary Brigade. Choosing a title for your group is important. It must resonate with echoes of the glorious past. The IRB shared initials with the Irish Republican Brotherhood, which was behind the 1916 Rising. The Irish Revolutionary Brigade became active around the border and Dessie O'Hare would eventually be awarded the media tag 'the Border Fox'. He would be at liberty for just thirteen months after his release from Portlaoise. Within that time, the obscure operator from a fraction of a faction would sum up in the public mind the strange and brutal thing that the INLA had become.

· · · · ·

They smashed the door open with a sledgehammer and came in flashing guns. Dessie O'Hare, Eddie Hogan, Fergal Toal and Tony McNeill. The Irish Revolutionary Brigade was in full cry, on a fund-raising raid.

It was Tuesday, 13 October 1987. Dessie O'Hare had been released from Portlaoise prison a year ago. That year had not been kind to O'Hare, and it had been even less kind to some others. In January 1987 two INLA leaders, John O'Reilly and Ta Power, had been shot dead at the Rossnaree Hotel outside Drogheda. The IPLO/Army Council faction was believed to have organised the killings.

Inevitably, retaliation was arranged, and the INLA GHQ faction used Dessie O'Hare's little gang to obtain revenge. Tony McCluskey, an IPLO activist who was believed to have helped set up the O'Reilly/Power killings, was the chosen target. A couple of weeks after the killing of O'Reilly and Power two men and a woman took McCluskey from his home in County Monaghan. At some unknown place, McCluskey's hands and feet were bound and he was badly beaten. A bolt-cutter was used to cut off the lobe of one ear and the tip of his right index finger. He was shot five times. His body was left on the south Armagh border.

Later, O'Hare would refer to this killing and say that he wanted McCluskey to have 'a hard death — I didn't want him to die lightly.'

The O'Hare gang remained active for some months. The RUC believed it was they who shot at an Ulster Defence Regiment member at his home, missed and killed his seventy-two-year-old mother. As the feud ended the INLA had no use for O'Hare and around September 1987 he was expelled. He claimed that he wasn't expelled, he walked out. It was around then that the Irish Revolutionary Brigade was formed. A handwritten statement was issued to the press, declaring the IRB to be 'a body of dedicated socialist revolutionaries committed to a path of armed revolutionary struggle'. The statement concluded: 'By our actions in future months we will be judged,' a true enough remark. The statement was headed 'Border Fox: The Truth', and was signed 'Little Bird'.

Nationalists such as O'Hare are steeped in the iconography and trivia of the glorious past. About ten years before he led his troops into the GPO for the 1916 Rising, Patrick Pearse had written a short poem titled 'O Little Bird'.

> O little bird!
> Cold to me thy lying on the flag:
> Bird, that never had an evil thought,
> Pitiful the coming of death to thee!

· · · · ·

O'Hare decided that he needed to put his organisation on a firm financial footing. There had been robberies, but very much small-time efforts. On 11 September, for instance, the branch of the Ulster Bank in Castlepollard was robbed of £3,000 and the gang fired shots at the police, narrowly missing a young garda. Similar jobs won the O'Hare gang similar amounts. They were taking huge risks for peanuts. O'Hare decided on one big score. He would organise a kidnap and demand a massive ransom.

O'Hare's 'organisation' was somewhat threadbare. Some who had worked with him on robberies and shootings over the past year were less than enthused by him and made themselves scarce. Some were dead. O'Hare's choice of operatives for his big kidnap adventure was limited. In June 1987 Fergal Toal, aged twenty-five, from Callanbridge Park, Armagh, was released from Portlaoise prison. Then, in

September 1987 Eddie Hogan was released from Portlaoise. Hogan, aged thirty-three, was from Kerryhall Road, Fairhill, in Cork, and had a petty criminal record as a teenager. He became involved with the INLA and in 1981 received an eight-year sentence for armed robbery. O'Hare, Hogan and Toal had served time together and shared an allegiance to the wilder shores of INLA philosophies.

Then there was twenty-five-year-old Tony McNeill from Fitzroy Avenue, Belfast, who had lived in Dublin for the past seven years. He had started off throwing stones at the British army in the 1970s, then joined the Fianna, the republican youth organisation. After allegations of threats from the RUC his mother put him on a train for Dublin, and he had been there ever since. The hunger strikes got him active in republican politics and in 1983 he joined the IRSP. He was politically active, but was not regarded as a 'soldier'. From there, after the ebb and flow of the feuds, he found himself alongside Dessie O'Hare on the periphery of armed republicanism. He had no criminal record. He lived in a flat at Montpelier Hill, with his girlfriend and three-year-old son.

To be active in such circles required courage to the point of recklessness, self-confidence to the point of ruthlessness. You set goals. Some vague (a socialist republic), some immediate (money to fund your organisation), and you went for them, knowing your life might be snuffed out in the process, ready to brush aside anyone who got in your way. The long-term work of building public support for political positions was acknowledged but not undertaken. The republican tradition of solving problems with a gun dominated everything, until it was hard for many to see that anything existed behind the gun other than a ruthless will to impose a half-thought-out political philosophy.

O'Hare considered kidnapping a Dublin businessman who had made millions in the construction equipment business in Britain. Then his sights fell on Dr Austin Darragh. That was someone worth taking, and it would be easy to put an ideological gloss on things. Austin Darragh owned a medical business called the Institute of Clinical Pharmacology. It tested drugs for dozens of drug companies, hiring volunteers to take drugs that had never before been tested on humans. The volunteers were paid £20 a day. About 1,000 volunteers a year took the work, mostly students and unemployed. The extremely successful business attracted little notice until May of 1984, when a student who took part in drug testing died. The ICP, situated in the grounds of St James's Hospital in Dublin, was one of the most successful of such companies in the world and Dr Austin Darragh was in the millionaire range. In 1985 he floated the company on the New York stock exchange and raised $8.5m for 20 per cent of ICP. He would be rich enough for his family to be able to raise a big ransom, and from Dessie O'Hare's point of view there was the added advantage that Darragh could be denounced as a lackey of international capitalism, making huge fortunes for big drug companies by testing drugs on the needy.

Where would they keep Darragh once they had him? They had the use of a garage on Dublin's northside to change cars and rest up after the kidnap, but it wasn't suitable for a longer period of imprisonment of their victim. A safe place was needed and the options were limited. The O'Hare gang wasn't too familiar with Dublin. Tony McNeill had become friendly with another drifter on the edges of republicanism, a barber with a shop in Parkgate Street. Gerry Wright had a basement under the shop, and he had a house in Cabra. He might be worth talking to.

Gerry Wright would later claim that he became drawn into the plot because the gang promised they would kill the man who twelve years earlier killed Billy Wright, Gerry's brother.

Now, the gang had come together, they had Darragh's address in Cabinteely, they had a place to hide their victim, they just had to set the date. They decided on 13 October as the big day.

Two days before that, gang member Fergal Toal went to a disco in the Imperial Hotel, Dundalk. In the bar he met a woman named Belinda Mulligan. Six weeks earlier she had broken up with a man named Sean Hughes, with whom she had been living for two years. Hughes, aged twenty-one, was at the disco, drunk and jealous. He asked Mulligan to dance and she refused. She danced with Toal. Hughes became belligerent and the two men left the disco and went out into the car park. A fight followed. Sean Hughes was stabbed with a knife, the blade plunging five inches into his chest, through his ribs and into his heart. He slid down a car and lay in a pool of blood, dead.

Toal went to Dublin where he stayed the following night in a spare room at the home of Tony McNeill. McNeill himself had been away from home for a week. He returned on the afternoon of Tuesday 13 October, the day after Toal stayed over at his flat, the day planned for the kidnap. He didn't tell his girlfriend where he had been; he didn't seem surprised to see Fergal Toal staying there. McNeill had brought two goldfish for his son, three-year-old Piaras. At around 6pm that evening, having eaten, McNeill and Toal left the flat. They drove away in McNeill's car. Before they left, McNeill borrowed a fiver from his girlfriend, for petrol. McNeill and Toal were on their way to meet Dessie O'Hare and Eddie Hogan, and three hours later they would go into action. The Irish Revolutionary Brigade, its plans unaffected by the fact that two days earlier Fergal Toal had killed Sean Hughes in the car park of the Imperial Hotel in Dundalk, was ready to launch its major kidnap operation.

· · · · ·

The O'Hare gang had some good luck and some bad luck when they smashed in the door. The large, six-bedroom, Tudor-style house on two acres of high-price real estate at Brennanstown Road, Cabinteely, appeared secure. It was behind a high teak gate that was electronically controlled, and had all the latest security devices. Fortunately for the gang, the alarm system had malfunctioned several times recently and tonight it was switched off. Otherwise, the kidnap might have ended shortly thereafter. The gang couldn't have known that the alarm was switched off and they didn't seem to have taken it into account.

The bad luck was that the millionaire doctor, Austin Darragh, hadn't lived here for four years. He lived in Anglesea Road, Ballsbridge. Although he still owned the house at Cabinteely, and his name was on a brass plate at the gate, it was occupied by his daughter and son-in-law, Marise and John O'Grady, and their three children. John O'Grady was a dentist, with a practice in Ballsbridge. He was thirty-eight, well off but not in the millionaire category. The children were Darragh, thirteen, Anthony, twelve, and Louise, six.

That evening, John O'Grady left his surgery at Wellington Road and arrived home early, at around 5.45pm. After dinner he phoned his mother, Kitty O'Grady, learned she wasn't feeling well and drove the couple of miles to her home in Blackrock. He arranged for a doctor to come see Kitty the following day. He arrived home some time before 9pm. His daughter Louise was already asleep and the two boys were preparing for bed. O'Grady and his wife went to bed shortly afterwards and they were in bed watching television at 9.30pm when they heard the thuds of the sledgehammer smashing open their front door.

The gang came in at high speed, armed and masked. There was another door, mostly glass, about four feet beyond the front door. They smashed through that too.

John O'Grady jumped out of bed and confronted them on the stairs. 'Don't panic, I'm not going to do anything,' shouted O'Grady when he saw the guns.

Dessie O'Hare said he wanted to know if there was anyone else in the house. He was loud and aggressive and threatening to blow John O'Grady away. O'Grady and his wife were forced back upstairs. Anthony came out of a bathroom and he too was held at gunpoint.

In his room, thirteen-year-old Darragh O'Grady tried to ring for help. He was down on the floor with the phone to his ear when Dessie O'Hare burst in and caught him. 'You little bastard!' screamed O'Hare.

The family was herded into Louise's bedroom and the door was closed. There was a phone in the room. As soon as the gang closed the bedroom door Marise O'Grady picked up the phone and dialled 999. She got through to the emergency exchange and was asked what service she required, and it was then that the gang remembered the phones and one of them came bursting in and grabbed the phone, ripping the extension off the wall. Dessie O'Hare ranted at Marise, calling her a bitch and a cunt.

John O'Grady was taken downstairs. His hands were handcuffed in front of him and he had to walk over broken glass in his bare feet as he was led towards the front doorway. He had to show the gang his home's security arrangements, the alarm, the switch that operated the front gate, the safe. O'Grady was taken into the kitchen. He asked for and was given tracksuit leggings and a towel for his feet.

The gang was confused, finding John O'Grady in the house, not Austin Darragh. They didn't seem to know what their intended victim looked like. Dessie O'Hare marched John O'Grady upstairs and into the bedroom and told Marise to identify him. She told him John was her husband.

'There's a fuck-up,' said Dessie O'Hare, 'we've got the wrong man.' O'Hare brought John O'Grady into the kitchen and sat him down. He walked up and down, went in and out of the kitchen, asking O'Grady about his relationship with Austin Darragh. O'Grady said he didn't know if his father-in-law was in the country or not, he hadn't seen him in a month.

Upstairs, Marise O'Grady and her children were being guarded by Fergal Toal. She tried to start a conversation. He put a finger to his lips and shook his head.

The gang sat around drinking tea and eating biscuits and discussing what they should do. They kept their balaclavas on all the time, so they couldn't later be identified. They tried to work out some way of getting to Austin Darragh.

At one stage Dessie O'Hare held a gun to O'Grady's head and told him to come up with some plan for getting Darragh to come to the house. 'Think about it,' O'Hare said, 'because your life depends on it.'

What if O'Grady rang Austin Darragh, one of the gang suggested, and told him Marise had fallen down the stairs? No, O'Grady said, he'd be suspicious, he'd never buy that. Another suggested that they take Marise.

'No,' said Dessie O'Hare, 'I'm not taking the woman.'

O'Hare told one of the gang to keep a watch on O'Grady. 'If he moves, blow him away.'

O'Hare went upstairs and took Marise O'Grady out of the bedroom and downstairs to an alcove. How would they get her father to come to the house, he wanted to know. Would Darragh come if he was told that one of the children was sick? No, Marise said, he didn't treat any of the children, or any of the family. Anyway, she didn't know if her father was in the country just then.

Where was her mother, O'Hare wanted to know. Marise O'Grady said her mother was at a fashion show. For some reason this infuriated O'Hare. He kicked Marise O'Grady on the backside, thumped her on the back and shoved her up the stairs, shouting that she was a lying cunt. He pushed her back into the bedroom with her children.

It was now around 11pm. The house, with its six bedrooms and two bathrooms upstairs, its one bathroom and one toilet downstairs, its corridors and two landings, its dining room, kitchen, breakfast room, living room, study, pantry, laundry room, boiler room, dogs' room, boot room and playroom, was a mansion far removed from anything in which any of the gang had ever lived. They indulged in a little plunder. They wore gloves all the time, so as not to leave fingerprints. They found a pearl necklace worth £1,000 and some bits and pieces of jewellery worth a total of £270. Dessie O'Hare stole a gold Cross pen. Fergal Toal tried on John O'Grady's cashmere overcoat and found it a good fit and decided to keep it. And they stole a Walkman radio belonging to one of the children, Anthony. The gang took everything from the safe, passports, baptismal certificates, pension policies, a TV licence, an innoculation certificate.

Dessie O'Hare came across John O'Grady's £450 Longines gold watch and took a shine to it. He stole it. Later, for some reason, he would replace the watch strap.

At around 12.30am, having been in the house for three hours, the gang told Marise O'Grady that they were going to take her husband and one of her children. The O'Gradys could decide which child. John and Marise lay side by side in their bedroom, trying to decide which of their children should be taken hostage.

An hour later John O'Grady was taken downstairs and a member of the gang produced a video camera. O'Grady had to stand in front of the camera and announce that he was being held for £300,000 ransom and that the police were not to be contacted. A member of the gang stood each side of him, masked and brandishing guns. As the camera recorded the scene, the two gunmen ejected shells from their weapons, to show the guns were real. They wanted to view their movie production and asked O'Grady where the video recorder was. He said he didn't have one. They couldn't believe it. John O'Grady said he didn't have a video because he didn't want his children watching video nasties.

John was brought back up to the bedroom and Marise was taken downstairs. John lay down on the floor beside his thirteen-year-old son Darragh and told him he loved him, not to worry, to be brave. After a while the two dozed off.

Downstairs, Marise was being told that she must tell her father that the gang wanted a £300,000 ransom. It should be withdrawn from a range of banks, and not more than £10,000 should be withdrawn from any one bank. Austin Darragh was to do this himself, the police were not to be informed, Marise should contact no one except her father. Dessie O'Hare said they needed the money for their army. They were up against big numbers, he said, but they were holding their own.

Marise asked them not to take any of her children. O'Hare agreed he wouldn't. He gave her code names, for use in the negotiations, John McCall, Pat McCormack and Sean Lennon. He said he and his men had messed up some kidnappings lately and their credibility was being doubted. They weren't going to mess up this one.

Marise was taken back upstairs. It was now about 2am. All five members of the family were held in the parents' bedroom. The three children slept on the bed, Marise and John slept on the floor. One gunman stayed in the bedroom, another outside the door.

• • • • •

The night passed. At around 8am the gunman in the bedroom switched on the television and began flicking from BBC to HTV, watching the breakfast news. The family was awake. There were things to be done. Marise was told to get some warm clothing for John. She had to phone his receptionist and tell her that John wasn't well, his appointments should be cancelled. She had to phone and cancel a school run, saying her children weren't well.

The gang began preparations for leaving. Marise and the children were herded into Louise's bedroom. The phone rang. Dessie O'Hare came into Louise's bedroom and told Marise to come answer the phone. He wasn't wearing his mask. Marise went into Anthony's bedroom and answered the phone. Dessie O'Hare, still apparently unaware that he was unmasked, came with her and stood nearby, supervising Marise's responses to the call.

The call was from a friend, Elizabeth Senier. She wanted to know if Marise and her family could come to lunch the following Sunday. Marise said they would be delighted. Dessie O'Hare suddenly realised he wasn't wearing his mask. He put his hand over his face. Marise talked briefly with her friend, then hung up. O'Hare said that she wasn't to look at him, and if she ever told the police she saw him without his mask and if he was arrested, his men would come and get her.

At around 9.30am John O'Grady was blindfolded. His handcuffed hands were placed on Dessie O'Hare's shoulders and O'Hare led O'Grady out of the house and to a car in the yard. The boot was opened and O'Grady was told to get in. A plastic box containing a pear, a banana and an orange was placed in the boot beside him. A litre carton of orange juice was also left in the boot. A duffle-coat was put over O'Grady, to keep him warm, and the boot was closed. O'Grady lay there for the best part of half an hour. He used the carton of orange juice as a pillow.

Dessie O'Hare was inside the house, telling Marise O'Grady that he would leave two of his men behind to ensure he made a clean getaway. There would be a phone call later in the day to say the coast was clear. This time he was wearing his mask. Marise and her children were all to stay in Louise's bedroom.

It was shortly before 10am when John O'Grady heard two gunmen get into the car. Dessie O'Hare was driving. Fergal Toal was in the front passenger seat. They set off. After a few minutes O'Hare stopped the car. He wasn't sure which way to go. He called back to John O'Grady. There was a T-junction and a signpost for Dun Laoghaire. He was heading for Dublin city. Which way should he go?

O'Grady had been keeping track in his head of the car's twists and turns. 'Is there a white house directly in front of us?' he asked.

'Yes,' said O'Hare. O'Grady told O'Hare to turn right and he'd find the Bray dual carriageway. They drove on for about ten minutes, through Stillorgan and down Booterstown Avenue, and again O'Hare had to ask O'Grady for directions. He wanted to go to the northside of Dublin, but the Border Fox was having a spot of trouble with his sense of direction.

'There's a pub called the Punch Bowl at the bottom of Booterstown Avenue,' said O'Grady.

O'Hare said he saw it.

'Turn left,' O'Grady called back, 'and follow the directions to the toll bridge.'

The car drove across the toll bridge and into the northside, to the private garage where a swop of cars would be made. O'Grady heard a roller door opening and the car was driven inside the garage and the engine was switched off. O'Grady lay there, waiting for something to happen. He ate the pear from the plastic box. More time went by. After a while he could hear that someone in the front of the car was snoring.

• • • • •

Hilary Prentice was a solicitor. She had known John O'Grady all her life and he had been her dentist for the past ten years. He was currently in the process of inserting a crown for her upper left pre-molar. She had attended his surgery the previous day, Tuesday 13 October, and her next appointment was for the following day, Thursday 15 October.

This morning, she got a phone call from John O'Grady's receptionist, Linda. The receptionist, acting on the telephoned instructions from Marise O'Grady, was ringing around the patients scheduled to see John O'Grady over the next couple of days. John had a cold and the Thursday appointment would have to be cancelled, the receptionist said. How about rescheduling for the following Tuesday, would that be convenient? That would be fine, said Hilary Prentice.

• • • • •

Back at the O'Grady house Marise was allowed leave her daughter's bedroom to make breakfast. She was allowed out to feed the family's two labrador dogs, who were kept in an enclosed yard. Some time after noon the phone rang and stopped after a few rings, then rang again a few seconds later. One of the gunmen picked up the phone.

At 1.40pm Marise was told the two gunmen were leaving now. In ten minutes she was to come down and close the front gate. They were taking her husband's Volvo and there would be a phone call later to tell her where it could be found. She wasn't to contact anyone until she got a phone call saying they were clear. At 1.50pm Marise closed the front gate. She waited, and at 4.55pm Dessie O'Hare rang. He called himself John. The car was parked at the Fairways Hotel in Dundalk, he said, and the keys were under the mat. Everything was going well so far. It was up to her now.

Marise O'Grady now rang her father, Austin Darragh, at Patrick Dunn's Hospital, and told him what happened. He drove to Garda Headquarters at Harcourt Square and reported the kidnap.

• • • • •

John O'Grady lay in the boot of the car, eating a pear. After a while he dozed off. Eventually he was allowed out, when he said he needed to go to the toilet. He was given a milk bottle, which he filled twice. He was put back in the boot. The garage doors rolled up and another car drove in. O'Grady was transferred to the second car, his blindfold was replaced by blacked-out glasses, which were strapped to his head. He could hear a Dublin Corporation bin lorry crawling past on the street outside, the binmen dumping the rubbish into the lorry, oblivious to what was going on a few feet away.

The kidnappers prepared to move on. Dessie O'Hare was behind the wheel, there was someone in the front passenger seat and now a third kidnapper got in beside O'Grady. The dentist was given an unlit cigarette, to make him look more relaxed.

The car was driven for about twenty minutes. O'Grady could feel the heat of the sun. It seemed to be a warm day, he remarked.

'Yes,' said Dessie O'Hare, 'it's a lovely day out.'

O'Grady was driven to 41 Parkgate Street, Gerry Wright's barber shop. One of the gang opened the car door and linked arms with O'Grady and brought him into the building.

Wright was waiting. He held O'Grady's arm. 'You're all right,' he said, 'don't worry.'

O'Grady could feel this new kidnapper's hand shaking.

O'Grady was taken down into the basement, a dusty and dilapidated room where he would spend the next four days. His handcuffs were taken off while he ate a meal of roast beef, turnips and peas, with mashed potatoes and gravy. He was asked if he would like something to drink with his evening meal. He said he'd like some Muscadet wine and some Ballygowan. That evening they brought wine and Ballygowan with a dinner of hamburger and chips from a takeaway. He was given a bucket to urinate in. At other times he would be taken upstairs to a toilet.

O'Grady was asked what kind of books he liked. Adventure thrillers, he said.

Meanwhile, Gerry Wright was dispatched to drive Tony McNeill's car, which the gang had used to get to the O'Grady house, back to McNeill's flat at Montpelier Hill. Wright brought a present for McNeill's son. He left it and the keys of the car with McNeill's girlfriend. She asked if he knew where Tony was. Wright said he didn't.

O'Hare was in no hurry to make a ransom demand. Perhaps he wanted to soften up the O'Grady family and the authorities by making them sweat for a while. That night O'Grady slept in a sleeping bag on a couch, one hand handcuffed to a chair. Fergal Toal and Tony McNeill stood guard.

Next morning O'Grady got two boiled eggs, tea and toast for breakfast. One of the gang gave him a copy of *The Power of the Sword*, by Wilbur Smith. It was one of a number of books the gang had acquired for O'Grady.

At around this time, back in the O'Grady home in Brennanstown Road, Detective Sergeant James Butler was arriving with a collection of photographs. The police knew who was out and about with guns, who had the nerve to pull a job like this. Detective Butler opened an album of twelve photographs of men, all about the same age, and asked Marise O'Grady to look through it. Without hesitation she pointed at one of the pictures, second row, second from the left. That was the leader, the one she had seen without his mask. Detective Butler knew the face. Dessie O'Hare.

Having identified the gang leader, the police began putting things together. Nine days before the kidnap a man named James McDaid had been taken from his Rathgar home and shot dead, his body dumped near the border. McDaid knew O'Hare, and had also done time in Limerick prison with a couple of unsuccessful kidnappers. The police suspected that the idea for the kidnap was McDaid's, and that the O'Hare gang had killed McDaid for some obscure reason, possibly because he was a petty criminal who sometimes used the INLA name. Among Dessie O'Hare's followers, the word was put out that McDaid had been guilty of 'extortion' of some kind.

News of the O'Grady kidnap leaked to the media on the Wednesday. The police asked for and were granted a news blackout. It was standard practice. The police had found that by keeping news of a kidnapping out of the media, the kidnappers could become unnerved and confused about what the authorities knew. Now, at around 3pm on the Thursday, two days into the kidnap, the police suddenly lifted the news blackout for reasons no one could discern. It was a local decision, made at Dun Laoghaire garda station, and not by senior headquarters police.

That afternoon, Hilary Prentice heard the news and realised that the reason her dental appointment with her friend and dentist John O'Grady had been cancelled had to do with something a lot more serious than a cold.

Among the stuff stolen by the gang at the O'Grady house was a Walkman radio belonging to twelve-year-old Anthony. The gang gave it to John O'Grady, to help him pass the time. He listened to a pirate station, Energy 103, and switched to RTE One for the news. He heard the news reports of the kidnapping.

That evening, Dessie O'Hare and Eddie Hogan arrived in the basement. 'Does he know?' O'Hare asked Toal and McNeill. They said yes, O'Grady knew the news was out.

O'Hare went to O'Grady. Think of someone, he said, who could be used to get in touch with Austin Darragh without the police knowing. O'Grady suggested the name of Hilary Prentice, his friend and patient. O'Hare asked for some details about her.

· · · · ·

Knowing who was involved was a start, but the police literally hadn't a clue as to where O'Grady might be held. Four days into the kidnapping, on the evening of Saturday 17 October, a conference of seventy detectives discussed the case at Dun Laoghaire garda station. They were given an intelligence briefing on the INLA and its spinoffs. They decided to concentrate the search for the gang in the Dublin area.

On the evening that conference was taking place, the gang decided to move O'Grady out of Dublin. He had spent long, dreary days in the dirty basement, reading and listening to the radio, and being supplied with takeaway food.

Late on that Saturday evening the gang handcuffed O'Grady and put the blacked-out glasses on his eyes. He was brought upstairs to the doorway of Wright's barber shop and held there for a few minutes until the coast was clear. Then he was hustled across the pavement to a waiting car. O'Grady was held in the back with one of the gang, probably Tony McNeill, while two others, O'Hare and Toal, sat in front. Eddie Hogan travelled separately. The gang was in high spirits, cracking jokes about the poor old Border Fox being blamed for everything that happened.

After a long time driving the gang stopped in a town. Dessie O'Hare got out and fetched fish and chips for everyone. Then they set off again, eating their takeaways.

About an hour passed and Dessie O'Hare suddenly shouted at O'Grady and the gang member in the back to get down. 'Brits!' he screamed, rolling down the window and firing two shots out into the darkness. O'Grady assumed they were now in the North.

In fact, they were in County Cork, near Carricktwohill. For the next few days O'Grady slept at night in a shed and spent the days sitting in the open, surrounded by thick brambles and gorse. He had his son's radio, and he was still reading *The Power of the Sword*. That Sunday he was given the *Independent, Tribune* and *Press* and read about his kidnap. By now the gardaí had confirmed that they were hunting Dessie O'Hare and his gang in connection with the crime.

Dessie O'Hare spent a lot of time away from the shed. He didn't seem to be in any hurry to negotiate with O'Grady's family. The idea seemed to be that he would let them, and the authorities, sweat. He may also have been wary of a garda trap, and may have believed that allowing a lot of time to go by without anything happening would take the edge off garda reaction. It would be a fortnight after the kidnap before O'Hare made a demand.

Gay Byrne was friendly with Austin Darragh and on his radio show one day he sent a message to John O'Grady, telling him that his mother, who had been ill and whom he had visited just an hour before he had been kidnapped, was now well and he shouldn't worry. O'Grady, listening on his son's radio, heard a reference to Byrne's message on the RTE news and took comfort in it.

O'Grady was being guarded by Fergal Toal and Tony McNeil. That evening, Dessie O'Hare and Eddie Hogan came to the shed.

O'Grady heard O'Hare ask one of the gunmen if O'Grady was handcuffed. 'Yes', was the reply.

O'Grady found himself announcing — and even as he did so, being aware of the stupidity of it — that in fact he wasn't handcuffed.

O'Grady had to leave the shed each morning by crawling through a two-foot square hole in the wall, while carrying out the bedding on which he slept, and had to climb back each evening.

'Is he getting in and out of the hole quick enough?' asked Dessie O'Hare.

'He's a bit slow.'

O'Hare got a long chain and wrapped it around one of O'Grady's wrists. He used a bolt and three nuts to secure the chain in place. He did the same with the other wrist, leaving a two-foot length of chain between the two hands. He wrapped the same chain around O'Grady's ankles, leaving a yard-long length of chain between each of O'Grady's feet. He then gagged O'Grady with a scarf.

'You're not getting out the hole quick enough,' said O'Hare. He began kicking O'Grady on his backside and legs. O'Grady lay on the ground, contracting his body, trying to protect his head with his hands. O'Hare kicked him in the back and the head, cursing as he did so. O'Grady tried to scream but the gag filled his mouth.

O'Hare stopped the beating. 'When I say go, you're to gather your mattress and get out of the hole,' he said. After a few seconds he said, 'Go!' and O'Grady hurried to gather the bedding together and scramble through the hole. He was brought back. O'Hare beat him again, kicking O'Grady as he lay on the ground. 'You're not quick enough!' he screamed. O'Grady, cowering on the ground, being kicked and cursed, found his eye drawn to a bright orange price tag stuck to the newly bought green rubber boots with which O'Hare was doing the kicking.

O'Hare made O'Grady scramble through the hole again, and this time he seemed satisfied. 'Leave the chains on,' O'Hare said. He ordered O'Grady to squat down on his hunkers and hold up the chains while he took two polaroid snapshots. Eddie Hogan held a gun to O'Grady's head, for the photographs. As O'Hare held up the camera O'Grady noticed that the gunman was wearing O'Grady's Longines gold watch. Pictures taken, O'Hare left with Eddie Hogan. O'Grady settled down for the night in his chains.

• • • • •

The gardaí still hadn't a clue. They speculated that O'Hare had joined up with a criminal gang to carry out the kidnap. They appealed to the public to search outhouses and derelict farm buildings. It can only be imagined what might have happened had members of the public stumbled across the gang in a derelict farm building.

O'Grady spent the following day outside, as usual. Tony McNeill, still wearing his balaclava, was for O'Grady the least frightening of the gang. He told O'Grady he sympathised with him, that he wouldn't shoot him. He asked O'Grady if he wanted to play chess. There, amid the brambles and the gorse, the masked kidnapper and his chained victim played two games of chess.

The days went slowly. Cattle came close to the hideout and one of the gang chased them away. The gunmen whistled signals to one another. On one occasion O'Grady witnessed the bizarre sight of one of the raiders answering a whistled signal, walking through the gorse, carrying a rifle, wearing a black balaclava and O'Grady's cashmere overcoat.

On the night of Thursday 22 October, O'Grady was driven to a new hideout. Before leaving the car, O'Hare gave him a felt-tip pen and a notebook. O'Hare shone a torch and told O'Grady he was to write a ransom note. He began dictating.

'For Godsake keep the light down!' said Eddie Hogan. Blankets were put over the car windows. The note was addressed to O'Grady's father-in-law, Austin Darragh, and demanded £1,500,000 ransom, in £20 and £50 notes, a million of it in sterling. There had been a five-fold increase in the ransom demand from the £300,000 mentioned to Marise O'Grady.

O'Hare dictated instructions for a courier to be sent to a hotel. The courier was to drive a car with a car phone, and when a Pat Murray was paged at the hotel he was to take the phone call and follow further instructions. O'Grady was then ordered to write a plea that the ransom demand be met.

O'Grady was then taken from the car, through wet grass to a cargo container. This was the gang's new hideout. It was in a field in an area called Ballymacsliney, just over two miles from the town of Midleton, Co. Cork. The thirty-foot by seven-and-a-half-foot container, with yellow paint obscuring an old Tayto sign, was a primitive prison. It stood close to a cottage in which lived an old woman. She had been persuaded by a relation to let him leave the container there. An electric lead was run out from the cottage to the container. The only heat came from the bar of an electric heater. The toilet was a bucket.

Having installed his victim in his new prison, Dessie O'Hare took off with Eddie Hogan. Toal and McNeill were left to guard the container.

The gang thought up a code. Anyone seeking entry to the container had to knock three times and say 'Geronimo'.

There was total darkness inside the container, except for the light from the bar of the electric heater. That Sunday, Eddie Hogan returned. Late that night he took O'Grady out into the fields, gave him some paper from a toilet roll and let him do the business. It was raining heavily. Hogan told O'Grady he could take off the blacked-out glasses, but not to look at anyone. He told him to walk to the end of the field and back.

For the next fifteen minutes or so O'Grady walked up and down, getting a bit of exercise, carefully not looking at Eddie Hogan and whoever else might be in the field. He noticed some lights in the distance. Normal life going on just a little distance away. Very near, very far. Hogan took him back to the container.

While Hogan, Toal and McNeill were left guarding the prisoner, Dessie O'Hare went in search of some rest and recuperation. The gardaí were keeping O'Hare's wife and daughter, at their flat in Bree Estate, Castleblaney, under close surveillance. Clare's every move, every visit to the shops, every journey to pick up her daughter from school, was carefully noted. At 5pm on the evening of Sunday 25 October, Clare O'Hare drove away from Castleblaney, towards Keady.

She was alone in her car and was spotted ten minutes later driving in the opposite direction. She wasn't seen again that day and wouldn't be seen by the police for over a month. At 7.20pm that evening the surveillance team carefully noted the arrival at Clare O'Hare's flat of an 'unknown man', driving Clare O'Hare's car. The man parked the car and disappeared through a side entrance. The gardaí on surveillance would watch in vain. Clare O'Hare had disappeared. According to her own account, she and Dessie spent that night in a cow shed.

· · · · ·

While Dessie O'Hare was attending to personal business, the rest of the gang were in trouble. The comings and goings around the container had attracted some attention. In or around noon of the following day, Monday 26 October, someone warned the police at Midleton garda station that there were armed men in the vicinity of a yellow container at Ballymacsliney. Three gardaí drove out and had a look around. The container was locked. They tapped on the door of the container and called out but there was no response. They reported back to Midleton that they were suspicious. This was around 2.20pm.

Over an hour later, at Midleton garda station, plans began to be drawn up for a raid on the container. A superintendent and a detective inspector decided to surround the field in which the container was sited. The police rang garda stations at Union Quay in Cork city, in Cobh to the south, Glanmire to the west and Youghal to the east, looking for backup. The superintendent phoned Collins's Barracks and asked for army support. He was told that would take two hours to arrange. Shortly after 4pm there was a call from Collins's Barracks saying that a captain and nine soldiers were on their way and would arrive in about forty-five minutes.

By then the gardaí had sixteen men available for armed duty. They were split into two teams of five and one of six and provided with armbands and flak jackets. They had revolvers or Uzi submachine guns. Eight uniformed gardaí were dispatched to set up four roadblocks. At around 4.30pm the three armed teams left Midleton for Ballymacsliney, under the command of the detective inspector. The superintendent stayed at the garda station, awaiting the arrival of the soldiers.

The police arrived at their destination at around 4.40pm, parked their cars half a mile from the suspect area and set out on foot, approaching the container from three directions.

Meanwhile, the army had arrived at Midleton garda station. It was 4.55pm.

The detective inspector, himself leading the team approaching the container from the west, checked by radio with the other teams. 'Are you in position?'

He then radioed Midleton garda station to let his superior know they were in the vicinity of the container. The superintendent told him he was about to leave for Ballmacsliney with another three gardaí and the detachment of soldiers. He just had to call the chief superintendent to let him know what was happening. He then rang the chief superintendent.

Ballymacsliney was covered in dense bushes, gorse and brambles. It was difficult terrain in which to move around. One garda in the team approaching the container from the north attempted to climb up on to a ditch. He grabbed at a branch and it broke, making a loud snapping sound. He immediately heard movement among the briars on the other side of the ditch. It was like someone running. Suddenly, a yellow van came along the narrow road, as if from nowhere, and pulled to an abrupt stop.

At Midleton garda station the superintendent had just hung up the phone, having briefed his chief superintendent, when the radio squawked.

'Help! Quick!' It was the detective inspector's voice. 'Under fire!'

• • • • •

The gang had that morning taken John O'Grady out of the container and held him in the open. He was taken to a kind of tunnel cut through brambles. There he was made sit, handcuffed, the blacked-out glasses on his eyes. Later he was moved through the bramble tunnel to another site. He was allowed to wear his son's Walkman radio. It was the October bank holiday and the Dublin City Marathon was under way and O'Grady was listening to the radio commentary. It was around 2.30pm, around the time the three gardaí came to investigate the report of suspicious activity at the yellow container.

Suddenly, the earphones were pulled off John O'Grady's head and he was hustled along the bramble tunnel and into the side of a field, where he was made lie on the ground. He was led along the side of the field, over some barbed wire, through some hedges, on to a roadway and into another field.

One of the gunmen said, 'There's someone at the far side of the field. He's seen us.'

The gang took O'Grady out of the field and back the way they had come, then he was made to crawl on hands and knees into another tunnel cut through a mass of briars. The gunmen joined him there. They sat there for a long time. One of the gunmen gave O'Grady a piece of currant cake. McNeill and Toal shared a cigarette between them.

Back at Midleton the gardaí prepared their plan, moved their three teams into place, awaited the arrival of the soldiers. In the tunnel through the briars the kidnap gang hid and waited, the afternoon ticking by.

As they sat in the briar tunnel, Hogan and Toal and McNeill and their hostage heard the squawking sound of a radio. It was very close, very clear.

'Are you in position?' a voice asked. The gang started moving, fast.

· · · · ·

Charles and Mary Terry were returning home to Kilva, having visited Mary's parents in County Limerick. They had been driving for over an hour now, in their yellow Toyota van, and it was 5.10pm. They intended picking up their daughter Maria as she left work in Midleton at 5.30pm. Charles stamped on the brakes as two armed and masked men burst out through the briars on the ditch to the left of the road and stood in front of the van.

Eddie Hogan waved a gun at Charles. 'Get out, get out!'

Charles got out. Eddie Hogan sat into the driver's seat. Mary Terry was in the front passenger seat, terrified. She asked Hogan if he wanted to be taken somewhere.

'Get out!' he said. He tried to open her seat-belt but couldn't. She opened it herself.

By now John O'Grady had been brought out from the briar tunnel.

And now there was another vehicle pulling up on the narrow road, immediately behind the Terrys' van.

Michael and Mary O'Brien were returning from Fermoy. Their daughter Patricia was driving their silver Renault. They knew the Terrys and had been driving behind the yellow Toyota van for the past ten or fifteen minutes. They couldn't figure out why Charles had suddenly pulled up his van in the middle of the road. Then they saw the people with the masks and the guns.

In the front seat of the yellow van, Mary Terry was asking Eddie Hogan, 'Can I get my bag?' He let her get her handbag, then she got out of the van. She was standing near a gate leading into a field and she appeared to be close to hysteria.

'Stay where you are!' one of the gunmen roared at her.

The gunmen decided to take the silver Renault car instead of the van. One of them ran back towards the car. 'Bring the hostage,' he shouted.

One of the police teams was within yards of all this. One garda, the one who had broken the branch on the ditch, had clear sight of one of the gunmen but Mary Terry was standing in between and he dare not shoot. He shouted at her to lie down. Terrified, she just froze. The gunman lifted his weapon and Mary Terry saw him point it in her direction. He fired towards the garda in the field behind her. The garda dived on to the ground. He looked up and the woman was still standing in his line of fire.

Another garda had flung himself behind a ditch as the shooting started. He couldn't see anything, any gunmen, and didn't know where the shooting was coming from or who was doing it. He could just hear the shots. He saw a lump of grass fly up from the ground a few yards ahead of him as a wild bullet hit the earth.

'Bring the fucking hostage!' a gunman screamed. John O'Grady was hustled along the road towards the silver Renault.

More shots at the gardaí.

Two of the gunmen were firing, one of them shouting, 'Get down, you fucking scum!'

The gang piled into the Renault and drove off, the right rear door swinging loose. Fergal Toal smashed the back window and began firing a rifle. John O'Grady was crouched down across the back seat, under Toal. Eddie Hogan was driving.

As the car sped by, the detective inspector caught a glimpse of the driver, his balaclava off. He recognised him. Eddie Hogan from Fairhill.

One garda ran into the road and, 160 yards behind the car, fired his Uzi submachine gun in an attempt to hit the tyres. He saw the bullets hit the rear of the car. Another garda fired two pistol shots from twenty yards.

A bullet clipped the right side of Eddie Hogan's head and pierced the windscreen in front of him. The car wavered and then drove on in the direction of Midleton.

· · · · ·

As word spread about the events at Ballmacsliney there was anger among senior gardaí in Dublin. The first suspicions about the yellow container had occurred in the early afternoon; by 3pm suspicions had been heightened to the point where the Cork gardaí fully believed that the O'Hare gang was in the vicinity; two hours had passed as the preparations were made for the raid, yet the gardaí in Dublin coordinating the hunt for John O'Grady had not been informed.

The Dublin gardaí complained that the Cork police's performance was less than impressive. They hadn't sealed off the area sufficiently to block the gang's escape; nor had they stopped civilians wandering into a dangerous situation. The Cork gardaí could argue that if Dublin had to be notified every time somewhere had to be checked out, nothing would ever get done.

In the aftermath of the shooting the Cork gardaí drove this way and that for a while, around the narrow country roads, in a vain effort to pick up the gang's trail.

· · · · ·

Mark Nugent steered his Datsun car into a layby. He was a private in the army, working at the barracks in Kilkenny. He was off duty that day and he and three friends had driven from Waterford to Turner's Cross, Cork, to attend a soccer match between Cork City and Waterford. The match ended at 4.45pm and the four left immediately to return to Waterford.

One of Nugent's passengers said he needed to pee. Nugent spotted an empty layby on the Waterford road, somewhere past the Youghal Carpet factory. All four of the young men got out of the car. They paid little attention to the silver Renault that drove by very fast, and seconds later all four were standing on a grassy mound, pissing into the ditch.

Mark Nugent turned around as he heard a car come to a stop. It was the silver Renault, which had doubled back. Hogan, Toal and McNeill were out of the car, waving guns and dragging John O'Grady.

Someone roared, 'Get down or I'll blow your fucking brains out!'

Three of the young men were forced to the ground, face down, by the men waving guns. Mark Nugent jumped backwards up on to the ditch as a gunman pointed a sawn-off shotgun at him.

'Get the fucking keys!' called one of the gunmen, who was standing near the car.

Nugent shouted that the keys were in the car. 'We have no money,' he said, 'take the car!'

John O'Grady was made lie down in the back of the car.

Eddie Hogan got into the driver's seat and called, 'Let's go!'

• • • • •

The gang had known they wouldn't get far in the stolen silver Renault, especially with the back window knocked out. They needed a swop, and Mark Nugent's car would do for the moment. They had no doubt that the hijack of this car would soon be reported (and back on the Waterford road Mark Nugent was already flagging down a garda car to report the robbery). Another car would be needed, and this time it must be possible to ensure that the robbing of the car wouldn't be reported for a while, to give the gang a little time to put some distance behind them.

The gang was by now headed in a north-west direction. Darkness came. Eddie Hogan mentioned that he thought he had been nicked in the side of the head by a bullet, but he didn't make a big deal of it. They were driving on backroads, bad roads. They were all the time on the lookout for another car, knowing that at any minute the Datsun could be spotted and identified. Near Mallow, at about 6.30pm, they spotted a car parked alongside a house, an Ascona. That would do nicely.

Inside the house, Nuala Hannon was sitting by the fire, feeding her seven-month-old baby, John. Her seven-year-old son Colin was on the sofa. Her husband John went to answer when the doorbell rang.

At first John thought it was friends, messing, when the two armed and masked men pushed their way in, one of them saying they were here to check the house. John Hannon laughed and grabbed at a scarf covering one gunman's face. Eddie Hogan pushed Hannon away, stuck a sawn-off shotgun into his chest and pushed him into the sitting room, past Colin, who had come out to see what was happening. John Hannon was pushed onto the sofa. Colin sat down beside his father and began to cry.

The gunmen demanded the keys to the Ascona. John Hannon got them from a coat pocket. Hogan left the room. Tony McNeill stayed, holding a rifle that he kept pointed towards the ceiling. There were lights up the road, he said. What was that? John Hannon said it was probably the sugar factory. Would there be people there? There would.

Fergal Toal was looking after John O'Grady out in the car. Eddie Hogan went outside and transferred O'Grady to the Ascona. On the way O'Grady asked if he could urinate. He was told to do it there on the ground, and he did.

Eddie Hogan went back inside and took John Hannon into the kitchen. 'We've nothing personal against you,' Hogan said, 'but we need your car to go on a journey and we have to have time. If you notify anybody about this we'll have your name and address and there'll be somebody to deal with you.'

Hogan and McNeill took John Hannon to a bedroom and made him produce several of his ties and then lie on the bed. His hands were tied together, and his hands were tied to his knees and his ankles were tied together. Colin was watching this. Then they tied Colin's legs to his father's legs. Nuala Hannon and her baby were brought in. A bedside locker was shifted so that the pram could be fitted in beside the bed.

Eddie Hogan was worried about the baby. He boiled a kettle of water and got a prepared bottle from the fridge, brought the lot to the bedroom and put the bottle in the kettle. The bottle was warmed up so the baby could be fed.

Nuala Hannon was told to lie on the bed and Tony McNeill began to tie her up. He was a bit hesitant. What about leaving her hands free, since she had to look after the baby?

'Tie her up,' Eddie Hogan said, 'and that's an order.' Fergal Toal came into the bedroom. Had the Hannons a Bible, he asked. John Hannon told him where the Bible was and the gunman went away but he couldn't find it. He asked then for Dettol. He was told it was in the bathroom.

Eddie Hogan showed John Hannon a business card holder they had found in his car. That's the information we need, he was told, your name and your address.

Before they left, the gang put Dettol on Eddie Hogan's head wound. They tore out the phones and stole a pair of binoculars. It was 7.10pm when they left the house.

The Ascona's petrol tank was half full. After a few minutes Eddie Hogan said they'd have to get petrol. They pulled into a petrol station. Where was the self-service pump? They were afraid that O'Grady, who was sitting in the back of the car, behind the driver, would be spotted. They drove out of the station and parked a few minutes away. O'Grady was taken out and shoved into a hedge. One gunman stayed with him while the others went back to fill up the petrol tank.

The car returned a few minutes later. O'Grady was put down behind the driver's seat and covered by a blanket. The car drove north-eastwards for three or four hours. The whole country was talking about the shooting in Cork; every garda in the land was on the lookout. And the gunmen drove through it all, back to Dublin, across to the northside again, this time further north, to Cabra West, a corporation housing estate. Gerry Wright had a house there, at 260 Carnlough Road. The house had been owned by Wright's father, who died a couple of years previously. Wright had been living there three or four years. Late that evening the gang arrived at 260 Carnlough, John O'Grady was brought upstairs and put to bed. One of the gunmen brought him a glass of water.

· · · · ·

Later, the police would ask Gerry Wright why he gave the gang the keys to his house in Cabra West. He said he was told the gang had caught the man who killed his brother and they needed somewhere to keep him. Asked what he would have done had that been the case, Wright said he would have got a statement out of him and then turned him over to the police.

The garda was sceptical and suggested Wright intended taking 'another course of action'.

Wright admitted, yes, he wanted 'an eye for an eye'.

It is certain that at this stage Gerry Wright knew that all of this had nothing to do with his brother's killer, if he had ever believed that. He would later claim that he was told that if he didn't cooperate he would end up like his brother.

The day after his arrival at 260 Carnlough Road, John O'Grady was moved downstairs to a small enclosed space under the stairs. There was a mattress on the floor and some blankets. The door was closed and he was allowed take off his darkened glasses. There was a light bulb hanging from a water pipe. There was a radio. The gang gave him some more Wilbur Smith books.

Later that day, Tuesday 27 October, O'Grady checked the bullet wound on the side of Eddie Hogan's head. It was up to half an inch wide and two and a half inches long, like a bullet had just missed taking part of Hogan's head away. O'Grady cut away the hair around the wound and advised Hogan to treat it with Sudocrem. O'Grady was given the three daily papers and read about the shooting at Midleton. He finally knew the name of the town he had seen near by while getting exercise in a field. The papers were full of the kidnapping and the Border Fox, and the police wanting to speak to a Dessie O'Hare.

That night Dessie O'Hare arrived at 260 Carnlough, accompanied by a woman. There was great excitement among the gunmen as they discussed the shooting in Cork. O'Hare and the woman went out looking for an off-licence. They stopped a couple of boys on Fassaugh Avenue and asked. The boys, Victor and David, said the local Londis off-licence was closed, but they offered to show O'Hare where there was an off-licence in east Cabra. The boys got into the car and showed the way to Reid's off-licence, on the Cabra Road. As it happened, Reid's was a few yards away from the hairdressing shop where Billy Wright had been shot dead back in 1975.

The woman went into the off-licence to buy beer.

'Anything going on about the place?' Dessie O'Hare asked. The boys said nothing much.

The woman came back out with the beer. She brought a couple of cans of Coke, 'for you and your little friend'.

At 260 Carnlough Road the O'Hare gang had a celebration that night, laughing and popping open cans of beer. Gerry Wright's cheerful Dublin accent rang loud. At some stage someone took out a polaroid camera and Eddie Hogan and Fergal Toal posed separately with a gun and had their pictures taken.

In his prison under the stairs, John O'Grady switched off his light and fell asleep.

· · · · ·

Two days later, on Wednesday 28 October, O'Grady was allowed to take a bath, his first since his kidnap fifteen days earlier. Gerry Wright was making daily shopping expeditions, bringing back provisions. He went to Kearney's, a local shop, where his habit was to make purchases worth £3 or £4. Now he was spending £10 or £12 at a time. One day he spent £25. The shopkeeper, John Kearney, asked him about the rise in purchasing power. Wright said he had visitors, he was having a party. He rented video tapes each morning — usually four at a time — and the gang whiled away the days watching movies. Eddie Hogan passed the time doing keep-fit exercises.

Dessie O'Hare needed to hide some documents. He went up to the front bedroom and removed a foot-long piece of wood from the base of a wardrobe. In this makeshift secret compartment he hid a white plastic bag, inside which were a cheque book, a lodgment book and a book of gift cheques from the Castlepollard branch of the Bank of Ireland, which had been held up a month before the kidnap. There were also driving licences, a passport and £75 worth of premium bonds belonging to a Dundalk family.

The house was somewhat dishevelled-looking, with shabby venetian blinds in the front windows. A local woman who was delivering leaflets almost passed by, then decided the place might be occupied after all and put a leaflet through the letter box. On one occasion two local boys knocked on the door. A woman answered. They asked if she wanted the grass cut. As it happened, one of them was Victor, one of the lads who had taken Dessie O'Hare and a woman to Reid's off-licence for beer on the night O'Hare arrived at 260 Carnlough. Now, the woman said yes, she'd like the grass cut. There was a three-year-old boy with the woman. Victor and his friend Jamie did the job and then told the little boy to go in and tell his Da that they were finished. The boy went inside and a man came out and gave the lads a pound and a small bottle of Bulmer's cider.

John O'Grady, in his makeshift cell under the stairs, was given a couple of pamphlets, one the writings of Bobby Sands, the other about Liam Mellowes. He was told to read them, that he would later be asked questions about their contents. O'Grady read them.

That evening Gerry Wright visited his girlfriend's home. He said he couldn't stay, he was doing a job as a security man at a gig that night.

· · · · ·

At around 3.30pm next day Hilary Prentice, the solicitor with Matheson, Ormsby and Prentice, and patient of John O'Grady, received a phone call at her Merrion Street office from a man calling himself John Mohan. It was Dessie O'Hare.

'You don't know me, but I know a friend of yours, John O'Grady.' O'Hare said he would 'authenticate' himself. O'Grady, said the caller, had been doing an upper left pre-molar crown job for Hilary Prentice. And he also knew that she had had a baby boy six months earlier.

He had a message. Prentice was to go to the home of a Dr Walter Doyle-Kelly, in Herbert Street. O'Hare gave Prentice the doctor's number. Then he said she was on no account to ring that number. Then he said he didn't know why he had given her the number. What she was to do was to tell Dr Doyle-Kelly that his wife Elizabeth, who was known to John O'Grady as Aunt Betty, was to go to Limerick city and look for an envelope underneath a statue of Our Lady beside the thirteenth Station of the Cross in Limerick Cathedral. She was to give the envelope to Austin Darragh's wife.

'John's life depends on it.'

Elizabeth Doyle-Kelly spoke with Austin Darragh that night, in the presence of Superintendent Noel Conroy of the Serious Crime Squad. She agreed to go to Limerick next day. Darragh provided her with a car, driven by his chauffeur, Peter Elliot. They arrived at St John's Cathedral in Limerick at about 2pm that Friday. Elizabeth Doyle-Kelly went in alone.

She knelt down and got her bearings. She looked for the Stations of the Cross and established where the thirteenth station was. She walked up the centre aisle, checked she was at the thirteenth station. She was standing in front of a huge, immovable solid stone statue of Our Lady of Perpetual Succour. It just wasn't possible to shift something like that to look for an envelope underneath. It didn't make sense. But they said John's life depended on it. Aunt Betty spent about twenty-five minutes in the cathedral.

She lit a candle at an altar and prayed. She came back to the huge statue and examined it closely. There was a small piece of folded writing paper at the base of the statue. She took it and left.

As she walked away she passed the nearby statue of St Teresa, facing the thirteenth Station of the Cross. Hidden underneath that statue was the envelope with the ransom note from Dessie O'Hare. O'Hare hadn't been able to tell the difference between Our Lady of Perpetual Succour and St Teresa.

Back at 260 Carnlough John O'Grady was in his cubbyhole under the stairs. He could hear Gerry Wright chattering away about how this wasn't a bad little place and when all this was over he was going to knock down a few walls and do the place up.

When Elizabeth Doyle-Kelly got back to Dublin she went straight to Austin Darragh and took the folded piece of paper from her handbag. A puzzled Darragh read the note: 'Dear Lady, cure Sean from his nerves and save us from our enemies, Dear Lady.'

· · · · ·

Meanwhile, the gardaí were combing through everything found at the container in Cork. There was a haversack containing documents, including some from the O'Grady house. These were catalogued and assessed for significance. Fingerprints were taken. A match was sought for a particular set of fingerprints and the police discovered that the prints matched those discovered in a current case. It was a murder case, involving the stabbing to death of Sean Hughes at the disco in the Imperial Hotel, Dundalk, just two days before the kidnap began.

That Friday night Gerry Wright couldn't come to see his girlfriend until 11pm. He explained that he'd been doing another security gig. They went to a Chinese restaurant.

Saturday, 31 October, Dessie O'Hare was back at 260 Carnlough, with the same woman as before. He brought a radio that picked up garda transmissions. He didn't go near O'Grady. That evening, perhaps annoyed at all the negative publicity he was getting, Dessie O'Hare decided to set the record straight. At around 7pm he rang the *Sunday Tribune*, announced himself and asked to speak to the editor. It was a busy time, as the final touches were being put to the next day's paper. The phone was answered by someone not up to speed on current events. She told O'Hare that the editor was at a meeting. Could Mr O'Hare leave a number where he could be reached, so the editor could ring him back? O'Hare declined the invitation and insisted on speaking to the editor.

In the subsequent phone interview O'Hare said that John O'Grady was not hurt during the shoot-out at the container, but added that if any of the gang had been killed, O'Grady would have been shot immediately. 'I don't know why they didn't kill a few cops. If I was there I would have got a few of them.'

He said that the INLA and the IRA were trying to kill him, but expressed confidence in his own abilities. 'I am called the Border Fox and foxes are very clever.'

· · · · ·

Government policy was against allowing ransoms being paid for kidnap victims. Such payments would help arm terrorists, went the reasoning, and that would lead to more deaths. Better to prevent such payments and save lives, even if the kidnap victim had to pay the price. Austin Darragh had put together the £300,000 which had been mentioned to Marise O'Grady by the kidnappers (unaware, as the note under the statue in Limerick hadn't been found, that the price had gone up to £1,500,000).

So far, the family had little on which to build its hopes. The only contact between the gang and the family had been the call to solicitor Hilary Prentice, several days earlier, and since the only outcome of that had been the discovery of the pathetic 'Sean's nerves' petition to the statue of Our Lady of Perpetual Succour, it had been concluded that John Mohan was a hoax caller.

On Sunday 1 November, the gang gave John O'Grady a copy of *Magill* magazine, which had a cover story on the 'Border Fox'. Gerry Wright took a break with his girlfriend and they drove to Fethard-on-Sea. Two more days passed.

· · · · ·

The police were sifting through the stuff found at the container at Ballymacsliney. Much of it belonged to the O'Gradys (birth certificates and the like, stolen by the gang) but some of it might lead somewhere. There was a garda case conference at Dun Laoghaire HQ on that Tuesday, 3 November, at which a number of leads were discussed. Sergeant Henry Spring was given details of a card found at the container. It was a Guinness Bicentenary admission card, an admission card for the Guinness leisure centre. It was being examined by the forensic people but he should get hold of it and check it out. This was eight days after the card was found.

· · · · ·

At around noon that Tuesday Hilary Prentice received another call from Dessie O'Hare. Again he was using the name John Mohan. Prentice had by now rigged up a dictation machine to record these calls. 'There's been a fuck-up,' O'Hare told her. The family's messenger would be sitting outside the Blarney Hotel in the car park, but the hotel was closed for renovations. Aunt Betty would have to phone the messenger at his car phone and tell him to go instead to the Killeshin Hotel in Portlaoise.

None of this made any sense to Hilary Prentice.

O'Hare hung up and rang back ten minutes later. 'When I rang the hotel where I was supposed to rendezvous with this man, the hotel is closed for renovation, so the chances is this man is sitting in the car park not knowing what's going on. He probably thinks the contact is to be made there but actually it isn't. Tell Aunt Betty that.'

Hilary Prentice, still without a clue as to what any of this meant, asked, 'Is John OK?'

'Oh, he's perfectly well so far,' said O'Hare. They agreed to talk again at around 2pm.

'All right, John,' said Hilary Prentice. 'Bye-bye.'

Dessie O'Hare replied, 'Cheerio.'

The mix-up with the statues in Limerick Cathedral was leading events in a dreadful direction. Underneath the statue of St Teresa were instructions that a messenger from the family was to bring the ransom money to the Blarney Hotel in Cork, where he would receive a phone call. The man was to have a car phone.

The idea was that O'Hare would ring the man at the Blarney Hotel, get from him the number of the car phone, direct him to drive away from the hotel and then ring him in the car with fresh instructions. O'Hare had just discovered the Blarney Hotel was closed for renovations and believed that this was screwing up the plan. The fact that he had got the statue's identity wrong when he placed the ransom note under the statue, mistaking St Teresa for Our Lady of Perpetual Succour, meant that John O'Grady's family knew nothing of the original ransom instructions. When Hilary Prentice rang them with O'Hare's latest orders they were puzzled. All they could say was that there was nothing under the statue of Our Lady, it was a massive thing that couldn't be moved. Hilary Prentice waited for O'Hare to ring back.

O'Hare returned to 260 Carnlough in a foul humour and had a shouting row with Eddie Hogan. 'Didn't I tell you to check out the Blarney Hotel?' he screamed.

Hogan shouted back obscenities.

O'Hare was seething. After the shouting match the whole house went quiet. O'Hare went away again.

At around 2.30pm he made another phone call to Hilary Prentice. 'Has there been any developments?'

'Ah now, look John, I've been in contact with Aunt Betty. Now, John, she says she complied with the last message . . . and she really doesn't understand what's happening, because there wasn't any message there.'

'There wasn't any fucking message there,' repeated O'Hare. 'I'm going to fucking chop his fingers off or something.' He began to rant. 'What do you mean there was nothing under the statue? Did you look under Our Lady's statue at the thirteenth Station of the Cross in the Limerick city, in the cathedral? How many fucking cathedrals is there?'

'Well, John, I passed on the message exactly as you've repeated it.'

'When she got to Limerick did she pick up any message underneath the envelope — underneath the statue?'

'Well, I'm told there was nothing there.'

'Did she fucking smash the statue up and look underneath it?'

'Well, I don't know, John.'

'Fuck this.' Dessie O'Hare hung up.

* * * * *

Dessie O'Hare opened the door under the stairs and handed John O'Grady a pen and a pad of Belvedere Bond notepaper. He began dictating another ransom note. O'Grady had to write that a messenger should be sent to the Silver Springs Hotel, Cork, with the money and a car phone. He would get a call there from a Pat Murray, and he was to follow the instructions he would be given. O'Hare took the note away and closed the door.

He came back minutes later with two pillowcases and put them over O'Grady's head. He handcuffed his prisoner's hands behind his back and brought him out to the kitchen and forced him face down on the floor. He tied O'Grady's legs together. He pulled off the pillowcases and put a cloth gag in O'Grady's mouth and tied it in place. He put the pillowcases back on. He opened the handcuffs and took O'Grady's left hand and splayed out the fingers, forcing the hand down on to a round wooden chopping board. One of the other gunmen stood on the hand.

O'Hare took a newly purchased chisel and a hammer and chopped off John O'Grady's left little finger, between the second and third joint. Blood gushed from the stump of the finger, staining the green carpet tiles. The gagged O'Grady threshed in agony. One of the gunmen used a red-hot knife to cauterise the wound and stop the blood flowing, touching the knife to the wound three times, causing O'Grady further agony.

O'Grady's right hand was then put on the board and the fingers were splayed. Again someone stood on his hand to hold it in place. He felt something cold on his little finger. The hammer made a loud bang as it hit the chisel and O'Grady's right little finger was gone. Again the wound was cauterised three times with a red-hot knife.

O'Grady's legs were untied, the pillowcases were taken off his head and the gag was taken out, and he was forced to hunker down near the back door. Dessie O'Hare, wearing a balaclava, took his time framing a shot with a polaroid camera. O'Grady was told to look into the lens, to hold his two hands up by his ears. He could feel blood trickling down his right arm.

O'Hare took off O'Grady's blacked-out glasses and began taking pictures. 'Think of the seasons,' he told O'Grady, 'think of spring.' He took three pictures.

Tony McNeill said maybe they should get some ice, put the fingers in ice, maybe they could be sewn back later on.

'Fuck him,' said O'Hare. Shortly afterwards he left the house. O'Grady was brought back in under the stairs.

Tony McNeill came in with a basin of hot water and some dressings. He gave O'Grady some Ponstan painkillers, a K50 sedative and Ampiclox antibiotics. McNeill started to dress O'Grady's fingers but he hadn't the stomach for it. 'Jesus Christ!' he moaned, 'Jesus Christ!' and left and went upstairs.

Eddie Hogan took over and dressed O'Grady's fingers.

• • • • •

At about 4.50pm Hilary Prentice got another phone call from John Mohan. 'I've just sent word to my men to chop off two of his fingers,' he said.

'Sorry, say that again?'

'I don't know what fingers they're going to chop off,' said Dessie

O'Hare. 'I'm going to pick up his fingers now, so give me your home number so that I can tell you where to get them.'

Hilary Prentice gave him the number and then tried to convince him again that Aunt Betty had followed his instructions. 'She spent twenty-five minutes searching and . . .'

'She searched nothing! All she had to do was to lean against the statue, bend it over.'

O'Hare tightened the screw. 'It's just cost John two of his fingers. Now, I'm going to chop him into bits and pieces and send fresh lumps of him every fucking day if I don't get my money fast.' Again he ended the call with the salutation, 'Cheerio.'

He called Hilary Prentice at home at around 7pm and told her the fingers had been left in Carlow Cathedral. He gave her detailed instructions on where the fingers were hidden. There was a message with them, and if they put that together with the earlier message, the one in Kilkenny, they would know what to do. 'That's only his two fingers,' he said, 'that's not so bad.' He said he believed 'yous are stalling to try and catch and kill me. Now, if they haven't got the ransom I don't know what I'll do. I'll chop this fucking bastard up! I'm reaching the end of my tether!'

The fourth time he mentioned Kilkenny ('Put the two notes together, the Kilkenny one and the Carlow one') Hilary Prentice interrupted and said, 'You haven't mentioned Kilkenny to me before.' The phone went dead.

Almost immediately it rang again. 'I made a mistake there when I said Kilkenny,' said Dessie O'Hare, 'I meant Limerick.'

Back at 260 Carnlough John O'Grady was worrying about infection. He asked the gunmen to cut up a linen sheet and boil it for an hour, and to boil a pair of scissors to sterilise them. They did this and Eddie Hogan again dressed the maimed fingers. O'Grady took another sedative and antibiotics and went to sleep under the stairs, holding up his hands in the hope of preventing bleeding.

Hilary Prentice passed on O'Hare's message to the gardaí and at 10.15 that evening Superintendent John McGroarty, in charge of Carlow District, received a phone call from Dublin, telling him to have a look in Carlow Cathedral. By 11pm Father Tom Dillon had been located and he took McGroarty and Detective Frank Duggan to the cathedral.

They followed the instructions O'Hare had given Hilary Prentice. ('When you go in through the main doors take a right, and then take a right again and you're into this wee grotty place. On the right-hand side there's a statue sitting on a plinth or something, that wooden plinth, that bench affair, the envelopes, three of them, sitting between it and the wall.')

Inside, wedged between the mortuary wall and a statue of St Teresa, they found a package and the gardaí and the priest took it back to the station. There, at around 11.30pm, they opened the package and found three buff manilla envelopes wrapped in several layers of black insulating tape. Superintendent McGroarty cut the tape and opened the bulkiest of the envelopes and found John O'Grady's two fingers wrapped in bloodstained tissue paper. The second envelope had a ransom demand and the third had two of the Polaroid photographs of John O'Grady holding up his mutilated hands. The package was quickly brought to Portlaoise, where a garda sent from Dublin was waiting to collect it. He brought it to Garda Headquarters in Harcourt Square, Dublin, where at 2 o'clock in the morning senior gardaí contemplated the stunning evidence of the kidnappers' ruthlessness.

· · · · ·

While the government was still opposed to the payment of ransom, the prospect of having John O'Grady delivered back to his family piece by piece was chilling. If the family wanted to pay, no effort would be made to stop them.

The next day, Wednesday 4 November, Austin Darragh made arrangements to ransom his son-in-law. A well-known priest, Father Brian D'Arcy, would deliver the money to the Silver Springs Hotel, in Cork, at 1pm the following day, Thursday. When he got there he would be contacted by the gang about the handover of the money.

That night the police were all over the Silver Springs, preparing a welcome for the kidnappers.

Elsewhere, ordinary decent criminals were annoyed at O'Hare, as constant garda activity affected their business. In one search gardaí stumbled across £60,000 worth of spirits stolen a few days earlier.

Peter Elliot, Austin Darragh's chauffeur, drove down to Limerick with another driver from Darragh's company, Michael Kelly. They went to St John's Cathedral and found the statue of St Teresa near the thirteenth Station of the Cross. Elliot tilted the statue backwards and Kelly looked underneath. There was nothing there. Kelly tilted the statue forward and Elliot looked underneath and found Dessie O'Hare's ransom letter. The family would now learn that O'Hare wanted £1,500,000 for John O'Grady.

Sergeant Henry Spring went up to the Garda Technical Bureau in the Phoenix Park that day and was given the Guinness Bicentenary admission card which he had been assigned to check out. He was accompanied by Detective Garda Martin O'Connor. Both of them were stationed at Dun Laoghaire and were working together on the kidnap investigation.

The Guinness card bore the name of Paul O'Sullivan, Traffic Department. A staff number, 237264, and pay number, 434, were on the card, so it would be easy enough to check out. The two gardaí set off for Guinness's brewery.

At 260 Carnlough John O'Grady changed the dressings on his maimed fingers, with Eddie Hogan's help. He noticed a large clot on the stump of his right little finger. He used the sterilised scissors to remove part of it. That afternoon he checked the dressings again and saw that the clot had grown bigger. It was dangerous. He cut the clot and there was a spurt of arterial blood, some of it hitting the wall of his cubbyhole. He squeezed the artery with his left hand and kept the pressure up for fifteen minutes. He removed the pressure and the blood was still flowing. He told Eddie Hogan the wound would have to be cauterised again.

O'Grady was brought out to the kitchen in his dark glasses, and was put sitting in a chair. A gag was put in his mouth. Drops of his blood fell on to a leg of the table and on to the handle of a chip pan kept underneath the table. One gunman held his left arm, another prepared a red-hot knife. O'Grady put his right hand on the table and wrapped his legs around his chair. Eddie Hogan cauterised the wound with the red-hot knife, five or six times. O'Grady was brought back in under the stairs and Eddie Hogan gave him a sedative, antibiotics and a couple of bottles of beer.

· · · · ·

Thursday 5 November. Gerry Wright was up early and down to the local shop by 8am, for provisions. He left back the previous day's rented videos and got two more, 'Heavenly Kid' and 'Escape to Victory'. John O'Grady woke at 8.30am and washed his maimed fingers in salted lukewarm water. He spent the morning listening to the radio and reading. The sad news of the day was that Éamonn Andrews had died.

Sergeant Henry Spring and Detective Garda Martin O'Connor were checking out the owner of the Guinness card. They had obtained from Guinness's an address for Paul O'Sullivan: 34 Parkgate Street. They arrived at O'Sullivan's address at about 11am and asked him about the card. Yes, it was his, but he had given it to a neighbour, a chap a few doors away, Gerry Wright, the barber at number 41. Gerry wanted to use the Guinness swimming pool.

The gardaí were in plain clothes. Gerry Wright was reading a newspaper when he saw what he took to be two customers entering his shop. 'Which of you is first?' he asked.

When the two introduced themselves as gardaí and Sergeant Spring produced the Guinness card, Gerry Wright just stared at it and shook his head. He couldn't remember anything about it, he said.

The card had been found at the scene of a serious crime, O'Connor said, and they had been told it had been given to Wright. 'Can you give an explanation?'

Wright said, 'Now I remember, I used it for the Guinness swimming pool.' He got it from Paul O'Sullivan a couple of years ago. He must have lost it.

'Where do you live?'

'260 Carnlough Road, Cabra West.'

'Is there anyone else in the house?'

'No, you can look if you like.'

Martin O'Connor said they'd need a warrant to search the house.

Wright said not at all, there was no need for a warrant, they could have a look. 'I'll go with you now and you can search it.'

It is possible that Wright, knowing that the ransom was to be picked up that day, believed that the gang had left the house. He must have been expecting them to leave early that day, as he rented only two videos instead of the usual four. Dessie O'Hare had, in fact, driven down the country to arrange the pick-up of the money, but

Eddie Hogan, Fergal Toal and Tony McNeill were in the house with their hostage.

Spring and O'Connor drove up to Cabra West with Gerry Wright. Spring was aged forty-five and was twenty-four years a garda. Normally he wouldn't be out in the field checking details. He was an information collator based at Dun Laoghaire garda station. O'Connor, aged thirty-six, had been a garda for sixteen years, nine of them a detective. Spring was unarmed; O'Connor had a pistol.

It was approaching noon when the gardaí and Gerry Wright arrived at 260 Carnlough Road. Father Brian D'Arcy was on his way to the Silver Springs Hotel in Cork, with another hour's driving ahead of him.

Having told the police there was no one in the house, it occurred to Gerry Wright that even if the gang was gone they would have left signs of their occupancy. As they walked up the footpath of 260 Carnlough Road, Wright remarked to the gardaí that some young people doing a course at the nearby AnCo centre were staying at the house but they would have gone to work by now. As Wright opened the door he made hard work of it, rattling the key in the lock. Inside the house, the gang scattered.

Eddie Hogan dived into the space under the stairs where John O'Grady was kept. He was breathing hard.

The living room was gloomy, with the venetian blinds pulled closed. There were papers burning in the grate, the television was on, there was a two-bar electric fire glowing on a chair.

'This is it,' said Gerry Wright. 'There's nothing here.'

Detective O'Connor crossed the room and pushed open the door to the kitchen. Fergal Toal stood there. He came into the living room.

Gerry Wright desperately tried to keep the AnCo story going.

'Didn't you go to work today?' he asked Toal. 'These are two guards, they're having a look around the house.'

'I believe you're doing an AnCo course?' said Sergeant Spring. Toal shrugged. Spring noticed a CB radio on a couch.

Detective O'Connor went upstairs with Wright. They found Tony McNeill in bed.

Wright said, 'This is one of the lads from AnCo, he mustn't have gone to school.'

O'Connor asked McNeill to get up. When McNeill threw back the bedclothes he was fully dressed. Detective O'Connor felt the bed and it wasn't warm. The three went downstairs to join Spring and Toal. The two gardaí exchanged uneasy glances across the darkened room. Tony McNeill walked into a corner and stood with his back to the gardaí. Detective O'Connor turned and left the house. Gerry Wright followed him out. O'Connor sat into the police car and radioed that Foxtrot Alpha Eleven needed urgent plain-clothes assistance.

When Gerry Wright heard this he ran back into the house and shouted, 'He's looking for reinforcements!'

In the living room of 260 Carnlough Road, Tony McNeill turned quickly, holding an automatic pistol in both hands, pointing it at Sergeant Spring's head. Both McNeill and Toal shouted at Spring, 'Get down, you bastard!'

Spring got down on the floor.

'Where's your weapon?' one of them screamed.

Spring said he wasn't armed.

The door of the closet under the stairs burst open and Eddie Hogan surged out.

McNeill and Toal screamed at Spring not to look. One of them kicked him in the head. 'Don't look, or we'll blow your head off!' Spring lay there, stunned from the kick.

Tony McNeill left the house and walked out to Detective O'Connor at the police car. He stuck his pistol into O'Connor's chest and told him to get out of the car. O'Connor grabbed the gun and turned the muzzle away from his chest and the two began to struggle. Fergal Toal came running out and began punching O'Connor. Toal grabbed the garda's head and pulled at his mouth.

Paddy McDermot, an ESB employee, was going from house to house on Carnlough Road, reading meters. From across the road he saw the three men struggling, two of them punching and thumping a third man. He crossed the street and said, 'What's going on?'

'Tell him to mind his own fucking business!' said Tony McNeill.

'He's trying to rob the car,' Fergal Toal said to the meter reader.

Paddy McDermot knew there was more going on than that. He started to back away.

Eddie Hogan came out of the house, holding a 12-gauge pump action shotgun, pushing John O'Grady, who was wearing the blacked-out glasses. Inside the house, Gerry Wright opened the back door and Sergeant Spring escaped into the back garden.

'Get his gun!' shouted one of the men struggling with Detective O'Connor.

The police car radio was squawking. Garda Control was calling back to Foxtrot Alpha Eleven. Detective O'Connor couldn't answer. Half in and half out of the car, the radio wire wrapped around one arm, he was still struggling with McNeill and Toal. Eddie Hogan pushed John O'Grady into the back of the police car and told him to lie down.

Hogan waved the shotgun and shouted at McNeill and Toal, 'Stand back! Stand back! I'll blow his knees off!' He pointed the shotgun at O'Connor. Toal and McNeill moved away.

'OK! OK!' said Detective O'Connor, 'I'll stand up!'

The detective got out of the car and backed away. He could feel blood on his face. He put his hands up to touch it. Eddie Hogan worked the pump action on the shotgun. Detective O'Connor backed up to the garden wall of the house next door to Wright's. From a distance of two feet, Hogan shot O'Connor in the stomach. O'Connor staggered back, a large hole in his abdomen. Still on his feet, he pulled out his gun. He fired one shot at one of the gunmen, and missed. O'Connor leaned on the garden wall, his left hand holding his belly. He could feel that he was bleeding heavily.

O'Connor cocked his weapon again, raising it towards one of the armed men at the car. He was immediately shot in the shoulder, this time by a handgun. The bullet shattered his collar bone. He fell down on to his back.

Eddie Hogan stood over O'Connor, wielding the shotgun. 'Give me your gun, you pig!' he roared. He kicked the detective.

O'Connor pleaded, 'Don't shoot me again!'

Hogan stooped and grabbed O'Connor's gun.

Already there were armed gardaí closing on Carnlough Road from several directions. John O'Grady was pulled out of the police car. McNeill hijacked a passing Liteace van from a double-glazing company. He called for Hogan and Toal to get into the van, but before they could drag O'Grady to the van the first garda arrived in response to Detective O'Connor's radioed appeal for help. As the gunmen scrambled for cover they dropped a radio scanner, used to listen to garda transmissions, and still turned on.

Detective Garda Gregory Sheehan was alone in his car when he got the call to assist a Foxtrot unit at Carnlough Road. As he arrived on the scene and stopped his car, he saw the three gunmen at the van, with all the doors open. There were two shots.

Detective Sheehan took cover behind his car and shouted, 'Armed gardaí! Drop your weapons!'

This drew several shots in his direction. A bullet shattered the window of 232 Carnlough.

Detective Sheehan pulled out his .38 Smith and Wesson and fired six shots at the gunmen.

As Sheehan reloaded, the three gunmen took off, abandoning their hostage. Unsure of what was happening, John O'Grady made a break for it. He ran, pulling off the blacked-out glasses. As it happened, he was running in the same direction as the gunmen.

Back outside Gerry Wright's house, Detective Sheehan had reloaded his pistol and was about to follow the gunmen when he saw Martin O'Connor lying on the ground. He went over and recognised him as a garda.

'I've been shot,' O'Connor said. Sheehan called for an ambulance.

Further down Carnlough Road, the three gunmen hijacked a red Daihatsu, an old banger with one green door. Just then Detectives Richard Fahey and Brian Coade arrived in an unmarked patrol car. Eddie Hogan jumped out of the Diahatsu and fired his shotgun at the police car. Fahey dropped low in the police car, reaching for the radio. Coade jumped out and fired his pistol. The Diahatsu reversed and slammed into a CIE bus. The three gunmen abandoned the Diahatsu, leaving a handgun behind, and in the confusion they split up. Hogan and Toal turned a corner and ran down Kilkiernan Road. Tony McNeill ran back up Carnlough Road. He stopped and leaned on a gate, unsure what to do. He spotted a blue Datsun slowly approaching.

Detectives Fahey and Coade advanced up Kilkiernan Road, guns at the ready, after Hogan and Toal. Two men stood at the side of the street, waving their hands in the air. They were local men, showing that they weren't armed. Detective Coade shouted at them to get down. Fahey and Coade continued up the street. Hogan and Toal, running from behind a garden wall to behind a car, fired shots at the gardaí.

Two more detectives, Michael Moone and John Burke, arrived and followed Fahey and Coade up Kilkiernan Road.

Meanwhile, a man named Patrick Donnelly was driving down Carnlough Road in his blue Datsun. He was taking a break from the nearby LenPak factory and was on his way to buy cigarettes. He slowed down as he found himself driving through a scene of bloody drama. Over here a man crouched behind a car, reloading a handgun, over there a man was lying bleeding on the ground. He continued on down Carnlough Road. From near by he could hear the sound of shots. There were police cars down the street ahead of him.

He stopped the car as a man appeared outside the front passenger door, pointing a gun and roaring at him, 'Open the fucking door or I'll blow your head off.'

Donnelly got out of the car and ran back up Carnlough Road. Tony McNeill got into the car and drove off, turning a corner and driving away from the scene.

John O'Grady had run for about sixty yards. There was shooting. He saw a man and woman standing in the doorway of a house. 'Can I come in?' he called. The pair, confronted by the dishevelled man, with gunfire in the distance, hurriedly closed the door. John O'Grady started running again.

Back on Kilkiernan Road Eddie Hogan and Fergal Toal carried out a military manoeuvre, one firing and the other retreating; the second then giving covering fire while the first retreated to a new firing position. The gardaí inched along, from cover to cover. Detectives Fahey and Coade could return fire, but Moone and Burke, some distance behind them, couldn't fire in case they hit their colleagues.

Fahey and Coade fired and saw one of the gunmen fall to the ground and immediately get back up. A bullet had grazed Fergal Toal's knee.

In the middle of all this a middle-aged woman came walking by, oblivious to it all, and walked past the two gunmen. Detective Burke shouted at her to take cover and she did, running into a nearby house.

Two more detectives, Joseph O'Connor and Gerard Russell, arrived at the junction of Carnlough Road and Kilkiernan Road and spotted the gunfight. They hurried to catch up with their four colleagues chasing Hogan and Toal. As they moved up Kilkiernan Road a man came running out from the right, across the road and into a garden. The man jumped over a plywood gate into the back garden. The two detectives ran after him. They crouched as shots came down the road from Hogan and Toal. Joseph O'Connor dived over a garden wall for cover, then cautiously made his way along the side of the house towards the back garden, where the running man had disappeared. Russell followed him. The garden was overgrown, full of brambles and small bushes. The two detectives, guns at the ready, waited and watched. They saw a bush move. O'Connor aimed at the bush with his Uzi submachine gun, while Russell moved closer.

Russell bent forward and saw an unshaven man crouched down on his hunkers, holding up bandaged hands. 'Don't shoot,' the man said.

'We're guards,' Russell said.

The man said, 'I'm John O'Grady.'

The two detectives rushed O'Grady to their car. He asked them to take him to the Blackrock Clinic.

Meanwhile, Hogan and Toal were trying to hijack a car. They ran to a yellow Hillman Hunter that was stopped on Kilkiernan Road, waved their weapons at the driver and shouted at him to get out. The elderly man inside pushed down the lock buttons on the doors and shook his head.

With their options running out, the two gunmen ran to a Dublin Corporation road-sweeping machine, from which the driver was getting out. 'You drive,' they told driver, Thomas Sutcliffe, pushing him back in. They got out of Cabra West in the road sweeper.

The detectives who had been following them on foot ran to find cars to continue the chase, but the gunmen had too big a lead. One of the detectives, John Burke, reached his car and drove around the area, in vain. Before long he spotted Sergeant Henry Spring. The sergeant's face, eye and hand were bloody, after the kicking he received inside 260 Carnlough. He had got out the back way and across a wall to another house. The woman who lived there spotted him coming across the wall and locked her back door, grabbed her child and ran upstairs to a bedroom. Spring found a yardbrush and broke a window to get into the house. He got through on to the street and went in search of a phone and called Garda Control. Spotting him, Detective Burke stopped the car and gave Spring a lift back to 260 Carnlough.

Detective Garda Martin O'Connor lay on the pavement near Gerry Wright's house, his stomach a bloody mess, his left hand raised, pawing at the air. There was blood coming through his clothing at his shoulder and waist. Gerry Wright went into his house, brought out a blanket and covered the detective. O'Connor shouted up at him, 'You bastard! You set us up!'

Sergeant Spring arrived and shouted at Gerry Wright, 'You walked us into this!'

'I don't know anything about this,' said Wright. 'There's been no one living in that house for ages. It's unoccupied for ages. I don't live there and I don't know who they were.'

Some locals gathered around.

'I'm finished,' Martin O'Connor said. He said he wanted to see his wife Roslyn and he began saying her name over and over, 'Rosie, Rosie, Rosie.'

Gerry Wright was arrested. Word that the kidnap victim had been found and that the kidnappers had escaped was flashed back to Garda Headquarters. Father Brian D'Arcy was on his way to a rendezvous at the Silver Springs Hotel in Cork, with £1,500,000 in the back of his car. His appointment was at 1pm. He was twenty minutes from the hotel when the police intercepted him.

Meanwhile, roadblocks had been thrown up all around Dublin, causing traffic chaos. Patrick Donnelly, whose car had been hijacked by Tony McNeill, reported the hijack to a garda on the scene. Instead of taking details and having them immediately circulated, the garda told Donnelly to contact the local garda station. Donnelly walked back to his workplace and rang Cabra garda station.

On his way from the shoot-out, Tony McNeill came to a checkpoint. Since Patrick Donnelly was still walking back to his workplace, the police didn't yet have a report that the blue Datsun that McNeill was driving had been hijacked. McNeill slowed down as he approached the checkpoint, smiled at the gardaí, and was waved through.

By now, RTE was broadcasting the news that John O'Grady was free. Somewhere on a country road, on his way to collect the ransom,

Dessie O'Hare heard the news on the car radio. Clare O'Hare watched as he began to rant and pound the dashboard.

• • • • •

At Blackhorse Avenue, near the Phoenix Park, Eddie Hogan and Fergal Toal spotted a man getting out of a car and decided to abandon the road-sweeping machine and hijack the man's car. While running across the road they saw an easier option, a woman in a red Fiesta. They pulled the woman, Anne Hand, out of the car, jumped in and then pulled her into the car, taking her as a hostage. They drove to Clondalkin with the terrified woman in the back seat.

As they arrived on a residential street in Clondalkin two women, Teresa Beesley and her friend Imelda Sheppard, pulled up in a Volvo. They were on their way back from a parent-teacher meeting. Imelda Sheppard noticed a red Fiesta near by with a woman in the back seat gesticulating frantically. Hogan and Toal had abandoned the Fiesta and they now approached the Volvo and began struggling with the two women. Teresa Beesley leaned her weight on the horn of her car, attracting the attention of several people. One of the gunmen grabbed her by the neck, pulled her out of the car and threw her on to the ground. Hogan and Toal took the car, reversed, smashing the side of another car as they did so, and made off.

• • • • •

At around 7 o'clock that morning Una Dermody, from Clondalkin, drove her husband to Heuston railway station so he could catch the train to Limerick, where he had business. She didn't know it then, but before the day was out she too would wind up in Limerick.

At about 12.20 that lunchtime she and a friend, Maria Hennessy, were sitting down to lunch when a red Fiesta pulled into the driveway. Una went to the front door. 'Yes?'

'O'Sullivans?' the man standing there said.

'You must have the wrong address.'

A second man came to the door and now both men were walking in, Una Dermody walking backwards, seeing now that both men were carrying guns.

'We're not going to harm you. We want medical help.'

Hogan and Toal spent an hour in the house. Maria Hennessy bandaged Fergus Toal's wounded knee and when he complained of a headache she gave him a couple of Disprin. He seemed very tense.

Toal had a cup of tea, Hogan had a coffee. They left their guns standing in a corner of the dining area of the kitchen. They got a map from Una Dermody and asked her to point out where they were on the map. She said she didn't understand maps. Hogan said he wanted the keys of the red Saab out front. He told the women they would have to come with them. They asked for changes of clothing, and Toal changed in the upstairs bathroom while Hogan changed in the hall.

They decided they would tie up Maria Hennessy and take Una Dermody. Una said she wasn't going to leave her friend tied up, she'd recently had an operation.

All four went outside. Hogan wanted to drive, but Una Dermody said she wasn't going unless she could drive herself. She drove, Hogan sat beside her, Toal sat in the back with Maria Hennessy. The two guns were left on the back seat, with an overcoat over them.

Somewhere near Robertstown they stopped for petrol. Una Dermody asked the attendant for £20 worth and was taking the money from her handbag.

'Give her the money,' Hogan said, and Toal gave her a £20 note. She said she needed some cigarettes and got out of the car and crossed the road to a shop, where she bought a packet. Maria Hennessy was kept in the back seat. Una Dermody came back to the car with her cigarettes. They headed off, taking backroads where possible, towards Limerick. Hogan told the women that if they were stopped by the police, Una Dermody was to say she was his mother, and the other two were friends. They listened to news bulletins on the radio and the registration number of one of the cars in which Hogan and Toal had made their escape from Cabra was read out.

Hogan ordered Una Dermody to stop the car. 'Get out and check the number of the car,' he told Toal.

Toal did so and reported back that it wasn't the number given out on the radio. They carried on.

• • • • •

The police, convinced that the gunmen were trapped in Dublin, were searching housing estates in the west of the city, while a police helicopter hovered overhead. Eventually, the Volvo stolen from Teresa Beesley was spotted outside Una Dermody's home and the house was surrounded by dozens of Special Task Force detectives. Dermody's car was missing, she was gone, and the police now knew the car in which the gunmen were most likely travelling.

Despite this, Hogan and Toal had an untroubled three-hour drive from Dublin to Limerick. Eddie Hogan talked about how lovely the trees were, changing with the season. He talked about how he liked art and said he had done some oil paintings. They arrived in Limerick at around 6pm and Hogan directed Una Dermody to drive the car to a secluded spot and up a laneway. The two gunmen got out and began walking back in the direction they had come. Dermody turned the car and drove back down the lane, passing Hogan and Toal. The gunmen waved her goodbye.

. . . . .

Up in Dublin, doctors were attempting to clean up the gunmen's mess. John O'Grady had been taken to the Blackrock Clinic, Detective Martin O'Connor to the casualty department of St Laurence's Hospital. The damage had been done to O'Grady. His two fingers were gone, but the worst was over. He was put under general anaesthetic and the stumps of his fingers were trimmed back and sutured. He was given intravenous antibiotics and the wounds were dressed.

At St Laurence's, doctors quickly assessed Detective O'Connor, decided his shoulder wounds were not life threatening but the wound in his abdomen was a dangerous mess. It looked for a while like his circulatory system was about to collapse, so transfusion lines were set up. He was whisked into the operating theatre and doctors found a hole in his stomach the size of a fist, with a section of his bowel hanging out. Gunshot and wadding from the shotgun cartridge were found in the wound and removed. The small bowel had been severely damaged in five places and had to be resectioned. Countless shotgun pellets had penetrated into the detective's stomach and each had to be removed individually.

. . . . .

At the Bridewell, Gerry Wright was telling lies. He needed to limit his involvement in the kidnap, so he left out the part about the basement of his barber shop being used to hold O'Grady and pretended that it was less than a week earlier that he had been drawn into the kidnap.

'Are you a member of the INLA?' he was asked.

'I'm a republican. I'm a sympathiser. I see no difference between the Sticks, Provos or IRSP. They all fight for the one cause. I'm not a member of any organisation but I believe in the cause.'

Later, Wright told the police he was obsessed with the gunman who had killed his brother Billy. He named the gunman. That this man was the killer of Billy Wright was well known in republican circles and well known to the gardaí. A man had come to his shop for a haircut and promised to get his brother's killer. He had given the man, whose name he wasn't sure of, a key to his house, so that his brother's killer could be taken there. He was obsessed with getting his brother's killer, he said.

'You know well he fucking shot my brother Billy, ye did nothing about it. Billy always said the police set him up.'

Gerry Wright's interrogation was just beginning. With John O'Grady free, and in a position to identify the basement where he was held, Wright was sewn up. In the hours and days that followed he fought a losing battle, smoking continuously, denying all but a peripheral involvement in the crime. To demonstrate his separateness from the gunmen he claimed at one point that when he looked into the alcove under the stairs, not knowing John O'Grady was there, he was pistol-whipped by the kidnappers.

'Where are the marks?'

'I have no marks,' he conceded.

'How are you feeling, Gerry?'

'I'm fucked.'

Wright asked how the detective was who was shot. A detective said he'd heard on the radio that Martin O'Connor was stable.

'Thank God he's still alive,' said Wright. 'I hope he'll be OK. I walked him into it.'

Eventually, Wright conceded that perhaps he'd been involved in the kidnap for more than a few days.

'I didn't buy any food or look after these men in any way. I don't know where they got their food.'

Eventually, talking about how he led Sergeant Spring and Detective O'Connor into Carnlough Road: 'I should have told them.'

'Who?'

'The guards, I should have told them. God, why didn't I? I knew O'Grady was there. On the way, I knew I was in trouble. I didn't know what to fucking do, believe me. I hope the guard is all right. I did what I could do for him when he was shot. I opened the back door for the other guard.'

'Would you know the gunman again?'

Wright wasn't going down that road.

'Listen, my brother was shot. I don't want to be, and I won't.'

· · · · ·

Eddie Hogan and Fergal Toal decided to abandon their guns. By now, Una Dermody and Maria Hennessy would have alerted the police that the two gunmen were in Limerick and two men moving around with a couple of guns wrapped in an overcoat were going to attract attention.

Hogan and Toal crossed a graveyard and walked along a railway line to a station. Somewhere along the way they dumped their weapons. About an hour had passed since they released the two women.

They got into a taxi at the railway station and told the driver, Denny Mulqueen, that they had missed their train to Tipperary. How much would the fare be?

'It's a long distance, it must be twenty miles. I suppose I'd charge £20.'

'OK,' said Eddie Hogan, and climbed into the front passenger seat.

Fergal Toal got into the back. His sister had a house in Tipperary, Hogan said, and they were going to stay with her.

There were police checkpoints all over the place. By the time they got to the first one, Denny Mulqueen had missed his turn for the Tipperary road. He got directions from a garda at the checkpoint. They passed through another three checkpoints safely. Hogan and Toal seemed relaxed and didn't show any sign of the pressure they were under. Again and again they were waved through. Hogan wondered aloud why there were so many gardaí disrupting traffic. At one checkpoint Hogan was asked for identification and he said he was Terry O'Sullivan and produced a driver's licence in that name.

At 8.15pm they reached Tipperary town safely. There was one last garda checkpoint.

· · · · ·

'Terence O'Sullivan,' Eddie Hogan said, handing over the fake driving licence.

The garda noted the Cork accent. Hogan explained he was visiting a friend, a friend who worked in a bottling plant. The garda was somewhat suspicious. Not enough for an arrest, but there was something that didn't look right. The man in the back was asked his name and he didn't reply.

'Have you any identification?'

'I might have some.'

The man was reaching down around his knees, as if searching for something.

There should have been an armed garda on the checkpoint, but arrangements to bring in an off-duty garda with experience in the use of an Uzi submachine gun hadn't worked out. The unarmed garda on the checkpoint decided to let the taxi go, not to arouse suspicion. He and a colleague would follow it in the next civilian car to arrive at the checkpoint. He waved the taxi through. As he did so, a garda patrol car with three members inside arrived to relieve the gardaí on the checkpoint. The garda explained his suspicions and the patrol car began following the taxi. The garda in the back of the car was in civilian clothes and had an Uzi submachine gun.

The driver of the patrol car radioed the station and asked that they check a taxi with registration 889 KPI. The patrol car passed other traffic until it was tucked in behind the taxi. The gardaí decided to wait until they reached a lit-up part of town. In the back of the patrol car Garda Liam Walsh took his Uzi out of its case and loaded it. When the taxi stopped at traffic lights in Main Street the patrol car pulled up alongside and the two uniformed police jumped out and approached it. The garda with the Uzi waited.

Eddie Hogan again introduced himself as Terry O'Sullivan. Fergal Toal was mumbling. A garda opened the right back door of the taxi and again asked Toal his name.

'Sean Murphy,' he said, 'from Cobh.'

The garda opened the back door of the patrol car, directly across from the open door of the taxi, and revealed the plain-clothes garda sitting there with an Uzi.

'Do you know anyone in Cobh?'

Toal didn't reply. The garda with the Uzi asked Toal if he knew where the cathedral was in Cobh.

'Up the hill, in the centre of town,' said Toal.

His attempt at a Cork accent wasn't very good, and his northern accent was coming through. Both men were taken out of the taxi and searched. They didn't match the description the gardaí had been given, and the fact that they weren't armed seemed to exclude them. But Toal's effort at a Cork accent was sufficient for the gardaí to decide to take them in, to check their identities. Hogan and Toal were cooperative. The three gardaí put the two suspects into the police car. They told taxi driver Denny Mulqueen to follow them to the local garda station.

It was now about 8.30pm. The area around the station was packed with parked cars. The nearest parking space the gardaí could get was about forty feet away from the station entrance. They took the two men out, neither suspect handcuffed, and walked them towards the station entrance. Just before they got to the gate Eddie Hogan suddenly bolted, just ran away, taking the gardaí by surprise. One garda ran after him, the other two grabbed Toal and hustled him into the station.

The garda running after Hogan found his garda cap a hindrance and threw it away. Hogan approached Clanwilliam rugby grounds. The garda shouted at two youths at the entrance to the grounds to stop the fugitive. The two looked blankly as Hogan shot past, the garda about six yards behind.

Meanwhile, the two gardaí with Fergal Toal hustled him into Tipperary garda station. On reaching the day room they were in haste to join the chase for the escaped prisoner.

'Hold him, hold him,' they instructed the three gardaí inside.

'There's another fella gone away!'

They then left Toal and hurried back out of the station and dived into their patrol car, to go in search of Eddie Hogan.

The gardaí in the day room had no idea who Toal was. One got the impression that he was some kind of mental patient.

'I'm on tablets,' Toal said. 'I want a glass of water, I have a pain in my stomach.' He was still using his version of a Cork accent.

'Hold on. When I search you I'll give you water.'

Eddie Hogan, running through Clanwilliam rugby grounds, pulled some maps out from under his jumper and threw them away, in an effort to distract the garda chasing him. The garda ignored them and kept after the fugitive. Hogan ran across the rugby pitch, where the Clanwilliam team was training. He ran along the end line, off the field and around the pavilion. He got over a six-foot high wall and although the garda followed he lost Hogan in the darkness.

The other two gardaí arrived, but Hogan was nowhere to be seen. Heavy fog was falling, which didn't help. The gardaí sought help from the Clanwilliam rugby team, about ten of whom were training at the grounds, and they joined in the search for Hogan. He was well away.

Inside the garda station the other gardaí had no idea who it was they were holding, or why.

'What's your name?'

'Murphy, from Cobh.'

Fergal Toal was told to take off his jacket. The garda took Toal's tie. Prisoners can't be allowed to keep items of clothing, ties and belts and the like, with which they can damage themselves. Particularly prisoners who may be mental patients. The garda spotted a bulge in Toal's trousers pocket. He reached in and took out a roll of money, over £200.

'What are you doing with my money?' Toal asked.

'You'll get it back when you leave the station.'

The garda had the money in his left hand and was removing Toal's belt with his right. The buckle caught in the final loop. The garda turned to put the money down on a table so that he could free the belt. In the second that the garda's attention was distracted, Toal made a run for it. The three gardaí ran after him but the corridor down which he ran was narrow, so they had to jostle into single file.

One garda was an arm's reach behind Toal and grabbed the gunman's shirt just below the collar. The shirt ripped down the back, a six-inch strip tearing free from collar to hem, and the garda lost his balance and fell against the wall of the corridor, grazing his knuckles. In the narrow corridor, the two gardaí following took precious extra seconds to get past the first garda. Toal jumped down the seven steps leading to the front door, ran out of the station and disappeared into the distance, the two halves of his shirt hanging off his shoulders, his back naked. He had been in the station for less than a minute.

Arriving at the garda station, as instructed, taxi driver Denny Mulqueen watched as his erstwhile passenger came running out of the garda station and off down the street.

Toal ran down Davis Street and through the town. He came to traffic lights which had just turned green and the cars were moving off. A beige Granada with two men in the front was moving out from the kerb and about to pass through the lights and Toal ran to the car, waving frantically. The driver, twenty-six-year-old Michael McCarthy, a farmer, thought this was someone needing medical help. He stopped the car. Toal opened the back door and dived into the car, slouching down out of sight.

'Keep going, the cops are after me,' he said. He had dropped his Cork accent.

Michael McCarthy immediately made the connection between this fugitive and the kidnappers. It had been all over the radio, the shoot-out in Dublin, the escape. He didn't know if Toal was armed, but he decided cooperation was the best course of action. He drove on.

His friend Timmy Ryan turned around in the front passenger seat and said, 'Who are you? Where are you going?'

'Get me out to the country,' Toal said. 'I'll pay you.'

Michael McCarthy was beginning to wonder if he'd made the right choice. Once they got out into the countryside this guy mightn't get out of the car. And outside the town, away from witnesses, who knew what might happen? Instead of heading out into open country, he turned into a street that would keep him within the town. He was heading towards the Old Monastery Road when he decided to make his move. He stopped the car and turned to Toal.

'Hey boy, this is as far as I'm going.'

Toal opened the back door and got out. He asked for a jacket or a jumper. McCarthy said he didn't have either.

Toal began running away. He turned and called back to McCarthy and Ryan: 'If you say anything about this you're in trouble.'

Michael McCarthy watched the man running away, his torn white shirt flapping from his shoulders.

· · · · ·

Catherine Ryan and Charles Barrett were saying goodbye to their friends in Ballinard, Co. Tipperary, about then. Catherine was from Tipperary town, Charles was from Buttevant, and they had spent the evening together, having a meal and then dropping off to see the friends in Ballinard. They then drove to Shaughnessy's lounge in Kilfinane for a drink. At around 10.30pm Catherine drove Charles home to Buttevant, stayed for about twenty minutes and then began the drive home to Tipperary.

Just before RTE Radio 1 went off the air at 11.50pm there was a news bulletin. The shoot-out in Cabra and the hunt for the kidnappers was big news. The bulletin said that the hunt was now centred around Tipperary town. Listening to this on her car radio, Catherine Ryan was a bit nervous. Thick fog had fallen and driving in such circumstances was unpleasant. She stopped at Ardpatrick and found a phone box and rang Charles Barrett in Buttevant and told him about the news report. He told her not to worry, everything would be OK. He said she should phone him as soon as she got home to Tipperary town and let him know she was all right. She said she would.

Radio 1 had closed down, so when she got back into the car Catherine switched over to Radio 2 and there was another news bulletin at midnight, with the same information about a hunt for the kidnappers in Tipperary.

About three miles from Tipperary town, where the road cut through a grove of trees, Catherine stopped the car suddenly. There was the long branch of a tree lying across the road. She got out and moved the branch on to the grass margin. There was a rustle of leaves and Fergal Toal came up over the ditch. Catherine turned and ran back to the car. She made it, slammed the door and reached to push down the lock button as the door was jerked open.

'Don't be afraid. I won't harm you if you do as I say and don't try anything smart.'

Fergal Toal had found a round-necked white jumper somewhere to replace his tattered shirt. He stood on the road, holding the door open, leaning into the car.

'You know who I am, you must know about the shoot-out today. I have to get out of here, my life depends on it.'

He told her he would drive. He grabbed her by the arm.

'Move over, Missus,' he said, and got into the car. He tried the gears, getting the feel of the car, then did a U-turn and drove back towards Kilross.

'Where did you come from?' he asked.

'Kilfinane.'

'If we drive back that way where will it take us?'

'Limerick or Mallow.'

'No.' They'd have to stay off the main roads, he said. 'I haven't a clue where I am.'

Catherine asked where he wanted to go. Toal said Dublin.

'It'll be difficult to get from here to Dublin by backroads,' Catherine said.

'We'll get there, and you're going to help me.'

Catherine decided that she should cooperate with the fugitive. If she cooperated, she believed, no harm would come to her. She took a road map from the open shelf at the front of the car and Toal stopped the car, turned on the internal light and the two spent several minutes choosing a route.

They set off again, through the villages of Emly, Hospital, Herbertstown and Caherconlish. It was now around 1am. Toal asked her to turn on the radio for the news and they listened to an account of Toal and Hogan's escape.

Catherine asked him was it true, about running out of the garda station.

'They tore the bloody shirt off my back,' he complained. 'My mate ran away out of the garda car and I haven't seen him since.' He said he'd been running through fields until he stopped her car. The two drove along in silence. Finally Toal asked her name.

'Catherine Ryan.'

'Do you live in Tipperary town?'

'Yes.'

'Are you working there?'

'I work at the hospital in Cashel.'

'What do you do?'

'I'm a nurse.'

Pause.

Still driving, Toal leaned across, holding out his right hand. 'I've a cut on my little finger.'

Catherine looked at it. There seemed to be a bit of skin missing off the knuckle. She said that it looked all right.

'I've a pain in the lower right side of my chest,' said Toal, intent on taking advantage of some free medical advice. 'What do you think of that?'

'Maybe you fell and hit yourself.'

They drove in silence a bit more.

'Are you married?' he asked.

'No.'

They were just turning on to the main Tipperary-Limerick road and as they did so they saw an army truck parked down the road.

'We have to get off this road fast,' Toal said.

Fearful that the fugitive might think she had tricked him into getting on to a main road, Catherine said that wasn't the turn they were supposed to take.

'That's all right,' Toal said. They passed a road sign for Thurles. Toal decided they'd have to avoid the town, but he didn't know what direction to take. They drove aimlessly around backroads. They turned a bend and through the fog they could see three gardaí manning a checkpoint.

· · · · ·

When Catherine Ryan didn't ring Charles Barrett that night he became worried. Unlikely as it might seem, perhaps something might have happened to her, perhaps she had stumbled into something. He rang the police, who checked her address at Lacey Villas, Tipperary, and found she wasn't home. It was possible that she was delayed by the fog, the gardaí considered.

At the garda checkpoint, Fergal Toal slowed down and prepared to speak to the gardaí. He hurriedly asked, for the second time, 'What's your name?' Catherine Ryan told him. Toal stopped the car and rolled down the window. A garda approached the car.

'Goodnight, guard,' Toal said.

'What's your name?'

'Peter Ryan.'

'Where are you from?'

'Thurles.'

'Please turn off your engine.'

'I will, certainly,' said Toal, accelerating away through the check-point. As the car surged away he switched off the headlights, disappearing into the fog and the darkness.

· · · · ·

Gardaí were setting up checkpoints here and there throughout County Tipperary. At 2.50am a radio message was sent out that a car had broken through a checkpoint at Dolla, near Nenagh. It was a grey Toyota Starlet 596 ZHI. And there was a possibility that this was a hijacked car owned by a lady. The hijackers could be expected to be armed. A number of patrol cars were asked to try to intercept this car, which appeared to be heading for Nenagh.

At a checkpoint on the Roscrea road, near Templemore, three gardaí heard the message and got into their patrol car and set off towards Nenagh, via Borrisoleigh. Garda Eamon McCarthy was driving, Detective Garda James Hession was in the passenger seat, and Garda Pat Phelan was in the back seat. Hession was armed with a Smith and Wesson .38; Phelan had an Uzi submachine gun.

About three-quarters of a mile from Borrisoleigh they came upon a car parked at a crossroads, a Toyota Starlet, 596 ZHI. The internal light was on in the car and the gardaí could see a man and a woman inside.

Fergal Toal and Catherine Ryan had stopped to try to figure out from the map where the hell they were. Toal had been driving sometimes with the headlights on, sometimes with them off, taking random turns, getting agitated and ending up he knew not where. Now, as the garda car pulled up fifteen yards behind him, he said, 'They have me.' He started the car and sped away into the fog.

'Maybe it's not the guards,' Catherine Ryan said.

'It is! It is!' Toal put his foot down and the car roared through the village of Borrisoleigh. Toal switched off his headlights as he left the village, ploughing into the fog, heading towards Nenagh. He switched the lights on again and then off again shortly afterwards.

'Slow down or we're going to crash!' Catherine Ryan called.

Toal ignored her.

In the darkness, speeding, Toal didn't see a leftward bend in the road and the right wheel of the car went into a ditch; and after the car had travelled for about twenty-five yards half in and half out of the ditch the right wheel hit a shore in the ditch and the car was sent flying into the air, turning over and landing upside down, and skidding sixty more yards along the road on its roof.

The patrol car stopped twenty yards behind the Toyota, its headlights lighting up the crashed car. The three gardaí jumped out and took cover behind their car. Detective Hession shouted that they were gardaí. There was movement inside the car. Detective Hession fired a shot in the air, to let the fugitive know the gardaí were armed. Garda Phelan fired a burst of about a dozen shots from his Uzi into the air.

Garda McCarthy had taken a walkie-talkie with him from the patrol car and he was now urgently calling for support.

Inside the car Fergal Toal ceased moving and shouted, 'Stop shooting! I have a female hostage!'

'How many of you are in the car?'

'Two.'

'Are you sure there aren't three?'

'There's the woman and myself. Keep back or I'll kill her.'

Toal and Catherine Ryan were hanging upside down, held in by their seat-belts.

'Can you open the door on your side?' Toal asked. Catherine tried, but couldn't.

Toal used his legs to push open the door on his side and said to Catherine, 'Come on.'

'No.'

'Come on, come on, they won't shoot.'

He pulled her by the arms, she opened her safety belt and he pulled her free.

From a distance the gardaí could see that Catherine Ryan was distressed. Garda Phelan said he was going to work his way around behind the car. Detective Hession nodded. As Phelan slipped away Hession fired a shot in the air, to distract the fugitive.

'I'm taking the girl out of the car,' Toal shouted. He guided her out and held her down behind the overturned car.

'Give yourself up,' Detective Hession called. 'Let her go and nobody will get hurt.'

Crouched behind the car, Toal assessed his chances. The police couldn't know whether he was armed; they didn't seem to know much of anything. They might even think that Eddie Hogan was in the car, with a weapon. They wouldn't want to risk the woman's life. Once beyond the blazing lights from the patrol car, Toal would be into darkness and fog and another chance to head off through the fields. Toal pushed Catherine into a standing position, put one arm around her neck and the other around her body, and edged her out into the middle of the road, into the glare of the patrol car headlights. He began walking backwards, keeping his hostage between him and the police.

'Back off. I'm telling you, I'll fucking kill her! I'm telling you, I'll fucking kill her!'

Behind Toal, Garda Phelan came out of the darkness, moving slowly forward as Toal moved slowly backwards. Phelan put the muzzle of the Uzi against Toal's back and said, 'Let her go and nobody will get hurt.'

'OK, OK,' Toal said. He released Catherine and she stumbled forward, almost collapsing. Garda Eamon McCarthy ran forward to assist her. Toal was handcuffed and placed face down across the bonnet of the patrol car.

· · · · ·

About fifteen hours later, someone reported a suspicious-looking man walking on a road at Ballydrehid, close to Cahir, Co. Tipperary.

Two gardaí, Detective Iggy Seery and Garda Jim Lynch, responded to the call. It was about 5.40pm. Darkness had fallen. Detective Seery was in plain clothes, Garda Lynch was in uniform. The detective was armed with a .38 revolver. The two gardaí, in an unmarked patrol car, had driven about four miles out of Cahir, on the Tipperary road, when they rounded a bend and came across a man walking towards them. He was wearing a cardigan and trousers and was carrying a rolled-up newspaper under one arm.

The gardaí drove past the man, stopped and got out of the car.

Detective Seery called, 'Garda Siochána! We want to talk to you!'

Eddie Hogan started running, dropping his newspaper. The gardaí ran after him. Detective Seery drew his revolver as he ran. Garda Lynch was ahead. The detective fired a warning shot into the air. Hogan kept on running, heading for bushes in the ditch on the side of the road and he almost made it. Garda Lynch brought him down and Detective Seery came running over, keeping his revolver pointed straight up, for safety sake. Garda Lynch twisted Hogan's right arm up behind his back.

'OK, you have me,' said Eddie Hogan. 'Mind my arm!'

The two gardaí lifted Hogan up and brought him back towards the patrol car, one arm still up behind his back. The occasional car went by.

As the police and their prisoner reached the patrol car, Eddie Hogan suddenly lashed out, brushing the detective aside, jerking out of the garda's armlock, striking out several times at the garda's head. Garda Lynch held on to Hogan's arm. Hogan kicked the garda on the legs and headbutted him in the chest. Detective Seery knocked Hogan to the ground. Both gardaí also fell to the ground, Garda Lynch losing his grip on Hogan's hand. As all three started to get up, Hogan headbutted the detective and grabbed the garda's shirt and tie and began twisting, turning and kicking with ferocity in an attempt to wrest himself free.

The three rolled on the ground, Detective Seery's head smacking off the road. The detective rolled over on top of Hogan, still trying to keep his revolver pointed up into the air. Hogan was reaching for the gun.

Detective Seery held his right arm outstretched, trying to keep the gun as far as possible from Hogan's grasp. Hogan gripped the detective's right forearm and began pulling it towards him.

'Look out, Jim,' Seery called, 'he's trying to get the gun!'

The gun was now between Seery and Hogan's faces, inches away from both. Hogan jerked his head up and tried to bite the detective's gun arm. The detective strained to push the gun away. The gun went off, twice. The bullets flew away harmlessly.

Seery wrenched his gun arm free. He was on top of Hogan, who was still struggling furiously. The detective had ended up almost astride Hogan's face. Hogan sank his teeth into Detective Seery's crotch. The teeth cut through the detective's trousers and into his flesh, at his upper right thigh. The detective screamed.

Garda Lynch had pulled himself free and was rising to his feet when Hogan lashed out with his feet, catching the garda in the chest, knocking him to the ground. Hogan was reaching for the gun again, his teeth still sunk into the detective's thigh, his head giving a violent jerk, causing the detective excruciating pain. Hogan grasped the detective's gun hand. Garda Lynch came up off the ground and grabbed Hogan's hand, tearing it free. Seery smacked the butt of his revolver off Hogan's head. The shock of the blow caused Hogan to release his bite on the detective. Seery scrambled to his feet and holstered his gun. Lynch was still rolling on the ground with Hogan, the two exchanging violent punches. Seery dropped on to Hogan. The gardaí managed to get Hogan face down and handcuffed his hands behind his back. Hogan stopped struggling.

Detective Seery told Hogan he was being arrested under Section 30 of the Offences Against the State Act. Garda Lynch went to the patrol car and radioed for backup. The two gardaí kept Hogan face down on the wet road. They decided they wouldn't chance taking him up to put him into the police car until some support arrived.

· · · · ·

Neither Toal nor Hogan were over-cooperative with the police. Eamon Ó Hogáin, said Eddie Hogan when asked his name at Cahir garda station. Hogan was searched and was found to have £290 in cash. Two doctors were brought to the station to check his health. He asked for a cigarette and a cup of tea. Garda Jim Lynch, who had been rolling around on the ground with Hogan, swapping vicious punches, went to the station kitchen and made a cup of tea. As he did so he noticed the buttons missing from his tunic, lost in the struggle.

Later, when Hogan was brought a meal of chicken and chips, Garda Lynch cut up the chicken for the handcuffed prisoner. 'Where have you been?' the garda asked. Where had he eaten last?

'In the hills and glens of Ireland,' said Hogan. 'I was only on the road for a hundred yards,' Hogan mused, 'and if I'd stayed off it I'd never be caught.'

Later, Garda Lynch made more tea for Hogan and he and another garda cleaned Hogan's face, which was cut and puffed.

Hogan said to Lynch that his face was all right. 'Don't worry about it,' he said, 'I won't be making any allegations. It was either me or ye out on that road.'

A garda asked him what was the difference between the IRA and the INLA.

'The INLA has a different emphasis,' Hogan replied.

The garda asked why different parts of the INLA were killing each other.

'There's a war on.'

What did he think about the cutting off of John O'Grady's fingers, and the shooting of Detective Martin O'Connor?

'Everything is justified when there's a war on.'

Was he involved with cutting off O'Grady's fingers?

'No comment.'

Did he ever shoot at a garda?

No reply.

The gardaí hadn't shot at him, a garda remarked.

'Ye didn't, fuck,' said Hogan. 'The gun went off four or five times,' referring to the two shots fired during the struggle out on the road.

'Where did this happen?'

'Forget about it.'

Meanwhile, across in Thurles garda station, Fergal Toal had tried to pass himself off as 'Jim McKerr', from Monaghan. It was a hopeless attempt at deceit. What was he doing in the Tipperary area?

'Socialising,' he said. He wouldn't account for his movements. 'I don't want to be ignorant but I won't say anything until I see my solicitor.' He was fingerprinted but refused to sign the fingerprint form. ('Och, I'll not bother.')

'Do you know Dessie O'Hare?'

'Yes.'

'Is he as dangerous as he's supposed to be?'

'Yes, I don't think he'll be taken alive.'

Eddie Hogan was taken to the Bridewell in Dublin in the small hours of the morning and his interrogation continued after he had got some rest. Sergeant Henry Spring, who had gone to 260 Carnlough with Detective O'Connor and who had been kicked and beaten by the gang, recognised Fergal Toal in a line-up but could not identify Eddie Hogan.

Later, Hogan remarked, 'Sure, yer man will know me.'

Who was that?

'That fellow that was shot.'

'Did you shoot the detective?'

'I'll say no more.'

Hogan gave a garda £40 and asked him to buy an anorak and a pair of underpants. What colour would he like the anorak? the garda asked. Any colour except green or black, Hogan said. It wasn't that Hogan wanted to make a fashion statement. He was already preparing for the next phase of his life. In Portlaoise prison, he explained, they don't allow dark jackets, because the prison guards wear dark blue. And it couldn't be green because Portlaoise is guarded by the army and that was the colour of the army uniforms. The garda went out and bought the clothing and brought Hogan back £13.12p change.

• • • • •

Five days after the arrest of Eddie Hogan, at 10.20 on the morning of Wednesday 11 November 1987, over a dozen armed gardaí arrived at 16 Le Fanu Drive, Ballyfermot, with a search warrant. Two gardaí went to the front door and knocked. There was no response.

Inside, Tony McNeill was fast asleep on a couch. He had been on the run and hadn't slept properly in almost a week, since the shoot-out at Carnlough Road. He was prepared for death, having written his goodbyes on a long strip of paper headed: 'To my loved ones and especially my Mammy'. On the reverse side of the paper he had written a poem, 'A Bright Star', for his three-year-old son Piaras. The piece of paper was in a pocket of his blue nylon jacket, hanging on an arm of the couch. In another pocket of the jacket there was a British Bulldog revolver loaded with four bullets.

The gardaí knocked again, twice. No response. Other gardaí now joined the two at the front door. At which point Detective Sergeant Michael Carolan kicked in the door and the gardaí went in fast, fanning out through the small house, some charging upstairs, some inside.

Detective Garda Thomas Costello, wielding an Uzi submachine gun, was first into the kitchen-cum-living room, where he saw a man lying on a couch, covered by a blanket.

'Gardaí!' Costello shouted.

Tony McNeill stirred.

'Stand up and put your hands over your head.'

McNeill looked up into the muzzle of the Uzi. Detective Inspector John McLoughlin was also crowded into the small room, pointing his handgun at McNeill. McNeill had thought about this moment and considered that he might raise his gun at the police, forcing them to shoot him dead. Better that than spend endless years in jail. Now that it had happened and they were here, the gun was out of reach.

The police found the revolver in McNeill's jacket. They searched the house, and up into the attic, in case anyone else was hiding.

'What's your name?' Detective Costello asked McNeill.

'Anthony Connolly,' McNeill said.

A garda held up the jacket with the revolver in it.

'Is this the only jacket you have?'

'Yes.'

The garda took out the revolver.

'That jacket isn't mine,' said McNeill.

McNeill cooperated with the police and went calmly, in handcuffs, to Ballyfermot garda station. He was perhaps still hoping — a ridiculous hope — that his false name would work wonders. At the station, after he was told that they knew he was McNeill, as handcuffs were being removed, he made an attempt to escape, although surrounded by five gardaí. He struggled in a last frantic bid for freedom or a panic welling up from the knowledge that he was going to prison for a long time. One garda held him by the neck, one by the leg, the others by whatever bits they could grab. A sixth had to join the affray before McNeill could be subdued and taken to a cell.

· · · · ·

They eventually got McNeill talking. He wouldn't implicate anyone else ('I don't want to get into specific things, I'll have to live in Portlaoise with these fellas') but he knew that as far as he was concerned the game was up. Now the job was damage limitation.

'I wasn't in Cabra,' he said. 'I had nothing to do with his fingers being cut off. You know the position I'm in.' He added, 'I wish I was dead. I suppose I'll not see the light of day again.'

He told the police that Clare O'Hare had not been at the house at 260 Carnlough.

McNeill said he wanted his mother and his family to know that he'd nothing to do with cutting off O'Grady's fingers.

'I was present when it was discussed and I was totally against it and when it happened I prayed for Dr O'Grady.'

McNeill seemed emotional, close to tears, and insistent that no one should think that he cut off John O'Grady's fingers.

A new garda came into the interrogation room. 'How are you doing?' he asked.

'Boys, I wish it never happened,' McNeill said. 'I expect to get two life sentences for this.' Later he said, 'I know I'll get twenty-five years.'

'Was it you cut off O'Grady's fingers?'

'No.' He seemed anxious. 'I hope people don't think I cut off his fingers.'

'Did you see Dessie cut off his fingers?'

'No, but when he gets wired up nobody can stop him.'

'How did you get entangled with Dessie O'Hare?'

'I thought he was a socialist, but now I know he's one dastardly bastard. I wish you'd shot me this morning.'

'What do you expect when you go on a job like that?'

'You take your chances.'

Later. 'You must have discussed cutting off O'Grady's fingers?'

'No. Dessie knows my politics. I knew something was going to happen, but I didn't know what.'

'Did you try to stop them?'

'No, I told you before how Dessie is all wired up, he acts like he's in Vietnam.'

'Well, what did you do?'

'If I was there I would have tended to O'Grady.'

'No ifs. Did you tend to O'Grady?'

'Ask O'Grady.'

The gardaí were taking all this down. When they read it back they asked McNeill if he wanted anything changed.

Just one thing, said McNeill. Could they change 'twenty-five years' to 'a long time'? He said, 'I don't want to give the judges any ideas.'

· · · · ·

Two days later John O'Grady began the unpleasant task of returning to the scenes of his incarceration, to help gardaí prepare a case against the kidnappers. He went to the basement underneath the barber shop in Parkgate Street and pointed out things he remembered. Likewise the container in Cork and Gerry Wright's house in Cabra. O'Grady had retained a remarkable amount of precise memories of his ordeal, consciously accumulating detail despite his knowledge that at any time something might go wrong and the gang would kill him. On dates in November and into December he methodically went through the garda evidence, identifying material that would help put his kidnappers away.

· · · · ·

Three weeks after the arrest of Tony McNeill, a strong force of armed police took cover at an area known as Minister's Cross, near Urlingford, Kilkenny. They were joined by a platoon of soldiers from Stephen's Barracks, Kilkenny. There were about fifty in all and they set up a roadblock, two police cars and an army Land Rover. They waited, alert and expectant. This was no routine roadblock. They knew Dessie O'Hare was coming.

Little had been heard of O'Hare since his gang had been captured. On the evening of Sunday 8 November, three days after the Carnlough Road shoot-out, Dessie and Clare O'Hare pulled up across the street from L'Orchidea chip shop in Dunleer, Co. Louth, in a Toyota Corolla. It was about 8.30pm. Dessie went into the chip shop. There were several youths in the queue; Enzo and Massimo Tersigni were serving behind the counter. O'Hare looked rough, a nervous wreck. There was stubble on his face, his hair was standing up on his head, he was wearing a dark jumper. There were blonde streaks in his dark hair, perhaps an attempt at disguise. He kept looking out the window, looking back at the counter, moving about. At least two of the youths in the chip shop assumed he was either drunk or on drugs.

O'Hare asked Massimo Tersigni for a can of Coke and a can of Fanta. He then said, 'Cancel the orange.' Massimo put the can of Coke on the counter and O'Hare, glancing out into the street, picked it up.

Outside, across the street, Clare O'Hare was getting out of the Toyota and hurrying away.

Dessie threw the can of Coke on the floor, yanked up his jumper and pulled a pistol out of his waistband. He pushed his way through the other customers and ran out of the shop in apparent rage. Holding the handgun in both hands, he fired a shot in Clare's direction. 'Stop, you bitch!' he screamed. 'Get back into the car!'

Clare kept running.

Dessie ran across the street and pulled a shotgun out of the car. He fired twice more in Clare's direction, then turned and fired at L'Orchidea, blasting the glass in the front of the shop. Customers scattered and hid behind the counter.

The owner of the Railway bar, Gerry Duffy, thinking there were bangers left over from Hallowe'en going off, opened the front door of his pub. He saw a man standing across the road, shotgun in hand. The man turned and looked at him. Duffy closed the door and ran to the phone and dialled 999. He then ran behind the bar and sought out his copy of that day's *Sunday Tribune* and checked the photograph. Yes, he told himself, it was Dessie O'Hare.

Outside on the street two people were passing.

'Get the fuck out of the way,' screamed O'Hare, 'or you'll get the same.'

O'Hare got into his car and drove after Clare. She was thirty yards up the road, at a pub called the Mill Race. She ran inside.

The owner of the Mill Race, Desmond Connor, didn't notice Clare O'Hare come in, but he had heard the commotion out in the street. He went to the door of the bar and looked out. Dessie O'Hare's car skidded to a stop on the wrong side of the street.

'Get the fucker out!' O'Hare roared.

Connor hadn't a clue what this was about. 'What?' he asked.

He saw O'Hare raise a shotgun from the car's passenger seat and point it at the pub. The gun went off. Connor felt the breeze of the shot pass him and heard the glass partition behind him shattering.

Connor ran back into the pub and shouted to his customers to get down, get out, head for the exit doors at the back of the pub. A second shot blew a hole in the window. Glass scattered over tables and chairs. Dessie O'Hare drove off.

When the police arrived Clare O'Hare was shaking, swaying and crying, apparently shocked. Her right thigh had been cut by glass. She was taken to the casualty department of Our Lady of Lourdes Hospital, where she was given a sedative and her minor wounds were treated. She couldn't be X-rayed as she was several weeks pregnant. When she was allowed leave the hospital a garda arrested her in the car park, under Section 30 of the Offences Against the State Act. She was taken into custody, where she was questioned. The gardaí claimed they wanted to talk to her about unlawful possession of firearms during an armed robbery.

'I never robbed anybody or ever had any guns,' she answered.

Was her daughter in the car with Dessie O'Hare? the gardaí asked. They needed to know, in the event of a show-down with O'Hare, if his child was in the line of fire. Clare O'Hare shook her head. No, she said, her daughter hadn't been with them. She said Dessie had come for her and tried to persuade her to come away with him. They had slept rough, in a cowshed.

'He tried to kill me,' she said. 'He doesn't care about man, woman or child, he will keep killing, he's gone mad now since things went wrong.'

Do you mean the O'Grady kidnap?

'Yes,' she said, 'he's gone crazy since that. He had me running across fields, carrying a heavy case, and he kicked me when I couldn't keep up.'

She said that Dessie had found out she had been seeing another man and was going to kill her and the man.

Some gardaí saw the whole event as a production, a PR job. They believed Clare O'Hare was part of the gang that held O'Grady. They told her that.

'He will kill me,' she cried, 'he will kill me.'

They showed her an album of photographs of the inside of 260 Carnlough Road. She was asked if she had ever been in that house. She studied the photographs closely and said no, she had never been there.

'I was never in a house in Dublin,' she said.

The police had established that her fingerprints were on doors and on various objects at 260 Carnlough. She was charged with falsely imprisoning John O'Grady at 260 Carnlough Road at a date unknown between 25 October and 6 November.

· · · · ·

During the kidnap, Dessie O'Hare had occasional support and cover from INLA sympathisers, but at its height the core activists of his Irish Revolutionary Brigade numbered less than a dozen, perhaps half that. Now, with the nucleus of his gang locked up and with the details of the O'Grady mutilation known, support was even weaker. The government offered a reward of £100,000 for information leading to O'Hare's arrest.

Someone gave the police a lot of information. It was known that O'Hare would be travelling through County Kilkenny, on the road between Freshford and Urlingford, that he would be travelling on the morning of 27 November 1987, and that he would be in a light green BMW, licence plate 220 EID.

Thirty-two troops arrived at Minister's Cross at 12.20pm. Two garda cars and an army Land Rover were parked across the road, with the gardaí and soldiers taking up positions behind the cars and to each side of the road. A garda car and three armed police took up a hidden position 400 yards down the road, with instructions to block off the road once they saw the green BMW pass through.

Some time after 1pm local people were told to stay inside their houses for the next half hour or so. No cars travelling towards the direction from which O'Hare was expected were allowed through the roadblock.

At 1.30pm a garda superintendent informed the army that the car would be along in about fifteen or twenty minutes. O'Hare's progress towards Minister's Cross was being carefully monitored. At 1.35pm word was passed from garda to soldier to garda: 'It's on.'

Ninety yards in front of the roadblock Garda Inspector Pat Moriarity and Detective Sergeant P.J. O'Rourke set up a checkpoint. They stood in plain view, everyone else was out of sight. Behind a wall on the far side of the road from Inspector Moriarity an army sergeant with an FN rifle prepared to give the two gardaí cover. There were other soldiers in nearby fields. Inspector Moriarity was in uniform, unarmed. Sergeant O'Rourke had a Smith and Wesson revolver in the pocket of his anorak. The function of the checkpoint was to identify the suspects, establish if they were armed, if they had a hostage, and if they could be arrested without a shoot-out.

The two gardaí stopped each car that came along, cleared it, and ninety yards down the road a garda car would pull back from the roadbock to allow the cleared car to go through.

Eventually, a green BMW came around a bend and swayed slightly, as if the driver momentarily hit the brakes when he saw the checkpoint. Then the car came on. Sergeant O'Rourke could see the registration, 220 EID.

'This is it,' he said to Inspector Moriarity. 'Here we go.'

The BMW, with two men inside, pulled up to the checkpoint and the driver lowered his window. Both men were well dressed. Inspector Moriarity didn't recognise them. He noted that both men were wearing seat-belts.

'How are things?' said the inspector.

Dessie O'Hare, the driver, just nodded. O'Hare was wearing a dark suit, with shirt and tie.

'Where are you coming from?'

'Kilkenny,' O'Hare mumbled, probably seeking to disguise his accent.

Ninety yards away, at the roadblock, a soldier trained his rifle on the BMW and used his telescopic sights to read the registration number. 'That's them,' he told the garda beside him.

Inspector Moriarity bent down further and spoke to the passenger on the other side of the car.

'Who are you?'

Martin Bryan, an INLA veteran suspected of one murder and one attempted murder, just grinned at Moriarity. It was more of a sneer, the inspector thought. Bryan didn't say anything.

'Where are you from?'

Still no reply from Bryan.

'Right, out of the car, get out!' Moriarity told Sergeant O'Rourke to go around the other side of the car and check out the passenger. Dessie O'Hare just sat there.

The army sergeant behind the wall called, 'That's O'Hare, get them out!'

As O'Rourke moved around the car, his hand on the Smith and Wesson in his pocket, he saw the passenger's hand move across his lap as if to undo his seat-belt. Then the hand was coming up from between the seats, clasping a handgun. Bryan pointed the gun across O'Hare and towards Inspector Moriarity. O'Rourke thumbed back the hammer on his Smith and Wesson. The army sergeant cocked his rifle and called, 'Watch out!'

Dessie O'Hare slammed his foot down on the accelerator and the car took off.

The two gardaí threw themselves back. Inspector Moriarity raised an arm in the air, signalling the roadblock.

'Stop them!' he shouted. 'They're armed!'

As the car wheels spun wildly and the BMW surged forward, the army sergeant behind the wall fired a shot into the passenger door, at handle height. He fired again at the front passenger side tyre, then two shots at the rear passenger tyre, bursting it.

From a field, an army corporal fired one shot through the driver's door. A private in a field fired two shots at the car tyres.

There was a pause in the shooting. A soldier at the roadblock, taking cover behind the Land Rover, focused his telescopic sight first on the right front tyre, then on the left, blowing them out.

The car kept coming, all four tyres burst. There was more gunfire, from a garda or a soldier using 9 mm Parabellum ammunition. The bullets struck one of the garda cars in the roadblock. One bullet clipped the blue beacon atop the car and sent it spinning through the air. Another bullet hit a drainpipe on a nearby house and fell down the pipe into a water barrel. It's probable that by now Martin Bryan was dead, another luckless travelling companion of Dessie O'Hare. As the BMW came at speed towards the roadblock, O'Hare crouched down towards the passenger side, possibly seeking cover, probably reaching to pick up Martin Bryan's gun. Two bullets broke the windscreen as they were deflected off it. The BMW rammed into one of the police cars and knocked it sideways, coming to a stop parallel to the police car. There was another burst of gunfire from a garda or soldier, and if Martin Bryan wasn't dead by then he was now.

O'Hare raised Martin Bryan's gun, a Colt semi-automatic, and stuck his hand out the window and fired at the soldiers behind the roadblock.

Inspector Moriarity and Sergeant O'Rourke were running down the road towards the roadblock, crouched over. They took cover behind the police car that the BMW had hit.

O'Hare fired again. A bullet grazed the left calf of Lieutenant Denis Harrington. Soldiers were returning fire now, and gardaí. All told, three dozen bullets hit the car. O'Hare took a bullet in each armpit and lead fragments punctured his right chest. He fired again. And again. His finger tightened on the trigger again and the semi-automatic pistol was in the process of transferring a fifth bullet from the magazine to the breech when O'Hare was hit by a burst of fire. He took wounds in each thigh and a bullet shattered his right forearm and another smashed into the gun in his hand, jamming the slide open. The gun fell from his hand, into the footwell of the car. Lieutenant Harrington gave the ceasefire order and there was silence.

The silence continued for about two minutes, and gardaí considered how to approach the car in safety.

Inspector Moriarity called to O'Hare to throw out his gun, to put both hands on the steering wheel. There was no response. Detective Garda Harry Mulhaire volunteered to approach the BMW.

'Go, but be very careful,' Moriarity told him. Mulhaire moved to within a few feet of O'Hare.

Off to one side, a garda crouching low on the ground, within sight of O'Hare, could see movement inside the car and called out, 'Harry, be careful, he has a piece in his right hand.'

Detective Sergeant O'Rourke moved to the rear of the BMW. He gestured to a garda lying on the ground to cover the passenger side with his Uzi. O'Rourke murmured, 'Keep him talking.'

Inspector Moriarty called repeatedly to O'Hare to put both hands on the steering wheel. O'Hare put his left hand on the wheel.

'Put your hands where we can see them.'

'I can't.'

'Put both hands on the steering wheel.'

'I can't, 'tis busted.'

Detective Sergeant O'Rourke ran forward and put the muzzle of his revolver to the back of Dessie O'Hare's head. Inspector Moriarty crawled alongside the car and reached up and opened the front passenger door. Martin Bryan's body fell halfway out of the car, restrained by his seat-belt. The inspector opened the belt and he and Garda Patrick Hassett laid the body on the ground. Garda Hassett said an Act of Contrition in Martin Bryan's ear.

Asked for his name, O'Hare replied, 'Agh, you know who I am.' Inspector Moriarty arrested him under Section 30 of the Offences Against the State Act, on suspicion of possessing firearms.

As O'Hare waited for an ambulance Detective Harry Mulhaire wet his lips with water from an army canteen.

'Fading . . . I'm fading . . . fading fast,' O'Hare said.

Inspector Moriarty travelled in the ambulance with O'Hare. The inspector had frisked O'Hare and found a pigskin wallet. Inside there was £100, plus fifty in sterling and a 1,000 peseta note. There were three photos of Clare O'Hare and one of John O'Grady holding up his maimed hands.

Back at the roadblock a doctor pronounced Martin Bryan dead and a Father Lambe from Gortnahoe anointed the body.

As the ambulance sped to St Luke's Hospital, Kilkenny, O'Hare remained conscious and complained of the pain. He held the inspector's hand all the way to the hospital. The inspector looked at the gunman's hand, and noticed the expensive Longines gold watch on his wrist.

· · · · ·

Six weeks later Dessie O'Hare was released from hospital and taken to the Bridewell in Dublin. He had had thirteen months' liberty since being released from Portlaoise prison. Fergal Toal had been out for five months. Eddie Hogan had been at liberty for two months.

Detective Garda Martin O'Connor was home with his wife and two children. He had spent six days in intensive care in the Richmond Hospital, and twelve days in a recovery ward. He would suffer six operations to restore his stomach and spend six weeks in the Blackrock Clinic. John O'Grady spent twelve days in the Blackrock Clinic.

When captured, O'Hare had on him several pages of notes, names, guns, transport and the addresses of safe houses. The gardaí now had a very complete picture of the Irish Revolutionary Brigade.

Just before 8pm on the day Dessie O'Hare was released from hospital, Inspector Pat Moriarity went to see him at the Bridewell. He introduced himself as the garda who had arrested him that day at the roadblock. O'Hare smiled and shook hands with the garda. Then, for no apparent reason, O'Hare suddenly stood up and clenched his left fist, a wild look came into his eyes and he began to shudder. Then, he just as abruptly sat down again and smiled. O'Hare didn't say a word.

Half an hour later Dessie O'Hare signed a statement. This is it in its entirety:

> I say that I am presently in custody in the Bridewell Garda Station under S.30 of the Offences Against the State Act, 1939 on suspicion of possession of firearms at Kilkenny in November 1987. I wish to say that I have said nothing to the Gardaí save to ask for a Solicitor. Further I wish to make it clear that I have nothing to say.
> Signed: Dessie O'Hare

Shortly afterwards, when a garda came to photograph him, O'Hare put a hand in front of his face. Gardaí took his hand away and held his head steady for the camera.

Left alone with O'Hare, Inspector Moriarity asked the prisoner why he wasn't talking. O'Hare pointed to the fly of his trousers, then made a zipping motion across his lips. In the days and weeks that followed, a procession of gardaí came to O'Hare to put before him pieces of evidence, to ask him to identify materials. On each and every occasion he remained silent. At one stage two gardaí had a kind of conversation with O'Hare about his injuries. He used sign language to convey his replies.

On the day after he was released from hospital Dessie O'Hare was asked to take part in an identity parade. His solicitor advised against it. O'Hare's face had been in newspapers and on TV for weeks, corrupting the identification process. A witness's memory of a face could be influenced by a newspaper photograph.

The police decided they would go ahead with the identity parade anyway, despite O'Hare's refusal to cooperate. O'Hare was brought to the room where the parade would be held. He took off his jumper and his shirt and sat down. Beneath his vest his wounds could clearly be seen. Ten volunteers, men roughly his age and build, were brought to the room to take part in the parade. They sat at random around the room.

The parade was about to begin. O'Hare stood up, lowered his trousers and turned to face a wall. The ten volunteers were asked to stand up.

Marise O'Grady was shown into the room. She saw eleven men standing. Ten fully-clothed volunteers, and Dessie O'Hare in his vest, shorts and socks, with his trousers down around his ankles, the wounds on his upper body and legs clearly visible. As directed by the gardaí, Marise O'Grady went around the room from right to left, from one man to the next, looking into each face. She came finally and last to Dessie O'Hare. He continued to stare at the wall. Marise O'Grady tipped him on the shoulder and quickly took her hand away.

'This is the gentleman that led the gang of invaders into my home in October.'

. . . . .

Three months later, in April 1988, Fergal Toal was convicted of the murder by stabbing of Sean Hughes at the disco in the Imperial Hotel in Dundalk two days before the O'Grady kidnap. A month after that Toal was back in the Special Criminal Court along with Dessie O'Hare, Eddie Hogan, Tony McNeill and Gerry Wright. The trial was expected to last weeks. Statements were prepared from hundreds of witnesses; elaborate security arrangements were put in place.

At 9.55am that morning two buses brought the accused and their guards to the Special Criminal Court in Green Street, Dublin. Land Rovers full of soldiers came barrelling into Green Street, the soldiers dismounting hurriedly and waving their weapons. A helicopter whirred overhead. It was like old times on a bad day in West Belfast.

The three judges, Liam Hamilton, Gerard Buchanan and Thomas Ballagh, mounted the bench at 11am and the prosecutor, Edward Comyn SC, asked for a short adjournment. Something was stirring. Behind the scenes the various parties were coming to an agreement. The court was to resume at 11.30am but the adjournment was carried on to noon. It was eventually agreed that the accused would plead guilty to a number of charges, and a *nolle prosequi* would be entered on the rest. The accused would have all but the main charges withdrawn. The state would be spared the expense of a massive trial.

When agreement was reached behind the scenes at the Special Criminal Court, and the judges returned to the bench at noon, Gerry Wright and Tony McNeill stood up and acknowledged the court. O'Hare, Toal and Hogan did not.

There was almost a last-minute hitch.

'Not guilty,' said Tony McNeill.

His barrister looked around at McNeill in the dock, surprise on his face, grimaced, looked up at the judges and back to McNeill and silently mouthed, 'Guilty, guilty.'

McNeill muttered, 'Guilty.'

'I want you to be clear,' said Judge Hamilton. 'It's count No. 14.' Falsely imprisoning.

'Guilty,' said McNeill. Judge Hamilton had some questions about the decisions made. For instance, why did the Director of Public Prosecutions enter a *nolle prosequi* when there was evidence that McNeill came out of 260 Carnlough waving a gun, and evidence that he shoved the gun in Detective O'Connor's chest? They're my instructions, said the prosecuting counsel. Hamilton shrugged.

The judge might have asked why McNeill was let off from threatening to kill Patrick Donnelly; why Hogan wasn't charged with another four counts of kidnap, and Toal another five (the hostages they took in their escape after O'Grady got away); why they didn't answer for their murder attempts on the gardaí on Kilkiernan Road;

the murder attempts in Cork; the threats to kill John Hannon; their roles in mutilating John O'Grady; and countless other crimes.

The state answer would be that since the accused were pleading guilty to serious charges, and would be going away for a long time, trying them on similar or lesser charges would not increase the actual time they would spend in prison, and would result in a marathon trial which would cost the state a lot of money.

Dessie O'Hare's lawyer, John Rogers SC, asked for leniency. He said that by pleading guilty, O'Hare had saved the state the great expense of a trial and had saved John O'Grady from the anguish of having to give evidence.

Before sentencing, Dessie O'Hare availed of the right to make an unsworn statement, the traditional republican convict's speech from the dock. It lasted ten minutes, as O'Hare read from typed pages. He took full responsibility for the kidnap, saying that his wife Clare 'was as much a hostage as O'Grady'. Hogan, Toal and McNeill were merely 'carrying out military orders in good faith', while Gerry Wright had been hoodwinked at first and then acted under threat of death.

O'Hare justified the kidnap on the grounds that the intended victim was Austin Darragh, 'a legalised drug peddler for mind-control in the interests of international capitalism'. He said that in Portlaoise prison he and his comrades 'suffered inhuman, degrading and barbaric treatment. If I appear brutal, it is the prison regime that has brutalised me.'

Although the mutilation of John O'Grady occurred eight days after the shooting at the container in Cork, O'Hare linked the two. He also ignored the mess made of the ransom instructions, the closed hotel, the wrong statue, and ascribed the blame for the mutilation to Dr Austin Darragh. 'The loss of O'Grady's fingers was a direct result of murder attempts by the gardaí on our comrades' lives. Were it not for Dr Darragh's selfish intransigence, these incidents would never have occurred.'

The Irish public was guilty of a cowardly and avaricious mentality. The time had come, in O'Hare's opinion, for republican freedom fighters to turn their guns on members of the Irish establishment, judiciary, prison warders, members of the navy, army and police. 'It will always be justifiable and morally right for Irish men and women to slay those who collaborate with British rule.'

O'Hare concluded in poetic style: 'May all my deeds reverberate until bloody war is waged against the Northern British and their Southern allies. Justice for the oppressed of Ireland can only come from the barrel of a gun. Victory to the armed enemies of Britain and especially to the Irish Revolutionary Brigade.'

Throughout this, the three judges of the Special Criminal Court looked up at the man in the dock, the man they were about to sentence, and who was calling for judges, along with sailors and prison warders and gardaí, to be shot.

As O'Hare finished, Eddie Hogan got to his feet. He said he considered it legitimate to attempt to 'prise some of that ill-gotten wealth' from Austin Darragh, 'to help the struggle of the Irish people'. About his act of shooting Detective Martin O'Connor in the stomach from a distance of two feet, Hogan said: 'I didn't intend to murder any member of the gardaí and I wish the injured man a speedy recovery and adequate recompense from the garda compensation fund.'

Detective O'Connor was in court. His expression remained neutral throughout Hogan's speech. While being interrogated by gardaí, soon after his arrest, Eddie Hogan was shown a copy of the *Irish Press*, with the headline: SHOT DETECTIVE STABLE. 'I'm glad of that,' Hogan had remarked. The sentiment wasn't exactly born of compassion. Hogan added: 'I was gone for forty years if he died.'

Dessie O'Hare was sentenced to forty years in prison, twenty for falsely imprisoning and twenty for mutilating John O'Grady. He was twenty-eight and had already spent a quarter of his life in prison. Eddie Hogan got forty years, twenty for falsely imprisoning O'Grady and twenty for the attempted murder of Detective Garda Martin O'Connor. Hogan, aged thirty-three, showed no reaction as he was sentenced. Sitting a few feet away, Detective Martin O'Connor also remained expressionless. Fergal Toal got twenty years for possession of firearms and falsely imprisoning. He was twenty-five. Tony McNeill got fifteen years for falsely imprisoning. He was twenty-five. Gerry Wright, aged forty-four, wiped his mouth as he was sentenced to seven years for falsely imprisoning. He was the only one to display any emotion.

· · · · ·

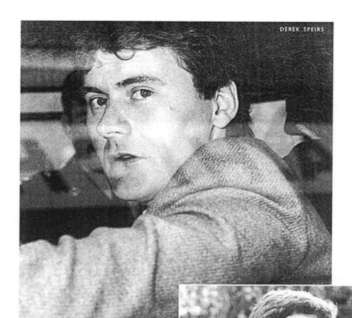

DEREK SPEIRS

Dessie O'Hare.

INDEPENDENT NEWSPAPERS

John O'Grady,
two years after the kidnap.

As the weeks went by, gardaí and troops mounted a widespread operation in search of John O'Grady.

Gardaí search bushes and brambles near the Midleton container site.

DEREK SPEIRS

DEREK SPEIRS

Dr Austin Darragh, kidnap target.

Manor House, the home of dentist John O'Grady.

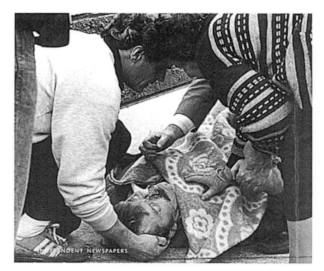

Detective Martin O'Connor is comforted by local people on Carnlough Road.

They went thataway.
Gardaí outside 260 Carnlough Road minutes after the shootout.

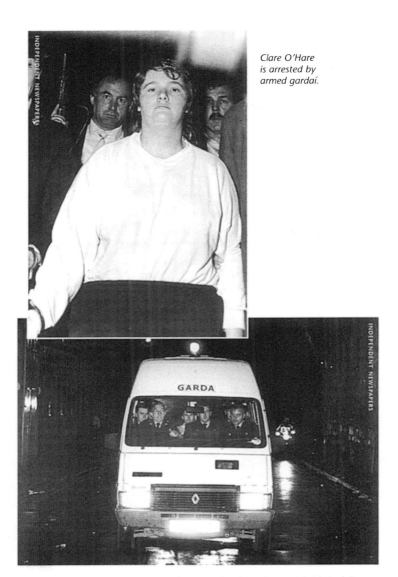

Clare O'Hare is arrested by armed gardaí.

Dessie O'Hare, in the centre at the back, is taken from the Special Criminal Court after being charged.

Detective Martin O'Connor.

Dessie O'Hare is taken away after sentencing.

A bearded Eddie Hogan after sentencing.

Clare O'Hare was tried separately, and when she appeared at the Special Criminal Court on 10 May 1988 she was seven months pregnant. Kevin Haugh SC, for the state, said in opening the prosecution case that Clare O'Hare 'was knowledgeable as to what was going on. She was a willing participant. She was acting in concert with them and the state is satisfied she was one of them.'

There was evidence of a woman being in 260 Carnlough Road when John O'Grady was held there, and Clare O'Hare's fingerprints were in the house.

After two days, Clare O'Hare's counsel, Paddy MacEntee SC, applied for a verdict of not guilty on the grounds that there was no evidence against his client. The state had brought no evidence 'that she was willing and participating, no evidence she was present at the kidnap'. He added, 'Her mere presence at the scene of a crime is not evidence of participation in the crime. There is not a pick of evidence that she wilfully encouraged any crime whatsoever. She may have been afraid of further enraging her husband, who might bring his wrath on her. This is a man who we know was armed to the teeth.'

The fingerprints at 260 Carnlough, MacEntee said, could have been left there at any time.

But she was there, as her fingerprints proved, so why did she deny ever being in the house? This denial, argued the state, implied guilty knowledge.

Paddy MacEntee said that Clare O'Hare may have thought that her mere presence in the house put her in trouble, so she denied being there. Maybe she denied being there out of revulsion at what happened in that house, and she wanted to distance herself from it. Perhaps she was in the house and was unaware that O'Grady was there, he said. There were a hundred and one reasons why she might have said she wasn't there.

Kevin Haugh, for the state, argued that Clare O'Hare 'at least provided aid, succour and comfort to those who were holding Mr O'Grady'.

Mr Justice Liam Hamilton retired to consider the defence application and came back twenty minutes later to rule that there were various inferences which could be drawn from the facts. He then quite properly noted that 'the court is obliged to draw the inference most favourable to the accused.' Clare O'Hare was acquitted.

* * * * *

In the years that followed, the INLA didn't greatly improve its reputation. There were constant rumours of simmering, deadly rows and enough killings to substantiate such rumours. The leader of one INLA faction, Jimmy Brown, was shot dead by a gunman from another faction in 1992. That year, one-time leader Dominic McGlinchey came out of Portlaoise prison and stayed away from the INLA. In February 1994 he was shot dead in a street in Drogheda by someone settling some score that no one outside the paramilitary world understood or cared about. 'Jesus, Mary, help me,' he cried as he lay dying. One of McGlinchey's sons, who in 1986 saw his mother shot dead, was also a witness to his father's killing.

It was five years after the acquittal of Clare O'Hare, in June 1994, that James Conlon came to court. He was the small-time knocker-off who was caught trying to shift a flat-ful of furniture from Gerry Wright's place, 41 Parkgate Street, where John O'Grady spent fearful days immediately after his kidnap. Conlon pleaded guilty. This was his thirty-fifth conviction. He was already serving a year for conviction No. 34. His barrister, Luigi Rea, pleaded with Judge Michael Moriarty 'not to unduly extend' his client's time in custody. The judge, a compassionate man, was as lenient as was consistent with enforcing the law. He gave Conlon another twelve months in jail, but backdated the sentence to coincide with the twelve months he was serving for conviction No. 34. He said that the building in question and the victim may have figured in a more celebrated matter, but Mr Wright had paid his price to society and he was entitled to have his property rights vindicated.

Two months later the IRA announced a ceasefire. The INLA didn't follow suit, but the group quietly suspended violent activities. Eight months after the ceasefire began, in April 1995, gardaí stopped a car near Balbriggan, heading north out of Dublin. There were four men inside. And two FN automatic rifles, two Kalashnikovs, two M3 submachine guns and twenty 9 mm Browning semi-automatic pistols. And 2,500 rounds of 9 mm ammunition. The four were, they claimed, on a mission of peace.

The four men were charged with arms offences and brought before the Special Criminal Court, where a solicitor acting for one of them, INLA chief-of-staff Hugh Torney, claimed that the INLA had begun its own ceasefire in July 1994, over a month before the IRA ceasefire. The INLA was leading the way again. They just hadn't told anyone until the four had been caught with an arsenal in their car.

A statement described the four as a 'delegation' charged with peace discussions. 'We concluded quite some time ago that a new non-violent approach was needed to address and overcome problems relating to Irish unity,' the statement said. The statement was the first public indication of yet another INLA split. Within days the INLA issued a statement denying that there was a ceasefire. The INLA, according to the statement, had merely suspended violence while awaiting developments. In truth, conflict about how to respond to the ceasefire was tearing the INLA apart.

In August 1995, two days before the anniversary of the IRA ceasefire, the IRSP, the long-silent political wing of the INLA, began to stir. It would, said a spokesman, relaunch itself as an alternative to Sinn Féin, it was opening an office on the Falls Road in Belfast, and it was reviving its newspaper, *The Starry Plough*. The INLA would maintain its suspension of armed activity, but violence would 'most likely be a part of the INLA's strategy at some stage in the future'. The INLA/IRSP seemed intent on making gains amongst Provos disenchanted by the ceasefire.

Within the INLA, however, the strains were leading inexorably to a new split. The INLA chief-of-staff, Hugh Torney, who supported the ceasefire, was expelled in November 1995, along with his supporters. A new chief-of-staff, Gino Gallagher, took control. Gallagher was firmly anti-ceasefire, and although the INLA remained militarily inactive, that remained a tactical decision rather than a strategic move away from killing.

In January 1996 a supporter of the Torney faction went into a Belfast labour exchange, where the new chief-of-staff Gino Gallagher was signing on, and shot him dead. There were the usual immediate denials that this was part of a new feud.

The Gallagher faction began seeking revenge for their leader's killing. A few weeks later John Fennell, an INLA member involved with the Torney faction, was taken captive at a caravan park in Donegal by the Gallagher faction. They tortured him, assuring themselves that he had a hand in Gallagher's murder, then they smashed his skull with a concrete block, killing him. In March 1996 the Gallagher faction fired into a Belfast home, killing a nine-year-old girl, Barbara McAlorum. Anyone thinking such a shocking deed might bring the feud to a sudden end was underestimating the INLA. The shooting went on and on. One of the four men arrested with a car full of guns near Balbriggan was shot dead while on bail, sitting in a restaurant with his girlfriend. Finally, Hugh Torney was shot dead.

By 2005, the INLA was on ceasefire, along with most other paramilitary outfits, and Dessie O'Hare had served seventeen years in jail. The political landscape had changed utterly since the events of 1988. Having made his peace with the INLA, O'Hare was deemed to qualify for consideration for release under the Belfast Agreement. He had reportedly become interested in art and had reportedly already been allowed out on temporary release, to prepare him for re-entry to civilian life.

John O'Grady never spoke publicly of his ordeal. Over the entire seventeen years he maintained a dignified silence, keeping his thoughts to himself.

❷ Doing Sharon's Da

Jesse and Sharon started going together in February 1988 and about a month later, according to Jesse's statement to the police, Sharon asked him to kill her father.

For reasons which will become clear, most of what we know about what happened comes from the statements which Jesse and his mates, Stitch, Anthony and Neil, subsequently made to the police.

Jesse O'Dwyer was eighteen. He lived in Saul Road, Crumlin, Dublin, with his mother and brother and sister Jenny.

Sharon Payne was aged fifteen. She was a friend of Jesse's sister Jenny. Sharon lived at 82 Rutland Grove, Crumlin, Dublin, with her parents, Christy and Philomena, and her thirteen-year-old brother, Christopher Jr.

Jesse was born in January 1970 and lived in England until he was four, when his parents were divorced and his mother came back to Ireland with her children. As a teenager, Jesse returned to Britain and spent some time knocking around the Birmingham area, living with relatives and in hostels, before returning to Ireland in late 1987. He had on occasion got jobs as a labourer or tyre fitter, but he was mostly unemployed, with no great prospects.

He wasn't long back in Ireland in 1987 when he was charged with stealing a bicycle. A couple of weeks later he was charged with taking a car. That was all dealt with in the Metropolitan Children's Court. A month later Jesse graduated to the District Court, charged with burglary. He got probation. It was all small-time stuff, the rites of passage of a petty criminal.

A couple of months later Jesse met Sharon Payne and the two started going together. The combination would catapult Jesse into a whole new league.

Jesse wasn't welcome at Sharon's home, but that didn't stifle the romance. He would arrive at 82 Rutland Grove and go around the back, then climb up on to the roof of the kitchen extension and tap on Sharon's bedroom window and she'd let him in.

Sharon's father, Christy Payne, aged fifty-two, didn't like Jesse O'Dwyer and tried to end the relationship between his daughter and the petty criminal. Christy Payne was not a well man. He had for many years suffered severe kidney failure and was physically very weak. To stay alive he had to regularly attend Beaumont Hospital for kidney dialysis.

Tales were told about Christy Payne, tales of him beating up his wife and his daughter, of how he molested kids, about how he fired an arrow at a kid. We don't know the truth of this, but there is no reason to believe any of it. The tales were being told for a purpose.

According to what a court would later be told, when Sharon first asked Jesse to kill her father, he refused. He was asked repeatedly over weeks but he wouldn't agree to do it. That was Jesse's story.

Jesse had a friend, Stitch McKeever. He was seventeen, his real name was Stephen, and he was a year younger than Jesse. Stephen McKeever was born in January 1971. He lived in nearby Drimnagh with his parents and sister. Like Jesse, he had a record of petty crime, just some small scrapes with the law as a juvenile, nothing serious. He too was unemployed.

According to what Stitch told the police, when Sharon got no response from Jesse she approached Stitch with her request that her father be killed. She repeated her request about a dozen times over the next fortnight, with Stitch always declining to oblige.

If they weren't into killing Christy Payne, the two young men were not averse to stealing from him. Their knowledge of the Payne house and its comings and goings, through their friendship with Sharon, made the enterprise a doddle. In April 1988, Jesse O'Dwyer and Stitch McKeever burgled the Payne house and stole a television set, two video recorders and a camera.

Jesse and Stitch discussed Sharon's request that they kill her father. 'What's in it for me?' Stitch asked. According to Stitch's statement Jesse revealed how there was money to be made from the killing. Jesse said that Philomena Payne, Sharon's mother, had said that she would pay Jesse £3,000 as soon as she got the insurance from the burglary they had carried out on the house.

Jesse began to put together some kind of a plan. It required the involvement of someone other than himself and Stitch McKeever. On an afternoon in May, Friday the thirteenth, a kid named Anthony O'Neill showed up at Jesse's house. He knew Sharon and he was a friend of Jesse's sister Jenny.

Eighteen-year-old Anthony O'Neill was the youngest son of a family of five from Drimnagh. He began getting into trouble when he was attending — or nor attending, as he frequently mitched — the Christian Brothers' school in Crumlin. In 1982, at the age of thirteen, he was sent to St Joseph's industrial school in Clonmel, having been sentenced to three years' detention for larceny. He was convicted in 1985 of being a passenger in a stolen car. He was sniffing glue, smoking cannabis, drinking heavily, taking pills and cider.

Anthony O'Neill wasn't so much a petty criminal as a screwed-up adolescent. The stuff he was taking was not physically addictive but O'Neill displayed a pattern of psychological addiction. He did a few AnCo training courses but remained unemployed.

When Anthony O'Neill arrived at Jesse O'Dwyer's house that Friday, Jesse was there with Stitch McKeever. 'I know where there's an easy touch,' Jesse said. The Payne house. Sharon's da's house. If there was any hassle from old man Payne, Jesse would hit him a few digs. Anthony O'Neill asked if Sharon knew about this. Jesse said yes, she wanted it done.

It would be cool, Jesse said. O'Neill left Jesse's house without agreeing to become involved in the burglary of the Payne house. At about 9 o'clock that evening he met a friend, Neil Kelly, also aged eighteen. The pair bought four cans of Holsten Pils lager from an off-licence on Sundrive Road and went to a field off the Old County Road.

There were about ten young people drinking in the field, which is known locally as The Plots. At The Plots someone gave Kelly some tablets, Roches, about eight of them. Roches are named for the drug company that manufactures them. They are usually Valium. In housing estates all over Dublin, at drinking parties such as this one, kids swallow pills of indeterminate dosage, mixed with drink (usually cheap cider) to make a powerful and immediate intoxicant.

Neil Kelly swallowed the Roches. He was not a regular user and became immediately spaced out. Kelly was an apprentice fitter. Six months earlier he had received his one and only conviction, being fined £20 for malicious damage to a car rear view mirror, and ordered to pay £5 to charity.

On that evening of Friday 13 May, Anthony O'Neill and Neil Kelly bought another two bottles of Holsten. They, along with the other teenage desperados in The Plots, were enjoying their drink when the guards raided the field. Everyone scattered and ran. In the panic, O'Neill and Kelly dropped one of their cans of Holsten.

After a while, the police left and O'Neill and Kelly returned to The Plots to continue their drinking. At about 10.30pm Jesse O'Dwyer and Stitch McKeever turned up and joined the other two.

Anthony O'Neill asked Jesse, 'Are you still going to do that?' referring to the proposed burglary of the Payne house. He was well on with drink and pills and it seemed to him that Jesse and Stitch were also a bit spaced. He said to Jesse that he didn't think they were in a fit state for the job.

Jesse said the burglary was on and O'Neill agreed to go along. O'Neill said they'd have to take his friend Neil Kelly as well, as he didn't want to leave him in The Plots on his own.

Jesse asked Neil Kelly if he was on for a stroke. Kelly asked how much it was worth. A few grand, said Jesse.

They went up to Jesse's house on Saul Road to make their preparations for the job. Jesse explained that all O'Neill and Kelly would have to do was watch the kids and the mother after they were tied up.

No, said Kelly, he didn't want to get involved in a tie-up job. Someone gave him a Roche and he took it and he didn't protest any more. He was given a grey track suit top to wear, and red and white BMX gloves.

They made ballys — balaclavas — by cutting the arms off jumpers. They cut holes in the arms to see through.

Jesse borrowed his brother Alan's white Hiace van and at around 11pm the four young men, Jesse, Stitch, Anthony and Neil, arrived at Rutland Grove. As far as Anthony O'Neill and Neil Kelly knew, they were out on a burglary. Only Jesse and Stitch knew that there were plans for Christy Payne.

As they passed the Payne house Neil Kelly, who up to now hadn't known the identity of the target, said, 'That's Sharon's gaff!'

'I know,' said Jesse, 'don't worry.' They parked the van about seven houses away from the Payne house and the four of them got out. 'Yous wait here,' Jesse ordered O'Neill and Kelly. Jesse and Stitch went off towards the Payne house.

There had been a stolen car around the area earlier in the evening and there was a squad car on patrol. The police spotted O'Neill and Kelly hanging around where Jesse had told them to wait, and the two were told to move on. O'Neill and Kelly walked down the road to a friend's house. The friend wasn't in, so the two decided to go back up and rejoin Jesse and Stitch.

There was no sign of the squad car, and the four young men gathered at the side of the Payne house. It was agreed that Jesse would go around the back, while Stitch knocked on the front door. The other two would follow Stitch. All four, standing at the side of the Payne house, began putting on their makeshift balaclavas. Neil Kelly was having trouble pulling the jumper sleeve over his head. Across the road a neighbour was staring at this carry-on. She reached for the phone and rang the garda station on Sundrive Road.

Sharon was upstairs when Stitch, O'Neill and Kelly went in. Her parents were out of the house. Her father Christy was at Beaumont Hospital having dialysis to clean out his blood.

The trio, Stitch, O'Neill and Kelly, tied up Sharon and Christopher Payne, Sharon's thirteen-year-old brother, in Sharon's bedroom at the back of the house, using telephone wire. One of the gang went to keep look-out at the front window. Minutes later, the police, alerted by the anxious neighbour, arrived outside 82 Rutland Grove.

Stitch untied young Christopher Payne and told him to go down and tell the coppers everything was all right. The gang stayed upstairs and took their masks off. If the coppers came upstairs, Stitch later told the police, Sharon would tell them everything was OK.

Just then there was a tap at the window and Jesse climbed in, using his usual mode of entry to Sharon's bedroom.

The gardaí insisted on coming in and looking around. Everything appeared normal; the police did not go upstairs. After a few minutes they left.

At around 11.30pm Mrs Philomena Payne arrived home. When she saw what was happening she started shouting at Sharon and she was taken upstairs to the front bedroom.

'You know what we're here for,' one of the gang said.

Mrs Payne said they shouldn't do it. 'No,' she said, according to Stitch's statement to the police, 'he's dying.' Jesse said he wanted a word with her.

'What's the story?' he asked. Should they do it?

The court was told she replied, 'Do it, but be sure you get away.' According to Stitch's statement she said, 'All right, but don't hurt the children. Do it quick, I don't want him to suffer.'

It was now pushing midnight and Christy Payne was due home from Beaumont Hospital. He would be arriving by taxi. Jesse kept watch at the front window.

Meanwhile, through the drink and the Roches, it was finally dawning on Neil Kelly that this was more than an ordinary burglary. What's going on? he wanted to know. Someone told him they were going to bump off the oul fella, Christy Payne.

'Me bollocks,' said Kelly. 'No way.'

Don't worry, he was told, it's all planned, just watch them, the ones tied up. Kelly went into the front bedroom, where Philomena Payne was tied up on the floor. She was crying. 'Are you all right?' asked Kelly.

'Don't touch the kids,' she said. Kelly put a pillow under her head. She asked for another pillow and Kelly got one. He lit a cigarette for her and put it in her mouth.

Kelly went into the back bedroom, to Sharon Payne.

'Forget it,' he said, 'we're going.'

According to Kelly's statement, later read in court, Sharon said, 'No, no, you've got to go ahead with it. Do it! Do it!'

Kelly left the bedroom and headed down the stairs.

In the front room Jesse O'Dwyer was turning away from the window, saying, 'Here he is!' A taxi had pulled up outside.

As Neil Kelly came down the stairs Jesse and Stitch came out into the hall, there was a noise at the front door, a key in the lock, the door opened and Christy Payne came in.

It was about twenty minutes past midnight. As soon as he saw the balaclavas Christy Payne jumped to the conclusion that there was a burglary going on.

'Right lads,' he said, 'if you leave now there'll be nothing more said.' Chronically ill, Christy Payne looked weak and ineffectual. He wasn't impressing the gang.

Jesse kicked the front door shut and told Christy Payne to get into the living room.

'I've no money,' Payne said. He'd been burgled three weeks ago, he said, and everything was cleaned out.

'We don't want your money,' said Jesse. 'We want your life.'

The gang bundled Christy Payne into the living room and sat him down in an armchair. Jesse had a hammer, which he had found in the house. Stitch had found a felling axe. It had a three-foot-long handle and the head weighed seven pounds. The four raiders stood around the seated Christy Payne. Stitch, with the axe, was standing behind the armchair.

Christy Payne kept telling them he had no money, asking them to let him be.

Jesse grabbed him and pulled him up, then pushed him down again. 'I heard you were a child molester,' he said, 'and that you shoot crossbows at kids.'

Stitch McKeever, standing behind the armchair, swinging the axe with both hands, brought the blade down into Christy Payne's head, splitting his skull open. Payne slumped forward and to one side. Stitch hit him again, this time with the blunt edge of the axe-head. Blood flowed, the skull almost cleft in two.

'He's not dead.' Jesse swung the hammer at the side of Christy Payne's shattered head. A piece of scalp flew up and stuck to the living room curtain.

Anthony O'Neill grabbed Neil Kelly and the two ran from the house. Jesse and Stitch ran out after them. The four got into the Hiace

97

van and drove off. After 'doing Sharon's da', Jesse O'Dwyer later told the police, they threw away the balaclavas and the hammer and they went home.

When the police arrived Christy Payne was still alive. He was unconscious.

The police had no trouble at all sorting things out. Christy Payne's family, wife Philomena, son Christopher and daughter Sharon, made statements that night about burglars invading the house at Rutland Grove. Next morning, having thought about the case, the police showed thirteen-year-old Christopher Payne his statement and asked him if that was the truth. He began talking to them again. Within hours the four members of the gang had been arrested and were being questioned. Within minutes they broke down and admitted their involvement.

Christy Payne remained in a coma for several months, severely brain damaged. When he regained some consciousness he was paralysed and was not fit to be interviewed by the police. He was little more than a vegetable. In November 1988, six months after the attack, he died. Professor John Harbison, the state pathologist, did an autopsy. He reported that Christy Payne's kidney failure was so gross that Harbison was not prepared to say that Payne died as a result of the injuries inflicted on him that night in May. Christy Payne might have died anyway. He wouldn't have been a vegetable for those last months but it wasn't possible to make a firm causal link between the attack on him and his death.

Charges of attempted murder were withdrawn and Jesse and Stitch pleaded guilty to charges of grievous bodily harm. Anthony O'Neill and Neil Kelly pleaded guilty to burglary. The four appeared before Mr Justice Henry Barron at the Circuit Criminal Court in Dublin in July 1989, fourteen months after the axing of Christy Payne and eight months after his death.

Detective Sergeant Gerry O'Carroll of Sundrive Road garda station, the garda in charge of the investigation, went to pains to differentiate between the roles of Jesse O'Dwyer and Stitch McKeever on the one hand, and Anthony O'Neill and Neil Kelly on the other. A court will often pay attention to a knowledgeable garda's interpretation of a case, and this case brought into the court a world of which judges have little personal knowledge. A garda giving a fair and thoughtful account of a case can influence the sentencing and thereby have a significant impact on the course of the accused's life.

Detective Sergeant O'Carroll pointed out that, unlike Jesse O'Dwyer and Stephen McKeever, O'Neill and Kelly had not been involved in violence and had immediately shown remorse for what happened to Christy Payne. He gave his opinion that O'Neill was 'not a hardened criminal' and could be rehabilitated. O'Carroll said that Kelly 'was very much out of his head' with a combination of drugs and drink and 'really didn't know what was going on'. Kelly 'happened to be in the wrong place at the wrong time', spaced out at The Plots, as the gang gathered for the job.

Jesse O'Dwyer, said O'Carroll, was 'persistently asked' by Sharon and Philomena Payne to kill Christy Payne. He was 'hounded' he said. He said that Jesse O'Dwyer resisted the suggestion of killing for some time, that he was manipulated, that he and Stephen McKeever were played off against each other, that Jesse O'Dwyer appeared to believe things he was told about how Sharon and her mother had been the victims of brutality by Christy Payne over long periods of time.

The obvious question was eventually asked. Was anyone else going to be charged in this case? The counsel for the state, Denis Vaughan Buckley, was asked to enquire this of the Director of Public Prosecutions. Several days later he reported to the court that two other persons were to be charged with grievous bodily harm and with intent to murder Christy Payne, but they had not yet been arrested.

Jesse O'Dwyer and Stephen McKeever were each sentenced to nine and a half years in jail. Anthony O'Neill was ordered to keep the peace for three years and to undergo drug therapy at Coolmine for at least a year. Neil Kelly received a suspended sentence of eighteen months.

Sharon and Philomena Payne were not at the house in Rutland Grove when the police went to arrest them. It was believed that they had gone abroad; there was a report that Sharon was in Germany, but nothing was confirmed. Gardaí would still like to question Sharon and Philomena about the events of Friday 13 May 1988.

❸ A Day
in Court:
George's Legacy

Declan Budd, Senior Counsel, took off his wig and threw it on the table. He bent forward and began writing on a piece of cardboard torn from the back of a jotter. It was just gone ten minutes to three on a June day in 1991, in Court No. 5 in the High Court, and a case was about to be settled out of court. Perhaps.

Many cases are settled before court proceedings conclude, even more are settled before the matter gets into court. One lawyer will say casually to another, 'Suppose . . .', and tentative suggestions become negotiations, which become settlements. And then the whole thing can fall apart at any time.

When Thomas and Susan Levingstone of Oldcourt, Co. Kildare, died within months of each other back in 1970, they left behind a sixty-six acre farm and three grown-up children, George, James and Vera. George and Vera had never married. James married a woman named Floss and they had no children. George, James and Vera were the last of the Levingstones of Oldcourt, Co. Kildare, a highly regarded Church of Ireland family.

Thomas and Susan had made a will fourteen years before their deaths. George was left the sixty-six acre farm. James was left some other property, an outfarm. Vera, the eldest, was to live on the farm with George, as his housekeeper. They lived there together into the 1980s, when George was in his sixties and suffering from epilepsy, sister and brother, nurse and patient.

George didn't get on with his brother James. Nor with James's wife, Floss. The enmity between the brothers went on for a long time, occasionally flaring up. George, now a man of property, had to make a will. There was no way he was going to leave the farm to his brother James. George made a will leaving everything he owned to his sister Vera.

Then, on 28 September 1986, Vera died. The conflict between the brothers flared again. Vera didn't leave a will and there was a row over her furniture and her clothes.

With Vera gone, George needed someone to look after him. Betty and Cecil Young, from Belfast, came to Vera's funeral. Betty regarded Vera as an older sister. Vera was godmother to Betty's daughter.

Cecil had to return to Belfast but Betty stayed on for some weeks to look after George. Betty then arranged for another couple, Roland and Winifred Cox, to leave their own home and move in with George. Roland had some years earlier lodged with George and was happy to be of service. Then the Coxes received an anonymous threatening letter and decided it was time to leave Oldcourt. Betty Young came back down from Belfast to look after George.

George had made a will two years after his parents died, in which he left everything to Vera. That will had remained relevant for fourteen years. Now, with Vera dead, it was out of date and would have to be changed. On 10 February 1987, during the period when he was being looked after by the Youngs and the Coxes, George visited John Aylmer, the family solicitor, and said he wanted to change his will, leaving half of his estate to his only surviving relative, his brother James.

Ten weeks later George came back to solicitor John Aylmer and changed his will, leaving the farm to the Youngs and the Coxes and leaving his brother James just £5,000. George had notes in a little diary, written in block capitals, to help him make clear his intentions. The will was typed up and read back to George and he said that was what he wanted.

The solicitor, aware of the difficulties and dangers of drawing up wills in such circumstances, had consulted Dr Joe O'Neill, George

Levingstone's GP. Dr O'Neill was of the opinion that although George was slow of speech he was perfectly capable of making a will.

The following month, May 1987, George was unwell and moved into Winchmore Nursing Home, Newbridge. It was not a happy summer for George Levingstone. The bitterness with his brother continued and there were rows and accusations, incidents and allegations. There was a suggestion from a friend that a local couple be asked to live on the farm and look after George, in return for being left the farm. George was unhappy with this suggestion and dismissed it.

George had asked an acquaintance, William Hanly, to look after some of the contents of his home. James and Floss were of the opinion that Hanly was looking after George's property a bit too well. They accused him of stealing George's grandfather clock. James and Floss made it clear that it was they who should get to look after George.

Three months later, James and Floss Levingstone called to see solicitor John Aylmer. James asked if George had made a will.

Yes, he had, answered the solicitor. Was James a beneficiary? Yes, he was. How much? James asked. Not a large amount, said Aylmer. A few days later, on 31 August 1987, eleven months after the death of his sister, George Levingstone died.

Four months after that, on Christmas Eve 1987, James Levingstone, the last of the Levingstones of Oldcourt, died.

Death made the brothers' quarrel meaningless, but there was debris left behind. James's widow, Floss Levingstone, subsequently alleged that undue influence by the Coxes and the Youngs had caused George to make a will against his intentions. She was of the opinion that George's earlier will, leaving everything to her husband James, should apply. She would then inherit everything.

George's will became the subject of a legal contest between the Coxes and the Youngs on the one hand, and Floss Levingstone on the other. The farm was going to be sold and the dispute revolved around who would get the proceeds. Eventually, the case came to Court No. 5 in the Four Courts, Dublin.

· · · · · ·

The case was a mere thirteen minutes or so under way when the court adjourned so that the lawyers could examine the diary/notebook which George Levingstone had kept. It contained some notes about changing his will, notes demonstrating his antagonism towards his brother James, and supporting the case that his last will, in favour of the Youngs and Coxes, should be upheld. It was a small hardcover notebook with a pastel picture on the front of a girl with a basket, a pretty notebook in which a twelve-year old might write her secret poems.

Ten minutes became twenty. It was now pushing 12.45pm. Outside in the corridor lawyers for the two sides were talking. Someone had said, 'Suppose . . .'

The lawyers asked Judge Murphy for another ten minutes. Judge Murphy said there wasn't much point in resuming at five minutes to one, so he'd resume after lunch, at 2pm. Judges will usually, if they feel that a painful conflict can be averted, give the parties every opportunity to achieve a compromise.

Calculations were being made. Financial calculations, multiplying sixty-six acres by the current price per acre for a farm in an area not the best part of Kildare. And calculation of odds, of how a judge might see the evidence. If the case went ahead, the chances were that someone would win everything, someone would lose and be left with a big legal bill.

Lunchtime ended, it was 2pm and still the case didn't resume. Judge Murphy, aware that a compromise was possibly within reach, stayed in his chamber and didn't push the lawyers to restart the case. By 2.20pm there were a lot of smiles in evidence. A settlement was at hand. Still, Judge Murphy waited in his chambers, to allow the dickering to conclude.

Floss sat outside in the hall, accompanied by a friend, a Protestant rector. The Youngs and the Coxes sat inside, at the back of the court. Lawyers moved between them, in and out, huddling and whispering. A sum of money was mentioned, £35,000, to be paid to Floss within fourteen days of the sale of the farm.

At 2.52pm Declan Budd SC, for the Youngs and Coxes, threw his wig on the table and began writing out a draft terms of settlement on a piece of cardboard torn from the back of a jotter. At 3.07pm he handed the piece of cardboard to solicitor John Aylmer. 'Run an eye over that.'

Floss's barrister, David Byrne SC, suggested a change. Declan Budd made the amendment and Byrne brought the piece of cardboard out to the bench in the hall to show it to Floss Levingstone.

Almost four years of conflict, half an hour of court proceedings, three hours of negotiation for a settlement.

Two minutes later the whole thing fell apart. Floss was asking about George's grandfather clock. When last seen it had allegedly been stolen by William Hanly, an unsustained accusation. But Hanly had since died. Hanly had said he had taken the clock sure enough, but he had been minding it for George. Now, Floss wanted the grandfather clock back, and the proposed settlement was about to collapse.

The lawyers huddled in various combinations. Twenty minutes of urgent consultation passed, but Floss wouldn't budge. If the ownership of the grandfather clock wasn't resolved there would be no settlement.

The case would have to go ahead. At 3.32 Declan Budd shrugged. His clients, the Youngs and Coxes, were ready to settle but Floss was holding out. 'All I can do is tell the judge . . .'

Judge Murphy came back, the court resumed. The case wouldn't finish before the court adjourned at 4pm and would run into the next day, at least.

Floss Levingstone's barrister, David Byrne, was still out talking to her in the corridor. In the courtroom, everyone moved slowly, awaiting Byrne's return.

Finally, it was too late, the court couldn't wait any longer. Declan Budd rose to his feet. 'I had thought that we had reached a settlement,' Budd told the judge, 'but I understand there is some matter that is still causing difficulty.'

Moments later David Byrne hurried into the court. He held up the piece of cardboard on which the agreement was written. 'In the historic words, my Lord, I have a piece of paper . . .'

Floss had given up on the grandfather clock. The court agreed that the will would stand, the Youngs and Coxes would inherit George Levingstone's farm, and a proportion of the proceeds from the sale of the property was to go to his sister-in-law Floss. The agony of a case fought in court, with an outright winner and a loser facing a legal bill on top of the loss of the legacy, not to mention the years of bitterness which such an outcome can cause in such cases, had been avoided. The lawyers had done their job, achieving a settlement in which no one was entirely happy but in which everyone won a little.

The technicalities were observed, the legal loose ends were tied up, and Floss Levingstone and her rector friend left the court, as did the Youngs and the Coxes. The lawyers gathered up the case papers, which would be filed away in some cabinet, unlikely to ever again see daylight until, perhaps, the day comes when all involved are long dead and no one remembers what the conflict was about and someone is cleaning out the debris of the past and the papers are destroyed.

Tucked in among the papers as they vanished into folders was the pretty little notebook that contained not winsome poetry but the block capital notes of a sad and angry old man taking a final swipe at his brother, both of them at death's door.

❹ Shercock

Peter Matthews went into Shercock leaning on a crutch and came out of the village in an ambulance. He was a weak man, a troubled man. He was hardly a pillar of society, he was not the stuff of martyrs, but he didn't deserve what happened to him. And when it happened and when people had finished wringing their hands, we backed away from the case, impotent and shamed. Then we put it out of our minds, life went on, and after a while we stopped thinking about what happened to Peter Matthews in Shercock.

Shercock is a small village in County Cavan, near the border with County Monaghan. On 22 April 1982 Peter Matthews came limping into Shercock on his aluminium crutch, larceny on his mind. He was accompanied by his wife Ann. They lived across the county border, in Monaghan, at a place called Lough Fea, near Carrickmacross, about ten miles east of Shercock. Peter had told Ann, she later said, that he was going to Shercock to buy some iron to do some scroll work. There's nowhere in Shercock that sells iron.

Peter Matthews met Ann in England in the 1960s and they married and came back to Ireland and set up home at Lough Fea. Ann had three children in three years. Peter was unemployed, apart from the odd bit of ironwork. He was a character, friends said. He did a bit of singing. Once he put together a dreadful little band and got them a booking somewhere in England. They were so bad they were thrown out. When they came back to Ireland he booked them into local halls, advertising them as fresh from their successful tour of England.

In April 1982, when they went to Shercock, ten years after they'd had their third child, Ann was pregnant again. Peter was in very bad health. Aged forty-one, five-feet-ten, very thin, he drank a lot and refused to go into hospital when heart trouble was diagnosed at the beginning of March. His wife wasn't well, he said, she had to spend some time in hospital, and he would have to look after the children. Perhaps recklessly, Peter Matthews was giving his family priority over attention to his own health.

Of the three main arteries in Peter Matthews's heart, only one was healthy. A second was narrowed and the third was completely blocked. He had suffered a mild heart attack and had pills he was supposed to take when he suffered chest pains. His condition and his lack of attention to his health meant that he could drop dead at any moment, particularly if suffering stress.

The reason he was on a crutch that day had nothing to do with his heart. Three months earlier, in January, not long after recovering from injuries he received in a car accident, Peter slipped in the snow and broke an ankle. Peter Matthews was running a streak of bad luck, and it wasn't finished yet.

Peter and Ann Matthews hitch-hiked to Shercock that Monday. They went to Frank Burns's pub and ordered drinks, a whiskey and red and a brandy. It was about 5pm. After a few minutes Peter got up and left the pub.

· · · · ·

Maureen Daly recognised the man who came into the post office in Church Street, Shercock, at about 5.15pm that day. She didn't know his name, but she had served him on two occasions that month and on two occasions the previous month. Each time he had withdrawn £30 from a post office savings account. Maureen Daly was a clerk in the post office. Today, the postmistress, Elizabeth Mullen, was at the counter when the man came to be served.

He produced a post office savings book in the name of P.J. McEneany and said he wanted to withdraw £30 from the account. He added, nervously, that he was usually served by 'the other girl'.

Mullen was suspicious. She got Maureen Daly to engage the man in conversation. She took the post office book aside and checked it against a list of stolen books. Post office book No. 554407 was not on the list. The man was allowed to withdraw the £30 from the account.

Peter Matthews took the money, took back the book, and left the post office. He returned to Frank Burns's pub.

Elizabeth Mullen was still suspicious. She rang the post office at Carrickmacross, where the book had been issued. She was told that P.J. McEneany was an old man, blind and infirm, unable to look after his affairs, who had for the past two years been living in St Mary's, the county home.

Elizabeth Mullen immediately rang Shercock garda station. There was no answer. She rang her husband Seamus. Seamus Mullen was a former garda, now a jobbing builder in Shercock. He had retired from the force three years before. On receiving the call from his wife, he rang the garda station in Carrickmacross and told them what had happened.

Elizabeth Mullen sent Maureen Daly out to look around Shercock in the hope of spotting the man who had posed as P.J. McEneany. Maureen Daly eventually spotted Peter Matthews in Frank Burns's pub. She reported back to the post office.

Meanwhile, two gardaí, Detective Joseph Sheehan and Garda Dennis Durkan, were driving the ten miles or so from Carrickmacross to Shercock. Detective Sheehan had taken the phone call from Seamus Mullen. He knew that the home of P.J. McEeaney had been broken into, that a trunk had been vandalised and a post office book stolen. The police 'had information' that made Peter Matthews a suspect.

At this stage, Seamus Mullen, the former garda, husband of the postmistress, who will weave in and out of this story, makes another appearance. His first significant act in the drama had been to ring the garda station at Carrickmacross to tell the police of the suspected post office fraud. Now, he appeared in Frank Burns's pub, where he pointed out Peter Matthews to the owner and told him to keep an eye on that fella, the gardaí would be coming for him.

Meanwhile, Maureen Daly, the post office clerk, having succeeded in finding the man who had posed as P.J. McEneany, was waiting at the post office when the gardaí from Carrickmacross arrived. It was now almost 6pm. Maureen Daly got into the garda car and directed the police to the pub. Detective Sheehan went inside the pub and found Peter and Ann Matthews drinking at the bar. There were two other customers. The detective asked Peter to come outside.

'For what?'

'Come on ahead.'

Outside, Detective Sheehan asked Peter to sit into the garda car for a minute. There, the detective told Peter Matthews it was alleged that he had used a stolen post office book to carry out a fraud. Garda Durkan drove the car to the post office, where assistant Maureen Daly was brought out.

'That's the man, there,' she said, pointing at Peter Matthews. Matthews didn't say anything.

Garda Durkan drove the car across the road and stopped outside the Protestant church. Detective Sheehan asked Matthews if he had the post office book.

'I don't know what you mean,' said Matthews.

He took a piece of paper from an inside pocket, unwrapped a white tablet and swallowed it.

'You're an awful man,' said Detective Sheehan, 'taking tablets on top of drink.'

He asked Matthews if he'd mind being searched at the garda station in Shercock. Matthews had no objection. Garda Durkan started up the car and they drove to the police station. It was closed.

• • • • •

The Garda station in Shercock was a part-time set-up. The sergeant in charge was Peter Diviney, a tall, balding man of forty-eight years of age. Diviney had joined the force in 1958, at the age of twenty-two. Three years later he got married. He and his wife had two daughters and after he was promoted to sergeant in 1967 he served in various stations around the country. In 1974 he was assigned to Shercock. Five years later his wife died. He married again in February 1982. That was just two months before Peter Matthews came to Shercock on a crutch.

There were just two gardaí stationed in Shercock, Sergeant Diviney and Garda Seamus Galligan. Garda Galligan was aged twenty-three. He had been a garda for less than two years. Just eight weeks earlier he had been transferred to Shercock. He lived in digs two miles outside the village.

Shercock is a quiet country village. The garda station was open only in the mornings. The rest of the day the gardaí would be doing administrative work, out serving summonses and the like. Two-thirds of the garda station building was Sergeant Diviney's private residence, the other third was the garda station itself. The station consisted of a day room, where members of the public came to do their business; the sergeant's room, which was Diviney's office, a store room and a cell. Untypically, the garda station had been very busy the previous day, when the bank in the village had been held up.

Now, on 22 April 1982, as the two gardaí from Carrickmacross arrived at Shercock garda station with Peter Matthews, the garda station was closed. Sergeant Diviney and his wife Margaret were planning to have a night out in Longford. Garda Galligan was off somewhere on duty in connection with the previous day's bank raid.

Detective Sheehan went around to the residence part of the station and met Mrs Diviney. He asked her to fetch the sergeant. Diviney was wearing a green blazer over the pants, shirt and tie of his garda uniform. He had been looking forward to the night out, but after his years as a sergeant he knew that you were never off duty and this kind of thing could happen at any time. He opened the station.

Peter Matthews was taken to the day room. He had less than three hours to live.

· · · · ·

Peter Matthews cooperated in the search, taking off his own shoes and socks. He was stripped, his clothes searched. There was no post office book. Sergeant Diviney found seven £1 notes. Detective

Sheehan found six £5 notes in Matthews's back pocket. £30, the amount withdrawn from P.J. McEneany's post office account.

Sheehan asked about the post office book. Matthews said he hadn't got it, knew nothing about it. As for the £30, it was part of the £75 social welfare payment he had received the previous day. Why was it separate from the other £7? He was keeping it apart in his back pocket to pay an ESB bill.

Detective Sheehan brought Sergeant Diviney out of the room while Peter Matthews got dressed. He told the sergeant he was going back to the pub to find Ann Matthews. Maybe she had the post office book. He and Garda Durkan left. At 6.20pm Garda Galligan arrived back at the station. He was due to go off duty but decided to stay on to see if there was anything he could do in this post office fraud investigation. It was all go in Shercock. A bank robbery the previous day, post office fraud today. Sergeant Diviney sent Garda Galligan out to have a look around the village for the post office book.

Diviney went back into the day room. He gave Peter Matthews a cigarette and sat on the window ledge. Matthews sat on a chair in a crouched position, his arms across his knees. Diviney asked him about the post office book but Matthews had nothing to say about that. The two had a fairly amicable conversation, according to Diviney. He asked the suspect where exactly Lough Fea, Matthews's home, was in relation to Carrickmacross. There was a strong smell of drink from Matthews.

Ann Matthews, left alone in the pub, had finished her drink and walked the 150 yards to Duffy's supermarket. While she was there, Detective Sheehan and Garda Durkan arrived at Frank Burns's pub in search of her. They decided to look for her around the town. When she came out and walked back down towards Burns's pub, she noticed Detective Sheehan and Garda Durkan from Carrickmacross driving by in their police car. She didn't know that they had already made a couple of circles around the streets of Shercock in search of her. She waved them down. She said she wanted to see her husband.

'Game,' said Durkan, and Ann Matthews got into the squad car and was taken to the garda station.

Detective Sheehan rang his own station, in Carrickmacross, and asked that a policewoman be sent to Shercock to search a female.

Ann Matthews was questioned about the post office book.

'Give me the book,' she later said she was told.

What book? she asked.

The post office book. 'Peter said he gave it to you.'

It was only a few pounds, give it over and there'd be no question of anyone going to jail for life.

She claimed that Garda Durkan said to her, 'Don't be acting the bollocks, you know all about it.'

Ann Matthews's handbag was emptied on to the table. There was £41. 'That's all the money we have,' she said. 'It's my money and it's not stolen.'

There was a knock on the door. Seamus Mullen, the ex-garda, husband of the postmistress, was standing there. He had a list of the dates on which a man had withdrawn money from P.J. McEneany's post office account. Detective Sheehan took the list and went back into the room. The list said that money had been drawn from the account on 15 March, 29 March, 5 April and 13 April. Ann Matthews was by now quite agitated and struck the piece of paper. Garda Durkan grabbed her hand to restrain her.

Ann Matthews, four months pregnant, indignantly threw open her coat and offered herself for a search.

Sheehan and Durkan told Diviney that they had to leave, to go back to Carrickmacross. Sheehan advised Diviney to ring Detective Tom Jordan, in Bailieborough, a town about ten miles south of Shercock. He was of the opinion that a detective was needed on this investigation. Sheehan and Durkan then left Shercock. It was now about 7pm.

· · · · ·

Ban Garda Michelle Mannion had joined the force just ten months earlier. She was stationed at Carrickmacross. She had been out on squad car patrol that afternoon and arrived at the station at 6.30pm for a meal break. She was told that Detective Sheehan had phoned from Shercock and he needed a policewoman to conduct a search of a female at the police station there. Mannion couldn't drive, so her partner, Garda Joseph Feely, drove her the ten miles to Shercock. They arrived at about 7.15pm.

There were now four gardaí in the station: Diviney and Galligan, from Shercock; Mannion, who was here to search Ann Matthews, and Feely, who was there because he could drive.

Diviney sent out his subordinate, Garda Seamus Galligan, along with Garda Joseph Feely, to search the litter bins in the village, in the hope of finding the post office book. He told them to look behind the wall of the Protestant church, across from the post office, because Peter Matthews might have thrown the book there.

The post office book had become the focus of the investigation, as though finding it would clinch matters. By now, there was certainly enough evidence to charge Peter Matthews. He had been identified by the postmistress, Elizabeth Mullen, as having presented P.J. McEneany's post office book, and as having withdrawn £30 from the account. Post office clerk Maureen Daly had identified him as having presented the book on four other occasions. Still, the police wanted the book, they wanted Peter Matthews's admission that he knew what happened to the book.

Sergeant Diviney phoned Detective Tom Jordan at Bailieborough and Jordan agreed to come to Shercock as soon as he could get the use of a car. Galligan and Feely came back empty handed from searching the litter bins.

The mix of gardaí in the station that night included the experienced and those still learning. Sergeant Diviney and Detective Jordan were old hands. Diviney was twenty-five years in the job, Jordan twenty-three years. Garda Galligan was new in Shercock and still only twenty-three years old. Garda Feely was a couple of years on the job, and Ban Garda Mannion a mere ten months. Not surprisingly, it was the more experienced who dominated the proceedings and there appears to have been a reluctance on the part of the younger gardaí to intervene to change the course of events. At some stage that evening Ban Garda Mannion was in the company of Garda Galligan and Garda Feely. They heard shouts from the cell.

Galligan's response, according to Mannion and Feely, was to say: 'I love to hear them roaring.'

It was a callous and shocking thing for a policeman to say, but it may have been mere bravado in the company of two fellow gardaí, equally young.

Sergeant Diviney went to the day room and had a talk with Ann Matthews. It was a friendly talk. She told him, according to the sergeant, that her husband drank a lot, that their marriage was not the best. Diviney told her about various facilities which might help Peter stay off the drink. Ann Matthews would say that the sergeant advised her to put Peter into a mental home.

After a while she asked to see Peter. Sergeant Diviney went out and brought Peter into the day room. This must have been around 8pm or 8.10pm, around the time Detective Garda Tom Jordan arrived at the police station. Garda Galligan told him why Peter Matthews was being questioned and Detective Jordan prepared to take part in the investigation.

Ann Matthews became agitated at the sight of her husband. She would give evidence that his hair had been torn out, that there were clumps of hair on his shoulder and sleeve. Sergeant Diviney would swear that there was no evidence of such hair.

'Jesus, Peter, who done that to you?'

Ann Matthews would later testify in court that Peter pointed at Sergeant Diviney, and that he told her that Diviney had knocked a tablet from his hand.

'He skited the tablet off my hand and he wouldn't let me take it.'

Ann Matthews turned to Diviney and said, 'You've been giving me a lot of soft talk about putting him into a mental — and you've been abusing him out there.'

According to Garda Joseph Feely, Peter and Ann Matthews whispered together. He heard Ann say, 'I know, I've got a pain in my head myself.'

The garda said Ann Matthews told her husband, 'Listen to what the garda told you,' that he should go to hospital to dry out.

Peter Matthews was taken back to his cell. Ann Matthews was taken to the privacy of the sergeant's room by Ban Garda Mannion, where she stripped naked and was searched by the ban garda. She was not concealing a post office book.

Peter Matthews was questioned in the cell by Sergeant Diviney and by Detective Tom Jordan. And somewhere along in here Seamus Mullen, the ex-garda and husband of the postmistress, makes another appearance. Garda Joseph Feely saw Mullen confront Matthews in the cell. Mullen told Matthews to stand up. Matthews just sat there.

Mullen put his hands under Matthews's arms and lifted him up. He said, 'I seen you coming into the post office. Why are you trying to deny it? Why don't you tell them where the book is?'

Ann Matthews was in the sergeant's office, next to the cell, with Ban Garda Mannion. Garda Joseph Feely was in the day room. Garda Seamus Galligan was also there.

Both Ann Matthews and the policewoman heard loud voices.

Ann Matthews heard Peter scream, 'Ann, Ann, help me!'

She heard a voice shout, 'Hand over the book, you bastard!'

She rose, but Ban Garda Mannion was in the doorway. The policewoman said, 'He'll be all right. I promise you they won't do him any harm. Why doesn't he give them the book?'

Garda Feely heard Peter Matthews say, 'Annie, Annie!' and 'Keep away from me.'

It appears that Peter Matthews told the police he had a weak heart. At perhaps a few minutes to 8.45pm Sergeant Diviney rang Peter Matthews's doctor. She confirmed that Matthews had a long history of heart trouble and had been in Drogheda Hospital recently. She asked Diviney to tell Matthews that she wanted to see him soon. Peter Matthews had less than ten minutes to live.

Garda Feely told Sergeant Diviney that he knew Peter Matthews, that he was familiar with his background. He might confide in me, said the garda. Garda Feely went into the cell to talk to Peter Matthews and was with him for about a minute. Matthews had a smear of blood on his cheek. Garda Feely asked if Matthews knew him, that Garda Feely often had a drink around Carrick himself. Peter Matthews didn't respond. He just sat there, crouched over.

It won't make any difference to your case, Garda Feely told him, it's in your own interest to tell where the post office book is. Peter Matthews just sat there.

At about this time, Sergeant Diviney's wife Margaret came around into the station part of the building and asked the sergeant about their planned night out in Longford. He told her it was too late now.

Sergeant Diviney went into the sergeant's office and told Ann Matthews she was free to go. She insisted on seeing her husband. Diviney took her to the cell. Garda Feely, who had been attempting to engage Peter Matthews in conversation, went out into the corridor. Peter Matthews was sitting at the end of the bed in the cell.

Ann could see he had a black eye and blood on his cheek. She ran into the cell and knelt in front of him.

'Jesus, Peter, what are they doing to you?' she asked. 'If you have the book, give it to them.'

Peter didn't answer.

Ann told him, 'They're putting me out now. I don't have any money, they've taken all my money.'

Peter gave her some change and asked her to call the family solicitor in Ardee and tell him, 'They're abusing me.'

Ann Matthews left the cell. As she walked down the corridor, Peter was standing outside the cell, downcast, wretched, heedless. He was five feet ten, but to those who saw him then he looked drooped and small. Sergeant Diviney was there and Seamus Mullen, the ex-garda. Garda Feely and Ban Garda Mannion also saw this.

They saw Diviney make some gesture with his fists and say something like, 'Of all the fucking bastards . . . If you were a man I'd hit you, but you're a miserable get.'

Ann Matthews left the station. Garda Feely and Ban Garda Mannion left to return to Carrickmacross, where they had to serve a summons. With Peter Matthews in the station were Sergeant Diviney, Detective Jordan, Garda Galligan and ex-garda Seamus Mullen.

It was now in or around 8.50pm. At some point that evening Peter Matthews had sustained a serious assault. There were also minor assaults. He was pressed back against something, a wall or a chair. He was slapped on the face. His eyelids were bruised. He was hit on the head, here and there, both sides of the head, on the right temple, behind the left ear, at the back of the head. The medical evidence suggests that most probably someone rapped their knuckles downwards on his cranium.

At least fifteen or twenty minutes earlier, perhaps 8.30pm, perhaps earlier, perhaps prior to 8pm, someone punched Peter Matthews in the stomach, very hard. Matthews wasn't expecting the punch. If you know your stomach is about to be hit, your abdominal muscles automatically clench and tense to take the blow, protecting your internal organs. When that happens the abdominal muscles will later show bleeding from the punch.

Peter Matthews didn't see the punch coming. His abdominal muscles remained relaxed. The pancreas is a narrow organ about nine inches long. It sits horizontally at the back of the stomach, just in front of the spine, at about navel height. It secretes fluids that aid digestion. The distance from the surface of Peter Matthews's abdomen to his pancreas was about four inches. A fist slammed into his abdomen; the force of the punch was carried past his slack abdominal muscles and right through to the pancreas, pushing it against his spinal column. The pancreas bled.

The pain and trauma of this assault, and the resulting stress, were precipitating factors in the heart attack that killed Peter Matthews at around 8.50pm.

Ann Matthews called a solicitor from a pay phone in Shercock, then she got a lift home to Lough Fea. She had just arrived home when a garda called to the house to tell her that Peter was dead.

· · · · ·

The cover-up began immediately. Sergeant Diviney phoned Dr Kieran McMahon, a local doctor. Dr McMahon was told that a man had taken a turn, went blue and fell forward. The doctor arrived at the station at 9.25pm and found Mrs Diviney hysterical, distraught that a man had died in part of what was her home. The doctor was taken to the cell. Peter Matthews was lying on the bunk. Sergeant Diviney told the doctor that while sitting in the sergeant's office the man had stumbled forward and turned blue, and he had then been taken to the cell. Dr McMahon pronounced Peter Matthews dead at 9.40pm. An ambulance was called to remove the body to hospital in Cavan.

Questions had to be asked. The explanations from Diviney, Jordan and Galligan didn't satisfy the garda investigators. There appears to have been at some stage that evening or the next morning an agreement reached between Diviney, Jordan and Galligan to tell a cover-up story in which Peter Matthews died of a heart attack in the sergeant's office and was taken to the cell. When he 'had a turn' he fell forward and hit his face on the table, which would explain any bruises. The three gardaí also appear to have conspired, for whatever reason, to conceal the fact that ex-garda Seamus Mullen was in the station that night and questioned Peter Matthews.

The day after the death, Sergeant Diviney was interviewed by Inspector Owen Manning. He stated that Peter Matthews was sitting in a chair when his face suddenly turned blue and he slumped forward and his 'head hit the table'.

Two days after the death Detective Tom Jordan made a statement to Superintendent James Hanrahan. This concurred with Diviney's statement. It had Matthews sitting in a chair in the sergeant's office and suddenly slumping forward. 'At no stage could I get a look at his face.' This was convenient, as it meant that Jordan wouldn't have seen the bruises.

Garda Galligan also made a statement to Superintendent Hanrahan. He stated that he witnessed no improper action towards the man who died. He heard no harsh words spoken. The statement was weaker than the statements of Diviney and Jordan in that it merely said that Peter Matthews's head 'rested on the table' when he slumped forward. Later, in a coroner's deposition, Galligan would adjust this to 'hit his head on the table'.

The fact that Peter Matthews had been beaten and the fact that ex-garda Seamus Mullen had been in the station and had at least to some extent taken part in the interrogation of Peter Matthews, were omitted.

On the day after Peter Matthews's death, Sergeant Diviney, who suffered heart trouble, muscular spasms, went into hospital where he stayed for nine days.

Incredibly, the cover-up held firm for the best part of a year. There was unease at senior levels within the force. It was known that lies had been told. The state pathologist, Professor John Harbison, carried out an autopsy and it became obvious that the three garda statements simply didn't explain the injuries which Peter Matthews had suffered. Harbison's scalpel probed muscle and organs, revealing bruising here and bleeding there, building up a picture of what happened. For instance, nothing in the story concocted by the three gardaí explained bruises on Peter Matthews's face and head. More important, nothing they said explained the damage to Matthews's pancreas or the circumstances in which he received such a devastating impact to his stomach.

Ann Matthews and her family and friends were demanding that some explanation of the death be given, that someone be made accountable.

Probably in an effort to shake the solidarity of Diviney, Galligan and Jordan, senior gardaí let it be known in March 1983 that serious charges would arise from the death. Word reached Sergeant Diviney. He went to see a local superintendent and asked if he was to be charged. The answer was yes.

Diviney, his wife Margaret and Garda Galligan all immediately went to a solicitor, Tom Fitzpatrick, and made new statements. This was on 7 March 1983. All three went to the same solicitor on the same day and made similar and corroborative, supportive statements. They would later claim that this was a coincidence, that they did not act in concert.

The cover-up was falling apart. Diviney and Galligan were laying the groundwork for an accusation against Detective Tom Jordan. The new statements pointed the finger at Jordan as having punched Peter Matthews in the stomach.

The authorities decided that Sergeant Diviney would be charged with common assault and false imprisonment, relatively minor charges. Common assault is the least serious charge of assault. It does not mean that you have hit someone; it can mean that you have put them in fear of being hurt (such as, for instance, by raising your fists and saying 'fucking bastard').

In October 1983, eighteen months after the death of Peter Matthews, the trial of Sergeant Diviney took place at the Circuit Court in Bailieborough, before Mr Justice David Sheehy and a jury. Because Diviney was charged with a very minor offence, common assault, details of Peter Matthews's damaged pancreas were kept from the jury. Ann Matthews told of seeing her husband bruised and hurt, of how he accused Sergeant Diviney of assaulting him. Had Diviney pleaded guilty to such a minor charge, the punishment too would have been minor, and that would have been the end of the matter. Diviney, however, was pleading full innocence, and he had the support of his subordinate, Garda Galligan.

Slowly, haltingly, seemingly reluctantly, Diviney and Galligan told their stories of what happened that evening in the police station in

Shercock. They absolved Diviney of any part in the assaults, they left Seamus Mullen out of the interrogation, and they piled the blame on to Detective Tom Jordan.

Their story went like this: not a finger was laid on Peter Matthews until Detective Tom Jordan arrived at the station. Tom Jordan became annoyed at Peter Matthews and began hitting him about the shoulders and head.

Sergeant Diviney tried to stop him. 'I pulled him back and told him very, very forcefully that that kind of conduct would not be tolerated.'

According to a statement made by Diviney, Jordan answered, 'Fuck him, he has the book and it will have to be got.'

The Diviney/Galligan version of events continued: Galligan was in the day room just before Matthews died. After Ann Matthews left the station, Sergeant Diviney went around to the residential part of the building and had a cup of tea and a slice of bread. Then he went back to the garda station part of the building. On his way back he heard screaming from the cell. Margaret Diviney also testified that her husband had come around to the residential part of the building and was there when the screaming from the cell began.

Diviney claimed that he ran into the station, that Galligan ran out of the day room, that together they ran to the cell and as they got there they saw Detective Tom Jordan assault Peter Matthews. The suspect's trousers and underpants were down around his ankles, they said, and Jordan was holding Matthews's pullover with one hand. Matthews looked 'very rugged, very shook up'. Just then, said both Diviney and Galligan, Detective Jordan delivered a hard punch to Peter Matthews's stomach.

'Go easy, that man is in bad shape,' Garda Galligan claimed to have said.

Peter Matthews fell to the floor. Diviney and Galligan lifted him on to the bed. He was unconscious.

Both claimed that Jordan then attempted to leave the station, that he took out car keys and said, 'I'm off now.'

And that Sergeant Diviney said, 'You're not leaving, you're staying here.'

Diviney said on oath that Ann Matthews's evidence was untruthful, that the young gardaí, Feely and Mannion, were inaccurate, that he didn't see Seamus Mullen in the immediate precinct of the cell. When it was put to him that his initial account of what happened in the station, given to the investigating officers, was not truthful or accurate, he agreed it wasn't accurate. He was just out of hospital when he gave that account, he said, and he had received drugs.

The evidence of two gardaí fingering a third member of the force was devastating. The manner in which Garda Seamus Galligan gave his evidence, with apparent reluctance, only added to Galligan's credibility. The judge had to remonstrate with Galligan to get him to give coherent evidence. Galligan appeared reluctant to name Detective Jordan and referred only to 'another person in the cell'.

'Was there someone else in the cell?' asked the judge.

'Yes,' said Galligan.

'Do you know who that was?'

'Yes.'

'Well, will you tell the jury?'

'Detective Garda Jordan.'

Pressed to give details, Galligan said that Peter Matthews was assaulted by 'the man who was in the cell . . .'

'Ah, come on,' said Judge Sheehy. 'Why are you so reticent about mentioning his name?' Eventually, the judge exploded at Galligan: 'Stop pussy-footing with the jury! Please give your evidence properly. No cover-ups, now, out with it!'

And Galligan, reluctantly, hesitantly, confirmed Diviney's account, pointing the finger at Detective Tom Jordan. It came across as a young garda regretfully being forced to tell the truth about a colleague's misdeed.

Diviney's counsel, Sean Moylan, told the jury that this case was 'a horrible, horrible example of a scapegoat. Sergeant Diviney may have been guilty of moral cowardice in not ordering Tom Jordan out of the station, of weakness in front of a detective', but that was all. He said, 'Sure, Sergeant Diviney blames himself for not ordering Tom Jordan out of the station, for not telling on him.'

He said: 'No one wants to squeal on a fellow officer.' He asked why a jury had not been empanelled in relation to another officer, why weren't others being charged? What happened was a matter of speculation, nobody saw Sergeant Diviney strike Peter Matthews.

Judge David Sheehy told the jury they were 'not concerned here with the unfortunate death of Mr Matthews. That is not an issue before you. It is a very sad state of affairs, which perhaps will be an issue in another court.'

The absent Detective Jordan, who was not called as a witness, took the rap. In the face of the dreadful story of a humiliated, battered Peter Matthews, his trousers around his ankles, being viciously punched by a sadistic detective, the charges against Sergeant Diviney seemed puny. After two hours, the jury found Diviney not guilty of common assault and couldn't reach a verdict on the charge of false imprisonment. Given the shocking evidence, the jury's verdict is fully understandable.

· · · · ·

So, the dirty little secret of Shercock garda station was out. It was all Detective Tom Jordan's doing, and Sergeant Diviney had been the scapegoat. Diviney's contact with Matthews, before the suspect died, stretched from 6.15 to 8.50pm, a period of two hours and thirty-five minutes. Jordan's contact began at about 8.10pm and lasted about forty minutes. If Jordan delivered the devastating blow to Peter Matthews's stomach he had to do it in the period between his arrival, 8.10pm or so, and the latest time the medical evidence allows for the blow to have been delivered, 8.35pm. But the outcome of the first trial was that all the blame rested on Detective Jordan.

The state was at liberty to re-try Sergeant Diviney on the false imprisonment charge, on which the jury could not agree, but the office of the Director of Public Prosecutions chose not to.

The matter could not end there, and it was only a matter of time before Detective Jordan found himself in the dock. A year passed and Jordan was charged and sent for trial in October 1984 in the same Circuit Court in Bailieborough in which Sergeant Diviney had been acquitted. The charges were more serious than in the Diviney trial: manslaughter, grievous bodily harm and assault and false imprisonment.

The trial opened on Wednesday 17 October, and lasted three days. The fact that the trial was held in the town where Tom Jordan was stationed meant that few local people attended the court. A typical remark from a local man was that he was curious, but he wouldn't really like to be seen to take an interest in such a matter.

The case was heard by Mr Justice Frank Roe and a jury. Michael Moriarty SC, later to become a judge, was the prosecutor, and Paddy MacEntee SC, one of the best courtroom lawyers in the business, defended Detective Jordan. It took a while to select a jury. The judge made the usual speech to the panel from which the jurors would be selected. No one with an interest in the case could sit on the jury, he said. And that meant that no one related to anybody involved, no one who did business with anyone involved, no one with any personal or social relationship with anyone involved, whether good or bad, could sit on the jury. A juror must not have an interest in the outcome of the case.

Twelve jurors were selected. The trial was about to start. A middle-aged juror, male, a bit dawny-looking, put up his hand. 'Your honour,' he said, 'I've no interest in the case.'

The judge looked at him in bemusement. 'Well,' said the judge, trying to find a form of words, 'that's proper, that's . . .'

'I've no interest in the case, your honour, I'm not interested.'

The lawyers looked from one to another, up to the judge and over to the juror. Did any of them want such an obvious gobdaw sitting in adjudication on a matter involving one man's death and another man's freedom? The looks said they did not. The juror was excused and a woman took his place.

· · · · ·

Paddy MacEntee's first move in the defence of Detective Jordan was to have removed from the court any witnesses scheduled to give evidence. Witnesses would not be allowed to observe the trial or hear the evidence of other witnesses, until they had themselves given evidence. MacEntee's task was to attack the evidence of Sergeant Diviney and Garda Galligan. Those two would have to be broken, their credibility shredded, if Detective Tom Jordan was to have a chance of escaping conviction. By excluding witnesses from the courtroom until they had given evidence, MacEntee was maximising his chances of exploiting cracks in their stories.

In addition, the court was to have the evidence of Seamus Mullen, the ex-garda, whose role in the events in Shercock on 22 April 1982 was obscure. On the Friday before the trial Mullen was served with a summons requiring him to attend and give evidence.

Prosecutor Michael Moriarty outlined the facts of what happened at Shercock garda station, in so far as the state knew those facts. In the opening evidence postmistress Elizabeth Mullen again told of Peter Matthews coming to the post office, and Ann Matthews told of what she saw in the garda station. The state pathologist gave his opinion that while Peter Matthews died of a heart attack his death was hastened by the shock of the assault he suffered.

Ban Garda Mannion and Garda Feely gave evidence next day and told of Garda Galligan's remark about loving to hear suspects roaring.

Then Garda Galligan took the stand and Paddy MacEntee took him through the events of the evening Peter Matthews died. Galligan denied the remark about suspects roaring and painted Mannion and Feely as perjurers. He did not explain why two young gardaí would perjure themselves to blacken a fellow garda.

MacEntee savagely attacked Galligan's weakness on this point. 'That,' he said, 'is a dispute between Galligan, the sadist and lickspittle of violence, and two perfectly responsible and highly reputable members of the Garda Siochána.'

MacEntee took Galligan through the events in extreme detail, seizing on contradictions in Galligan's account. He pushed Galligan to explain why there were no entries in the station diary for 23 April, the day after the death. Galligan said he was too busy answering the phone and opening mail. MacEntee immediately produced a second station diary with entries for 23 April in Galligan's handwriting.

How come, if Garda Galligan arrived back at the station at 6.20pm on the evening of 22 April he signed himself off in the station log at 6pm? Galligan said he signed off at 6.20pm but he entered 6pm in the log because that was the time when his shift ended. Wasn't this unusual, MacEntee asked, a garda passing up twenty minutes overtime? And when Garda Galligan became involved in the investigation, and went searching litter bins for the post office book, why hadn't he signed himself back on duty?

MacEntee handed Garda Galligan the station log. He pointed out where Garda Galligan had signed himself off duty at 6pm. 'You say you made that entry at 6.20pm?'

'Yes.'

'Do you see the next entry?'

The next entry was Sergeant Diviney's: 'Coming on duty at 6.15pm re: Peter Matthews.'

'Your entry,' said MacEntee, 'should follow, not precede Diviney's.' How come, he wanted to know, the note that Galligan went off duty at 6pm, supposedly written at 6.20pm, came before Sergeant Diviney's 6.15pm entry?

'I don't know.'

Was Diviney's 6.15pm entry there when Galligan signed the book?

'It wouldn't have been.'

MacEntee was seeking to show that there had been messing with the times in the log book, that a sequence of events had been worked out and entered later on. Whatever the truth of this, MacEntee's ability to trip up Galligan on such points was damaging the young garda's credibility.

The entries, said MacEntee, had been 'manifestly falsified by you or some other person'.

'No.' Galligan appeared evasive. His evidence was peppered with 'I don't recall' and 'I don't remember'.

MacEntee asked a simple but crucial question. What was the time interval between Detective Jordan punching Peter Matthews in the stomach, as Diviney and Galligan alleged, and Peter Matthews dying?

Galligan didn't know. Was Matthews dead within a minute of the blow?

'I don't know.'

What was the time interval?

'I couldn't say.'

Was it three weeks? Was it an hour?

'I couldn't say.'

'You were there. What was the time interval?'

'I don't know.'

Judge Roe intervened. Surely Galligan could give the court some idea of the amount of time between the alleged punch and the death?

He couldn't.

'Were you there?' asked MacEntee. 'It's my instructions that you weren't.'

Why not tell, if he was there, what the time interval was? Galligan couldn't remember.

'Was it eight minutes?' MacEntee asked.

'I don't know.'

'Was it one minute?'

'I don't know.'

The fact that Galligan had misled senior gardaí investigating the death left him vulnerable.

MacEntee asked, 'For a year, for no reason whatsoever, you conspired to pervert the course of justice, simply to help someone from another police station?'

Galligan said this was untrue.

'What's untrue about it?'

'That I perverted the course of justice.'

'Between April 1982 and May 1983 did you not pervert the course of justice?'

'No.'

'What's untrue?'

'I don't know.'

'I suggest you have great difficulty distinguishing truth and lies when your self-interest is at stake.'

Galligan was a huge chunk of the state's case against Jordan, and that case was falling apart.

Sergeant Peter Diviney took the stand. He hadn't been in court for Garda Galligan's evidence and Paddy MacEntee took the sergeant through the events of the day of Peter Matthews's death, relentlessly exposing contradictions between his evidence and Galligan's. Diviney too accused Ban Garda Mannion and Garda Feely of lying. He accused them of perjury in their evidence about the presence of Seamus Mullen in the station that evening. He didn't explain why two young gardaí with accidental and peripheral involvement in the case should decide to commit perjury on this point.

How come Diviney and his wife and Garda Galligan all went to the same solicitor, on the same day, with the same story? It was coincidence, said Diviney.

'I knew I was innocent. Why should I carry the can?'

The fact that Sergeant Diviney had at first, when giving a statement to superior officers, given a false account of the events left him extremely vulnerable. He had to admit his lies.

'I was trying to cover up for Detective Jordan in case he got into trouble. I didn't want to bring trouble to a fellow member of the force when it might have been needless.'

Given Diviney's admission of giving a false statement, MacEntee could routinely refer to Diviney as a liar. He did so repeatedly. He remarked that he understood why Diviney was 'in the forefront of the liars'. Because, he said, 'You had most to lose, you had most to cover up and you had most to hide because you were the killer!'

Diviney replied, 'I was not the killer!'

By the time Diviney left the stand the case against Detective Jordan was in flitters.

Margaret Diviney took the stand. She was nervous. She described herself as an honest and religious person. She claimed that her husband was in the kitchen of their home when the screaming started in the station cell. MacEntee pressed her about the presence of Seamus Mullen. She couldn't remember. He pressed again and again. Again and again she couldn't remember.

MacEntee bored in, taking Margaret Diviney back through her evidence in exquisite detail. She was collecting flowers when she heard the screams, or she was getting a trowel? Which was it?

The relentless questioning broke Margaret Diviney. She began crying. She stood up, on the verge of hysteria. She wasn't a liar, she said. 'Just leave me alone!' she sobbed. She stumbled from the witness stand and ran from the court, wailing, 'You can arrest me, but I'm not saying any more.'

It might have been instructive to hear Paddy MacEntee apply his skills to the evidence of Seamus Mullen, the ex-garda. But that was not to be. The court was informed that on Wednesday, the day the trial began, Seamus Mullen was admitted to Ballinasloe Mental Hospital. His wife Elizabeth was called to the stand.

'When,' asked Paddy MacEntee, 'can we expect him to discharge himself?'

'He can't discharge himself.'

'I understand he can.' MacEntee told the court he understood that Mr Mullen had admitted himself voluntarily.

'Who committed him?' MacEntee asked. Mrs Mullen said that in the early hours of Wednesday morning she sent for Seamus's brother.

'Did he commit him?'

'He drove him.' Mrs Mullen didn't say who had committed her husband to the mental hospital.

· · · · ·

The state's chief witnesses, Diviney and Galligan, had been shown to be liars. Their stories were riddled with contradictions. When the state finished presenting its case Paddy MacEntee asked the judge to withdraw the charge of manslaughter. The medical evidence was that the punch which traumatised Peter Matthews's pancreas was delivered at least fifteen minutes before his death. Given the amount of bleeding from the pancreas, Peter Matthews had to have lived at least fifteen minutes after receiving that devastating punch. It was impossible to say exactly when the blow was delivered, it could have been some hours earlier, but it wasn't less than fifteen minutes before Peter Matthews died. Even if Diviney and Galligan were to be believed when they said that they saw Detective Jordan punch Matthews in the stomach, that could not have been the punch that caused the damage to the pancreas. That punch was, according to Diviney, delivered just before Matthews died.

Judge Frank Roe agreed with the defence application and withdrew the charges of manslaughter and false imprisonment. Detective Jordan now faced charges of grievous bodily harm and actual bodily harm.

Paddy MacEntee addressed the jury on the remaining charges. 'I do not pretend for one second, nor is it the case that anyone can possibly attempt to stand over what was going on in Shercock. There was an outrage perpetrated on Peter Matthews. There was an outrage perpetrated on Peter Matthews's wife, and I accept that the attempts to cover up that outrage scream to heaven and to the law for vengeance.'

If Peter Matthews hadn't died, MacEntee said, 'it would all easily have been hushed up.' The allegations of beatings would involve a conflict of evidence involving the word of a 'criminal drunk against that of a group of gardaí. And we all know who would win that.'

Detective Tom Jordan had not given evidence, nor had his account of what he claimed happened in the station that night been made public. MacEntee, in an account that could not be cross-examined or tested, put forward Jordan's story. MacEntee said his instructions were that Sergeant Diviney assaulted Peter Matthews initially. And later, in the cell, Diviney threw 'violent punches into Mr Matthews's stomach'. Jordan was now claiming that he put himself between Diviney and Matthews and received 'a violent flake' from Diviney, which nearly winded him.

If this was so, why didn't Jordan arrest Diviney for assaulting both Matthews and Jordan? The question begged to be asked but could not be put to Jordan since he didn't take the stand.

MacEntee portrayed Jordan as 'the victim of a conspiracy to pervert the course of justice'. He said that Detective Jordan had been 'the scapegoat in the affair'. He lacerated Sergeant Diviney, Margaret Diviney and Garda Galligan. 'This is a perfectly simple case. Here were three sad people so deranged that they no longer knew what was lies and what was the truth. Finding themselves in dire trouble, they hunted around for a scapegoat.'

MacEntee throughout the case referred to the sergeant as 'Diviney', and sometimes as 'the liar Diviney'.

At one point Margaret Diviney could take it no more. She stood up in the body of the court and screamed, 'It's Sergeant Diviney, not Diviney!' and was removed from the courtroom.

MacEntee told the jury, 'You would not hang a cat on their evidence.'

Judge Roe told the jury, 'It comes down to what do you think of the evidence of Garda Galligan and Sergeant Diviney. You must have no doubt that the sergeant and the guard told the truth. I offer no opinion.'

After an absence of thirty-nine minutes the jury returned with a verdict of not guilty.

· · · · ·

Sergeant Diviney was described, at his trial, as the 'scapegoat', and he was acquitted. And at the second trial it was Detective Jordan who was the 'scapegoat', and he too was acquitted. Both took turns pointing fingers at the other. Seamus Mullen went into a mental hospital and couldn't testify or be cross-examined. No one was guilty. There is no doubt that Judge Frank Roe was right, on the evidence before him, to withdraw the charge of manslaughter from the jury. There is no doubt that, on the evidence before them, both juries were not alone entitled to reach the verdicts they did but duty bound to do so. Which is not to say that they came close to the truth of what happened that day in Shercock garda station.

The description given by Diviney and Galligan of Peter Matthews's trousers having been pulled down was bizarre and was dismissed by Paddy MacEntee along with the rest of their evidence. The forensic evidence points to the possibility that Peter Matthews's trousers were indeed at some stage pulled down and that he fell on the floor of the cell. We can speculate on this because during the autopsy Professor Harbison found some grease stains on Peter Matthews's right wrist and hands, on his right knee, inner shin and thigh. There was, according to an independent garda witness, 'sticky, dirty, greasy oil' on the floor of the cell, as at one stage a motorcycle had been stored there for some length of time. This suggests that Matthews's leg came in contact with the oil or grease, and for that his leg would have had to have been bare. There might be another explanation of how the grease got there, but no one has suggested what it might be. The evidence does not, of course, tell us when Peter Matthews's leg might have been bared, when he might have fallen to the cell floor and made contact with the oil. Nor have we any reliable evidence of who might have been responsible for this happening to him.

Ann Matthews received compensation from the state. Diviney, Galligan and Jordan left the police force. Diviney, at forty-eight, was just two years short of retirement on a decent pension. He had a clean disciplinary record before the Matthews affair, and now it was all gone.

There was a lot of disquiet over the fact that a man could die violently in a police cell and his death could remain unexplained and no one would be made accountable. But no further avenues were explored, no further charges were laid. No one in power made any fuss, there were no lessons to be learned, no changes to be made. Pressing too hard on such an issue might bring whispers of anti-police tendencies, perhaps even suggestions of a whiff of subversion. For the authorities, the case was over. The media moved on to other matters. It was as if nothing at all had happened.

⑤ Family Values

She hid in the long grass and looked back at the house. She could hear him screaming abuse, she could hear the crockery being smashed. She lay there for a while, shivering in the January night, a twenty-six-year-old woman hiding from her father.

She was wearing just trousers, a T-shirt and slippers. He had pulled the bra off her earlier and made her stand half-naked in front of her nine-year-old son.

Suddenly, someone appeared from behind her, up over the wall. A man stood there on the fence, a stranger, a few feet away. She lurched down in fear. If her father came out now he'd see the figure and he'd think it was her and he'd come running this way.

She got up fast and ran. Her hair was caked with blood. Blood was running from her head and from her arm, where he had hit her with the bottle. She ran and ran. This was on the evening of Thursday 16 January 1992.

We will call her Mary, we will call her son John and her sister Linda. We will call her father Peter and her mother Ruth. None of those names are the real names of these people.

• • • • •

The water and electricity were disconnected and they couldn't get anyone to fix them up. It was Christmas 1975 and the family had bought a house and a farm of five acres, near a village in County Kilkenny.

Peter and Ruth were both from rural backgrounds in England. Both of them became farm workers when they left school. They met in 1962 and in January 1964 they married. Peter was nineteen, Ruth was twenty-two. In November 1964 their first child was born. They lived in a two-storey farm cottage and one night, about a month after the birth of the child, they went upstairs to bed and left the baby downstairs in a carry-cot beside the open fire. During the night a spark or ember from the fire landed perhaps on a rug, perhaps on the baby's clothes, causing smouldering. Ruth came down to feed the baby during the night and found the room full of smoke. She picked up the baby. The little body was so hot that Ruth had to drop it. The baby, impregnated with smoke and overwhelmed by heat, died.

The couple left the farmhouse and went to live with Peter's parents. They kept their grief to themselves. 'We didn't let it out,' according to Ruth. Their doctor advised them to have another child as soon as possible. Mary was born a year later, at Biddlescombe Hospital, in Ilfracombe, Devon. Linda was born two years after that. During the period of Linda's birth Ruth had a minor heart attack and her doctor advised her not to have any more children, and prescribed the contraceptive pill.

Peter and Ruth got their own place, in a village in Devon, but it meant giving up farm work. Peter drifted from job to job. He worked on a building site and later drove a bread van. Ruth got work as a cleaner in the local school. They had, according to Mary, a happy family life.

Peter always had a longing to have a farm of his own, but various attempts at purchasing land in England came to nothing. They made visits to Ireland, scouting out the possibilities of buying land. They had no prior connections with Ireland. Peter fancied Belfast, but Ruth was afraid to go there. Towards the end of 1975 they took a ferry to Rosslare and roamed around Wexford and Carlow, keeping an eye out for land for sale. They had no plans. They came across an estate agent who showed them a site in County Kilkenny, five acres with a prefab building. They immediately purchased it. They moved in after Christmas 1975. Peter was thirty, Ruth was thirty-three. Mary was ten, her sister Linda was eight.

There were a lot of creative people living in the area, and there was an awareness of the need for community development. A major industry had recently collapsed and unemployment was high. Social workers noted an increase in drinking and domestic violence. There were a lot of inter-related marriages.

The nature of the community was of little interest to the new family. They were loners, they might as well have settled in a desert or on the moon. Their contact with the rest of the community was minimal. Their standard of living was atrocious. There was no electricity in the prefab building, no water or toilet. They used a camping gas cooker and a neighbour loaned them a gas heater. Sometimes it seemed like they mostly lived on pancakes. Peter's mother came with them, to spend the New Year in Kilkenny, and stayed on into January. One morning, a few days after granny went back to England, Mary was at home with her father. Her mother was out.

Peter shoved his daughter on to his bed and began tearing at her clothes. He broke the waistband of her skirt, ripping the garment down the middle. He pushed his daughter's pants aside and raped her.

Peter was a few days short of his thirty-first birthday. Mary was two months past the age of ten. She didn't know what was happening, why her father was moving up and down on top of her. He didn't say anything.

Mary didn't say anything, she was too frightened. She could only think that she was being punished for doing something or not doing something. It hurt terribly and when he finished with her she was bleeding.

Four or five weeks later she was still sore, and he raped her again. 'You're a very naughty girl,' he said.

Mary struggled to get up and her father kept knocking her back down, slapping her face and chest. The overwhelming question that dominated Mary as a result of the rape, and that would dominate her life for years to come was, 'What did I do wrong?'

After that he raped her every two or three weeks. He prefaced his rapes with the demand, 'I want a bit of sex,' then he'd push Mary down on the bed. If she struggled he hit her. She came to accept that all she could do was lie there and get it over with.

Ruth did an AnCo course and got shiftwork in a nearby factory. Peter got a job as a hotel porter but it didn't last long and apart from that he couldn't find work. He got Home Assistance of £6 a week and whatever could be earned from the five-acre farm.

· · · · ·

Mary and Linda went to the local convent national school. Two years later Mary went to secondary school. She mixed more easily with boys than girls and played football and rugby. Girls talked about boring stuff such as hair and make-up, boys talked about real stuff, farming and cows. Neither Mary nor Linda were allowed out to play or mix with other children after school. The school authorities noted Mary's inability to make friends and referred her to an educational psychologist. Mary often missed school, sometimes for weeks. She told lies to her classmates and this made her unpopular and led to even more isolation. She received remedial help from her teacher.

The family lived in the prefab building for four years, then they moved to a terraced house in a nearby townland. They held on to the five acres, keeping two cows and some sheep, chickens and ducks, and raising turkeys for the Christmas market.

Meanwhile, the rape of Mary continued. Ruth would be at the factory, on shiftwork, Linda would be at school. Peter would tell Mary she had to stay home to help on the land. He called her a whore, he hit her, he raped her. Sometimes he had drink taken, just as often he was sober. For Peter and Mary the rape became as routine as feeding the chickens, just a part of the family's cramped little life. At some stage Mary told Ruth that there was something wrong. Daddy is doing something wrong, she said. Her mother, who was herself receiving occasional beatings, just said things would be OK.

Ruth said something to her husband, something along the lines that he couldn't carry on with that crack with Mary. Peter didn't rape Mary for a couple of months, then he started again.

· · · · ·

In the summer of 1981, Mary would sometimes spend the day with her father. He would tell her to stay home from school on Thursdays and he'd collect his dole between 10 and 11am and take her to a local pub.

Peter would drink his dole money and at about 3 or 4pm he'd bring his daughter home. His wife was sent out to the farm to do chores. Linda might be kept back at school, or if she came home she was sent out to the farm to help her mother. Peter had Mary alone. No matter what Mary did or didn't do, Peter would become violent. Perhaps she had talked to someone or even just said hello. He called her a whore and raped her. This happened most Thursdays.

Mary was fourteen and attending the Presentation convent. Peter was thirty-four.

Sometimes there was violence without rape. He told her the tyres on her bike needed pumping up and she delayed too long before doing it, so he threw a hammer at her, hitting her on the side of the head. He once whipped her and sent her to bed for three days, with nothing to eat or drink. She felt dizzy as she crept out from her bedroom to the bathroom. She'd flush the toilet and hurriedly sneak a drink of water from the tap, the flushing noise covering the sound of the running water. Her mother, when she got the chance, would sneak in a slice of bread or a sausage.

Linda too was beaten. A fox stole two hens when the two girls were off riding their bikes. Peter wore a belt cinched tight around his waist, outside the loops of his trousers. There was a metal buckle on the belt. He took the belt off, made Mary and Linda lower their pants and bend over and he lashed them with the belt. On one occasion, while helping her father clear ditches, Linda complained about the cold. He made her take her clothes off and stand in the field wearing only a vest.

Mary once told Linda that her father had tried to have sex with her. Linda laughed at the idea of sexual abuse. He hadn't tried sex with her, she said, she was just a punchbag.

The assaults left Mary with bruises and abrasions, and visits to doctors followed. Peter ensured that Mary didn't go to the same doctor too often. Mary, from within her closed, traumatised little world, saw the assaults and abuse as retribution for some unspecified wrongs she had done. From childhood, broken in spirit and suffused with the shame and guilt whipped up by her father's degradation of her, she saw the outside world as something to be feared, not a place of help.

When teachers asked about the black eyes, the broken arms and the bruises, Mary always had a detailed and convincing story prepared. She had slipped, fallen, tripped or been kicked by an animal. She just had a lot of accidents.

· · · · ·

Mary, forced to submit to sexual demands from the age of ten, knew little about sex. There was no sex education at school. Her mother told her a little about menstruation. After Christmas 1981 Mary had pains in her stomach. She had missed three periods, she was unable to zip up a pair of her jeans. Her mother took her to a doctor in the village. The doctor said Mary had wind, from eating too much at Christmas.

They went to another doctor, who confirmed that Mary was pregnant.

Driving back from the examination, Ruth asked Mary, 'Is your father the father of your baby?'

'Yes.'

'Don't worry about it, everything will be OK.' It was the first clear acknowledgment between them of what was going on.

When they got home Peter told Mary to go lie down. He and Ruth talked about the pregnancy but Mary wasn't told what was discussed. Knowing now that Mary was pregnant, Peter stopped raping her. If it was a girl, he told her, the baby would be placed for adoption. If it was a boy he would adopt it. He had always wanted a son.

Although he wasn't raping Mary, he continued to beat her when he felt a beating was merited. Given the job of feeding the lambs, feeling cold and hungry herself, Mary had something to eat, intending to feed the lambs later. Her father found her eating in the kitchen, remonstrated with her for feeding herself before feeding the lambs, took off his belt and beat his four-month-pregnant daughter.

Mary gave up school. Baby John was born in May 1982. Mary was sixteen. Ruth took care of filling in the necessary forms and registering John's birth. Mary stayed a week in hospital. There were three other women in Mary's ward, two of them also single parents. When she was asked about the father of her baby, Mary said she had a boyfriend but he was in England at the moment. Peter had prepared Mary to refuse to name the father. If she was pushed she was to stand firm and say, 'I don't want to tell you.' The prepared version that the family would give if anyone asked was that Mary had been made pregnant by a local married man.

About a week after Mary came home from hospital, two weeks after giving birth, Peter went into her bedroom and pushed her down on the bed. 'I want a bit of sex,' he said. Mary struggled this time.

'Don't do it, this is wrong,' she cried. Peter hit her about the face and breasts until she was subdued. She just lay there as he raped her.

A short time later she was eating in the kitchen when her father said to her, 'You'd better go on the pill now.'

Her mother took her to a doctor, who took down their medical card number and wrote a prescription for the pill. For the next ten years Mary was on the pill.

There were two bedrooms in the house, a bathroom and a kitchen/sitting room. Peter and Ruth had one bedroom, Mary and Linda the second. Baby John was kept in a pram in the kitchen.

Mary claimed Lone Parent Allowance and received £42 a week. Each Thursday she would go to collect the money at the post office. Her father waited outside and when she came out she had to give him the money. When she asked him for a fiver one week, he thumped her and left her with a black eye.

Now that she was finished with school Mary's world became even more enclosed. She had no contact with former schoolmates. There was a neighbour she got to know and trust and there was another family which lived some miles away which she came to know and like. The father of that family became godfather to her son, John.

Linda didn't know that her father was the father of her sister's baby. She believed the story about the local married man being the father. Linda couldn't take the beatings any more. She was fourteen when Peter beat her with a carpet sweeper, breaking it across her back. She ran away twice and was brought back, once with the help of the police. The third time, when she was fifteen, she stayed with a neighbour. The family was known in the area to be odd. They didn't mix, they weren't part of the community. Linda's running away was accepted. Linda stayed with these people and for the next eight years never saw any member of her family.

With Linda gone, Mary was able to take baby John, now aged two, from his pram and keep him in a cot in her bedroom.

With the birth of John, the family came to the attention of the state services, in the form of nurses and social workers. A public health nurse visited the home to advise Mary on feeding and hygiene. A student social worker, on temporary placement with the South Eastern Health Board, visited Mary when John was three weeks old. She was alone in the house when he called. She stuck to the cover story, that the baby's father was a local man, married with two children, and she was no longer seeing him. She had a boyfriend now, she said, a boy of her own age. She would stay home and look after the baby, she said, no more school, no work. She had great support for the baby, she said, great support at home.

The social worker thought Mary seemed ambiguous when she spoke of her parents' support. He returned to the house several times over that summer of 1982. Mary's stories were a mixture of truth and fantasy. She was covering up, but bits of the truth were mixed in with the stories. She told the social worker that when her father found out she was pregnant by a married man he beat her with a poker. She said she cried in hospital when her father didn't visit her, that she was discharged early after the birth because she missed her daddy so much.

On one occasion Mary told the social worker she didn't get on with her sister Linda. On another occasion the social worker noticed the two girls getting on fine. He wrote in his notes: 'I am not sure if Mary has been telling me lies, but she certainly hasn't been telling me the whole story.'

Mary, traumatised by years of abuse, locked into the tiny world of violence, conditioned to protect the family's dirty little secrets, was saying whatever her confused mind thought sounded right. Her performance was good enough to protect the family's secrets from the social worker, but it had gaps through which he could see that there was something wrong.

After the summer, the student social worker's placement was finished and he moved on. When he didn't contact her, Mary rang the social work department several times, asking to speak to him. She was offered contact with another social worker but she declined.

The public health nurse continued visiting Mary. Because Mary was a teenager and unmarried, because the house was in a state of poor hygiene, baby John was listed as 'At Risk', and noted for monitoring.

• • • • •

Within the family, there was talk of Peter and Ruth adopting little John. Mary's attitude to this seems to have been ambiguous. When John was six months old Mary contacted a senior social worker and asked him to come to the house to discuss John being adopted by her parents.

Mary and Ruth met the social worker together. Would she have any say, asked Mary, in where the baby might be placed for adoption? Her parents wanted to adopt John, she said. And then she said something that might have blown the whole thing wide open. In getting John adopted by her parents, she asked, would it help that her father was John's father?

The social worker was taken aback. He asked Mary to confirm what she had just said. Mary said yes, her father was John's father.

The social worker asked Ruth if she knew about this. Yes, Ruth said, she knew what had been going on. Mary and Ruth told the social worker about the violence against them both. The social worker told them they didn't have to go on living like this, they could go to the police and complain, go to a solicitor and get a barring order from the courts.

They said they didn't want to do either of those things. Could the social worker help? He replied that he had no power to intervene unless the baby was at risk. Mary and Ruth said that Peter doted on the child. John was not at risk.

The social worker went to the police in Kilkenny. He didn't identify the family, he just asked in general terms what the police could do. Not much, it turned out. There had to be a complaint from a member of the family. Anyway, they said, cases of incest are very hard to prosecute.

Mary visited the social worker at his office. Now she was worried that she might be pushed out of the family home and separated from her baby. The social worker told her that wouldn't happen. He tried to persuade her to leave home, but Mary said things were better now and she'd stay.

· · · · ·

One day, Peter sent Mary into his bedroom and told her to strip. He took off his clothes. He instructed his wife to bring in a polaroid camera and to take a photo as he posed as if performing oral sex on his daughter. Ruth stood there, unable to do it. Peter got up and beat her around the face. Then he got back down and his wife took the picture. Mary then had to take pictures of her parents in various sexual positions.

In May 1985, in the midst of one of his furies, Peter tore a metal bar from a Rayburn cooker and struck out at Mary. She raised an arm in fear and the bar lashed into her wrist, breaking it. She had to go to the casualty department of St Luke's Hospital in Kilkenny. She explained the injury by saying she fell while playing football with her three-year-old son. Her hand was in plaster for six weeks.

Three months later she was back in St Luke's, with injuries to her face and her left foot. She had been referred by a doctor. Mary's stories to the doctor and later to the nurses in casualty were confused. She was either punched or kicked in the face and two days later was either kicked on the left foot or had a concrete block dropped on her toe. No one picked up on the discrepancies. For the first time, Mary was admitting publicly that her injuries were not the result of an accident, that she had been assaulted. What she said was confused, but it clearly indicated trouble. No one followed up on this, no one asked any further questions.

Rumours about the family had grown. A public health nurse and a neighbour had both passed on their worries to social workers. There was a lack of coordination and exchange of information between different social workers who had made contact with the family. Mary's statements about what was going on within the family continued to be contradictory and fragmented. Mary would reveal some of the secrets, then back off, make appointments and break them. A social worker met Mary outside her house one day in June

1985. Mary said no, she couldn't ask the social worker in. Her father was cruel, she said, he kept raping her and he took her unmarried mother's allowance.

The social worker noted: 'It was very difficult to know how real any of this was and how much of it was a combination of Mary's fantasy and imagination . . . I told her that I was unwilling to be dragged into a situation of listening to her stories and then not being allowed or placed in a position to do anything about it.' The social worker arranged to meet Mary the following week in Carlow. Mary didn't turn up.

Social workers walk a fine line. They rush in too soon and they are home wreckers making false accusations. They hold back and they are neglectful, standing idly by while children are abused. Knowledge of child sexual abuse was less widespread in the Ireland of the mid-1980s than it might have been. The whole concept of child abuse was regarded as one of violence and cruelty to children. Official Ireland had always shied away from accepting that sexual abuse and incest happened in the island noted for its family values. It would be two years later, in 1987, before the Department of Health Guidelines on Child Abuse dealt fully with the subject of child sexual abuse. Five years after that, many professionals would admit to being unfamiliar with the guidelines, some didn't know they existed, some had heard of them but had not seen them.

Violence in the home had for long been regarded as a private affair. The Constitution identifies the family as the bedrock of society. Domestic violence was a family matter, and the state had no business poking its nose into the family. From the late 1960s onwards, the women's movement had dragged domestic violence into the light of day. Attitudes had changed, but many still regarded the roars and the screams coming out through the cracks in the family circle to be no business of outsiders.

In Mary's case, several official bodies, medical, health, social welfare and police, had bits of the truth, but the coordination needed to put the jigsaw together didn't exist. And no one was sufficiently aware of the signs of sexual abuse, or confident enough in their understanding of what was going on, to intervene.

Meanwhile, with Ruth out of the house a lot, doing shiftwork at a factory, Mary continued to be raped about once a week. She got thumped and clattered, black eyes and broken ribs. When Mary turned eighteen the rapes increased to an average of twice a week. In November 1985, when she was nineteen, Mary attended a GP for bruises on her wrist and arm. She told the doctor that her father was having sex with her and beating her. The doctor, rather than engaging the help of the social services and involving the state in the matter, decided to handle things himself. He would admonish Peter. He wrote to Peter and Ruth, asking them to come see him. They did so. He sat them down and told them that Mary had said her father was interfering with her. Peter didn't say anything. He just stood up and walked out. That was the end of the doctor's involvement.

At home, there was a row. Peter said to John, now aged three, 'Your mother wants to put me away.' Peter wouldn't talk to Mary. Ruth said to Peter that it had to stop. He said it wouldn't happen again.

The next morning, when her father and mother were up at the farm, Mary took her son John and, with the help of a social worker in Carlow, she left the area and went to stay in a hostel in Dublin.

Five days later, Ruth went to a social worker in Kilkenny and complained that Mary had left home. She didn't mind if Mary didn't want to come back but she wanted John brought back. Mary, she said, wasn't caring properly for the child.

Peter and Ruth contacted the police and reported Mary missing. The police obligingly traced Mary to the Dublin hostel and informed her parents of her whereabouts. Peter went to the hostel and stood outside, demanding to see his daughter, intimidating other occupants.

Ruth went to see Mary. Mary told her, 'I don't want to be living like that.'

Ruth said she would talk to Peter. Mary bowed to her parents' wishes and returned to the family home. Peter had promised Ruth there would be no more abuse. After a while Ruth asked Mary if there was anything happening and Mary said no. And nothing happened for a while. And then it started again.

On 4 September 1985 a public health nurse found Mary living in the prefab house on the five acres. She said she was on bad terms with her parents. That day, at the South Eastern Health Board offices in Kilkenny, at the end of a case conference about a child in the locality, social workers discussed Mary and her child. Information was so fragmented, Mary's allegations were so tentative and contradictory, that the meeting could not come to a firm conclusion about what was going on or what needed to be done. A public health nurse noted the meeting's decision: 'Get garda to keep a watch if necessary and see for ourselves if someone is being battered.'

Mary ran away again, this time to her granny's in England. Peter came after her and brought her home and beat her with his belt and raped her twice within two hours. She lay there under him wishing him dead, wanting to kill him but too afraid to fight back.

In 1987, when John was five, Peter insisted that the child be moved into a bed in his and Ruth's bedroom.

In 1988, when she was twenty-three, Mary again ran away to her granny's in England and again her father brought her home. Subsequently, he raped her anally. She screamed with the pain and he slapped her face and told her to shut up. She bled badly for three days and had to use sanitary towels. Peter wouldn't let her go to a doctor. The anal rape scared him. What if the bleeding hadn't stopped and it led to the discovery of what was going on? He didn't rape her anally again. But he did continue the usual routine of beatings and rapes.

It had been going on for twelve years now. It would continue for another four.

· · · · ·

One morning in May 1990, after a row about milking a cow, Peter beat his daughter, now aged twenty-five, with his belt. He got a hammer and made her hold out her left hand, palm down. He hit her hand with the hammer again and again. Each time he hit her he remarked that she wouldn't touch anything again for a while.

Mary went to hospital in Kilkenny, and was sent to St James's in Dublin, for treatment to the nerves of her left index finger. She explained the injury by saying she'd been kicked by a cow.

On 6 December 1991, Peter was drinking, as usual. He had received his dole cheque that day and he and Mary went into the village to cash it. He stayed in a pub for a while, then they returned home.

Peter was standing by the fire, Mary was sitting at the table. Peter began complaining that Ruth and Mary wouldn't let him go back to England for Christmas. He started beating Mary and Ruth. He took off his belt and began swinging it. Mary took injuries to one eye and to her nose. Her top lip was swollen. Peter threw an electric kettle at Mary. She avoided it and this made him even more angry. He threw a can of peas. Mary ducked and the can smashed a window. Peter chased her out into the hall and she crouched down as he beat her.

Peter told Ruth to fetch a neighbour named Mick, a handyman, to fix the window. Mary and Ruth left to fetch Mick. When Mick arrived at the front door Peter went out the back door and across the fields. Mick and Mary measured the glass, went and bought it and put it in. When Mick left Mary rang the gardaí in Kilkenny. She told them she was a neighbour of Peter and Ruth's and there was a row going on in that house and she thought someone was hurt.

Peter returned to the house at around 7pm. He beat Mary again and ordered her to take her clothes off. She was sitting in the freezing cold kitchen in bra and pants, her nose bleeding, her mother's eye cut, not knowing if Peter wanted her clothes off because they were bloody or because he wanted to rape her. After a while there was a knock on the door. It was a garda.

When the garda came in Peter ordered Mary to go put on a dressing gown. She did so and returned to the kitchen.

The garda said he had a complaint about a row in the house. He looked at Mary and Ruth, both beaten and bloody. He asked Mary, in front of her father, if she wanted to make a statement. She knew the minute the garda left she'd be beaten again, so she said no.

Her mother refused to make a statement to the garda. 'We thought we probably would have got worse once he'd gone,' she said later, 'and we didn't want to talk ourselves into any bother.' The garda offered to take the mother to a doctor. She said no.

The garda suggested that Peter go to bed and sleep it off, and Peter agreed. The garda left.

Mary went to take a bath. As she lay in the water she heard her father go to bed.

Two weeks later, five days before Christmas 1991, Mary was in the kitchen when her father stood in the doorway and said, 'I want a bit of sex.' He took her to her bedroom and told her to strip from the waist down, not to bother with taking off her jumper or bra, and he raped her. Then they went up to the five acres to kill the turkeys to sell them for Christmas. Her father did the killing, Mary pulled the feathers off.

Two days later Peter brought Mary to his mother's home in the Devon village, for Christmas. Christmas Day was fine, everyone enjoyed themselves. On Boxing Day, Peter took Mary to a local pub, where he got into the company of men he knew. He had told his mother he would be home at around 11.30pm. At around that time she came to the pub looking for him. His mates slagged him off, seeing his mother come to pull him out of the pub. He went home with Mary and his mother. On the way he wanted to go into another pub but his mother refused. They went home, Peter got some money and went out again.

After a while the phone rang. It was the landlord of a local pub. Peter was in no condition to go home himself, could someone collect him. Mary went and with great difficulty brought her father home.

When he arrived home Peter's mother made some remark to him, out of Mary's hearing. Peter exploded in rage and said they were going home. It was now the early hours of the morning. Peter demanded that Mary find out the time of the next train. Mary rang the local station, where a machine played a message that said there would be no trains until next day. Peter threw their belongings into their bags and said they were going home. Mary pleaded with him, told him there were no trains, but he wouldn't listen. The two left the house.

They walked through the village and up a hill, Mary carrying the bags. Peter was behind her, shouting and cursing. He suddenly kicked her in the back of the leg and she fell down. He was wearing steel-capped boots. As she tried to get up he kicked her in the eye. She felt blood running down her face from her eye.

They came to a phone and she tried to call a taxi, with no luck. She rang a doctor and got another answering machine. They walked for a long time. They came across a couple pulling into the driveway of a house. Peter asked them for a lift to the nearest hospital. They had been mugged, he said, further down the road, and they were trying to get to a hospital. The couple drove them to a hospital, where the story of a mugging was repeated.

Mary's eye injury received five stitches. It would be at least two days before she was able to open her eye. When they left the hospital in the middle of the night they went to a B & B but were refused admission when the owner saw Mary's eye. Father and daughter spent the rest of the night sleeping back to back on the platform of the railway station.

Back in Ireland, Peter continued to rape his daughter. 'I want a bit of sex,' he would say. 'Get them off.'

Mary's vision had been severely affected by the kick to her face. The sight in her right eye was gone. She could see darkness or light but couldn't make out shapes. She went to a GP on New Year's Eve 1992. She told him her father had kicked her in the face. The doctor wanted her to contact the police or a social worker but Mary wouldn't. The doctor called an ambulance and had her admitted to the casualty department of Waterford Regional Hospital. There, her mind zigging and zagging between fear and shame and the need to seek help and the urge to cover up, she told staff she had been mugged in England. An eye specialist found that her right eye was severely damaged. The prognosis was poor for getting her vision back.

Less than two weeks later, on the evening of Sunday 12 January 1992, Ruth put her young grandson, John, to bed some time between 7.30 and 8pm. She read him a story.

Mary was up in her bedroom when the door opened and Peter came in. He said nothing, just pushed Mary on to the bed. Mary said nothing, just lay there looking up at him. 'Get them off,' Peter said.

Mary pulled down her trousers and pants, Peter lay on top of her and raped her. Afterwards, Mary got a glass of water from the kitchen and went to bed.

Two days later, on the morning of Tuesday 14 January, Mary was in the kitchen, John was at school. Peter came into the kitchen. 'I want a bit of sex,' he said. He went down to Mary's bedroom. Mary went down and took off her trousers, shirt and pants. She left on her bra. She lay down on the bed. Peter got on top of her and raped her.

Afterwards, Mary went to the bathroom and washed herself. Then, she and her father went about their work, feeding the animals.

Two days later, on Thursday 16 January 1992, Peter was drinking poteen. Two local lads came looking to buy some spare parts for a car.

Peter had two old cars and the lads wanted to buy them. After some dickering they agreed on a deal and the two lads gave Peter £20 as a deposit. Whether it was just sheer drunkenness, whether the casual deal with the two lads made Peter feel bested and inadequate, we won't know.

Mary and Ruth had been in the nearby village. When they returned Peter seemed 'to go haywire all of a sudden'. He began ranting about how his family didn't trust him and they thought he couldn't make a deal. He hit Mary first with his hands and then with his belt. He threw into the fire the £20 the two lads had paid him. He hit Mary on the hand with a salad cream bottle and the bottle broke. Peter picked up an empty vodka bottle from which he had been drinking poteen. He swung it at Mary, hitting her twice on the head. Blood ran down the back of her head. Peter was shouting at her, drunkenly demanding she answer some question, but she didn't know what he was talking about, so he kept hitting her.

He pulled off her jumper and T-shirt and tore away her bra and made her stand there in front of nine-year-old John. 'This is the difference between men and women!' he roared at the child. He threw the jumper and bra in the fire and told Mary to put on the T-shirt. Then he began beating Ruth.

There was a knock on the door. A neighbour named Dinnie had come to visit. Peter locked Mary in her bedroom and let the neighbour in. Civilities were exchanged, Dinnie had a cup of tea and left.

When the visitor had gone Peter told Mary she could come down for a cup of tea. She had taken two mouthfuls of tea when he erupted again. He beat Mary and pushed her out the front door. 'If you want to go whoring I want the money!' he roared, then he slammed the door.

Mary hid in the garage. She heard him smashing crockery and she heard her mother say, 'You've hit her enough, leave her alone!'

Mary thought this meant her father was coming out to get her. She ran and hid in the long grass.

· · · · ·

She ran and ran and she found a group of young people just hanging out. She told them what happened, her head and her arm bleeding, shivering in slippers and T-shirt.

Suddenly, one of the kids spotted Peter approaching in the distance. Mary ran and hid and the kids waited until Peter came along and they said hello to him and behaved as though nothing was wrong, and when he was gone they went and got Mary from her hiding place. One of them walked with her to a neighbour's house. Neighbours washed her wounds but they couldn't stop the bleeding, so they took Mary to a doctor, who called an ambulance and sent her to St Luke's Hospital. The GP rang the hospital and asked them to contact the police. Mary had five stitches in her head and three in her arm and a fractured finger. The loss of sight in her right eye was noted.

She told the nurses that her father had been beating her up for about fifteen years. She told them he had sexually abused her for years. Mary's injuries were photographed, the police were contacted and a note was made that Mary's father was not to be told that Mary had been admitted to the hospital.

The next day, a social worker and a garda came to see Mary. Mary was at first uneasy at the prospect of police intervention. Without the patience of the police it is possible that Mary might yet again have pulled back from the brink and told another contradictory story and allowed herself to be sucked back into the family.

Mary was discharged after four days and taken to a refuge in Waterford. By now, Peter and Ruth were claiming that they had adopted young John. On the way to Waterford with a social worker, Mary picked up John from school and took him with her.

During the four days she was in hospital Mary was approached by Garda Agnes Reddy. The police had realised that there was something more going on here than just an isolated assault. Over the next few days, as Garda Reddy patiently and gently drew her out, Mary revealed the existence of other, older injuries. She eventually showed Garda Reddy two of the obscene photos she and her mother had been forced to take, which she had recently found at the back of a drawer.

Garda Reddy fetched Mary and John's clothes from her home and continued her chats with Mary. Gradually the full horror of those years was extracted from Mary. Garda Reddy took a twenty-page statement from Mary. It is customary when such statements are made for the garda to read back to the witness what has been written down. Having delivered herself of the catalogue of horrors Mary said no, she didn't want the statement read back to her. She signed it. Superintendent Vincent Duffe began checking hospital records, uncovering the history of injuries, all ascribed to accidents.

The police went to take a statement from Linda, Mary's sister. Since running away eight years earlier, Linda had had no contact with her family. She had married. Her family were not at the wedding. She had three children. Peter and Ruth had no contact with their grandchildren. Only now that the family had been broken open was some contact resumed.

Peter, suspecting what was coming, decided to go to England. He had no money. Ruth was ill and out of work, and therefore without income. She borrowed money to pay Peter's fare to England. After a while, Peter, no longer with any roots in England, had to come back. He returned to Kilkenny but stayed inside the house for ten weeks, afraid to be seen outside. He believed that if the police knew he was back they would arrest him. It was Mary who heard that he had returned and who told the police.

Peter, now forty-eight, was arrested in September 1992 and charged with fifty-six counts of rape, incest and assault. Faced with the evidence of Mary's injuries, the evidence Mary could give, the corroboration of the hospital records and the two obscene polaroid photos which Mary had found, Peter caved in. In January 1993, at the Central Criminal Court, he pleaded guilty to six specimen charges, comprising two counts each of the crimes of rape, incest and assault.

Mary was by now receiving continuous attention and support from the social services. Accommodation was found for her and she began to put down the foundations of an independent life for herself and her son.

On 1 March 1993 Peter appeared before Mr Justice Paul Carney for sentencing. The judge had options. Peter had pleaded guilty to both rape and incest. Rape had a maximum sentence of twenty years. Incest had a maximum sentence of seven years.

'The prosecution have accepted,' said Judge Carney, 'that while rape is in the indictment, I can treat this matter as being one of very violent incest.' He sentenced Peter to terms of seven years on each of the two incest charges, and seven years on each of the two rape charges. Peter was also sentenced to five years on each of the two assault charges. The sentences were to run concurrently, so the total sentence was effectively seven years. 'In view of the fact that he has been in custody for six months awaiting trial,' said the judge, 'I will suspend the last six months of the sentence.'

There was public uproar. Six and a half years seemed a small price for the depravity of Mary's treatment and the sixteen years of abuse. Judge Carney, one of the more thoughtful and conscientious judges to be appointed to the bench in recent years, came under withering attacks for the leniency of his sentence. The use of the lesser charge to set the level of sentencing disturbed politicians. They reacted to public unease by rushing through a change in the law, increasing the maximum sentence for incest to twenty years.

A few days after the sentencing, gardaí were called to the Shelbourne Hotel after midnight, where a man who seemed less than sober was found kicking the doors and demanding to be admitted to the bar. He was arrested and taken to Store Street police station. It was Mr Justice Carney. The judge later apologised to the hotel staff and explained that he had been under severe pressure lately, dealing with a very difficult case. No charges were preferred.

Mary gave interviews about her experiences but retained her anonymity and that of her son. She was said to have formed a healthy relationship with a local man and was planning marriage, but that's another story and a better one and none of our business. It was reported that Peter sent her threatening letters from jail.

Ruth continued to visit Peter in jail, once or twice a month, and to send him cigarette money every week.

⑥ The Death of Father Molloy

The priest had been hit in the face five or six times when he started dying. One of the blows split his lip, another gashed his left jaw. He went face down on to the bedroom carpet. Most of the blows were probably caused by fists, but the nature of one of his wounds suggests that as he lay on the floor the priest may have been kicked in the face. There was a blow to his back that left a kidney bleeding and that too might have been a kick delivered as he lay face down.

Lying on the floor, the priest was now unconscious and that was a small mercy. As a result of his head injuries his brain began swelling, there was subdural bleeding and his lungs began filling with fluid. Saturation of the lungs is called pulmonary oedema. The priest's fluid-laden lungs struggled to breathe, less successful with every breath. The priest was suffocating. White foam emerged from his mouth.

It's not known how long it took for the priest to die. Minutes, at least, as his bloated lungs laboured to suck in air. Perhaps a lot longer. As he lay there dying someone began dragging him across the bedroom. They may not have known he was dying. They may have been trying to drag him to a bathroom, to clean him up. They may have known that the priest's injuries were serious enough to require medical treatment and perhaps they were trying to get the priest out of the bedroom before calling for an ambulance.

Whatever the reason, by the time they dragged the priest across the bedroom as far as the door, a distance of about eight feet, whoever was doing the dragging appears to have given up. Father Niall Molloy was turned over on to his back.

It was there, as he lay on the floor of the bedroom of two of his closest friends, that the tiny air sacs in Father Niall Molloy's lungs filled to the point where he just couldn't breathe any more and he died.

· · · · ·

He was, in one part of his life, a simple country priest, a curate in a small County Roscommon parish, carrying out the mundane duties that involved. Father Niall Molloy was fifty. His priestly career had been a modest one and he was well liked by his parishioners.

He was from a family that farmed near Roscommon town. There were eight children. Niall was from very early on interested in horses. He won an under-12 showjumping title at Claremorris and later formed a pony club. In 1957 Niall was ordained a Catholic priest and served as a chaplain in the army. He was attached to Custume Barracks in Athlone and for a while served with the army on peace-keeping duties in Cyprus. In 1975 he was appointed curate to the parish of Feurty, in his home county of Roscommon.

All this time Niall retained an interest in horses, in pony clubs, showjumping and hunting. He was Chef d'Equipe for the National Hunt and was involved in the Pony Club of Ireland. While working as an army chaplain in Athlone he had a fair amount of free time and attended lots of hunt and showjumping events.

It was through his interest in horses that he came into contact with Theresa Brennan, daughter of a Galway merchant family with involvement in showjumping and hunting. When she married businessman Richard Flynn in the late 1950s the priest and Theresa and Richard became firm friends. Over the years, as the friendship deepened, Niall Molloy and Theresa Flynn went into partnership in the horse business, opening a joint account in the Bank of Ireland in Moate in 1972.

Richard Flynn was in the process of building up a number of businesses, including a chain of motor accessories shops. Richard and

Theresa had four children, Maureen, David, Zandra and Anita. The Flynns lived in Tober and in the late 1970s, as they prospered, they decided to move to a somewhat bigger house. The house in Tober would eventually become the home of their son David, when he married Ann Williams, daughter of another well-to-do family.

The Flynns decided to buy Kilcoursey House, in Clara, Co. Offaly, one of the homes owned by the wealthy Goodbody family. The Goodbody family's jute bag factory, once the dominant employer in Clara, had fallen on bad times, a victim of the rise of the plastic sack. The Flynns bought Kilcoursey House for a reported £500,000.

By any standards it was an extraordinary house. Large drawing room, large dining room, large study, playroom, kitchen, pantry, a china room and a laundry room. It stood on sixty acres, with accommodation for horses, so the main house also had a tack room and a boot room. There was a two-bedroom gate lodge and in the main house there were nine bedrooms, three of them en suite and two of them to accommodate staff. There were two front entrances, one for the Flynns and one for the staff.

Father Niall Molloy was so regular a visitor to the Flynn home that he had his own bedroom. His horses were allowed the run of the Kilcoursey land. When, in July 1985, the Flynns' daughter Maureen was marrying Ralph Parkes, of the well-to-do Parkes family, it was natural that Father Niall Molloy would join the celebrations. Before the confetti had time to blow away, Father Niall Molloy would be beaten and would die in the bedroom of his two close friends.

$\cdots \cdots$

The marriage took place at noon on Saturday 5 July 1985, and the wedding celebrations lasted two days. A marquee was erected in the grounds of Kilcoursey House for the wedding reception, which began about 1.30pm. The meal started at 3pm and after that a band started playing and the guests danced. Father Niall Molloy arrived in the late afternoon. He stayed at the celebrations until about 10.30pm, then had to return to his parish in Castlecoote, in order to say Sunday Mass the following morning. The festivities continued into the small hours.

The next day, having attended to his parish duties, the priest returned to Kilcoursey House. Theresa and Richard Flynn were hosting a buffet lunch for the family and friends of the groom and Father Molloy was invited. He would join the celebrations through the day and stay over with his friends that night.

The lunch started late, about 3pm, because of the revelries the night before. Douglas Goodbody, an old friend of the Flynns, left at around 4.30pm and as he went he invited the Flynns over to his house for drinks that evening. By around 5pm the bulk of the guests had left and the whole thing was over by 7pm. Father Niall Molloy helped clear the tables.

At around 7.30pm Father Molloy and Richard and Theresa Flynn drove to the home of Douglas Goodbody, in the town of Clara. The priest, the Flynns and Goodbody had been friends, sharing an interest in horses, for about fifteen years. The Goodbody family had owned Kilcoursey House before the Flynns bought it. That evening they spent about ninety minutes chatting about the wedding and, inevitably, about horses. They went outside and Douglas Goodbody showed them a horse he had recently acquired. Father Molloy and Theresa Flynn were drinking gin and tonic, Richard Flynn was on Power's whisky. They each had three drinks. It seems to have been a typical easygoing evening, friends relaxing together after the excitement of the wedding. Goodbody didn't notice any tension or friction.

The visit ended shortly after 9pm and the Flynns and Father Molloy returned to Kilcoursey House. The priest and Richard Flynn went to the sitting room and had a drink. Theresa Flynn was feeling tired after the exertions of the weekend. She made herself a cup of tea, then went upstairs. After that, there is little independent evidence of what happened. Theresa Flynn said she took a sleeping pill and fell asleep.

This would have been around 9.30pm, certainly no later than 10pm. Two of the Flynn daughters, Maureen and Anita, had been in the house when Richard and Theresa arrived home from Goodbody's. They then left to go drinking with the rest of the younger Flynns, at a pub in Clara.

At some stage, Father Molloy got himself a glass of milk and went to his bedroom. He finished off a Pikeur cigar and crushed it in the ashtray by his bed.

In the village of Clara, in White's pub, the three Flynn daughters, Anita, Zandra and Maureen, and Maureen's new husband, Ralph

Parkes, were finishing off an evening's drinking. The Flynn son, David, was there with his wife Ann. After closing time, the six of them went to David and Ann Flynn's home, in nearby Tober, for coffee and sandwiches.

Back at Kilcoursey House an elderly aunt of the Flynns, May Quinn, went to bed before midnight and slept through everything that was to happen. Apart from her, Richard and Theresa Flynn and their old friend Niall Molloy were alone together in the house. Some time between 11pm and 2am Niall Molloy was beaten and died.

· · · · ·

We know little for certain. At some stage, Father Molloy left his bedroom and went into the Flynns' bedroom. He was still wearing his slacks, shirt and pullover, so he hadn't had time to undress for bed. It must have been shortly after he came upstairs. Theresa Flynn claimed she woke up at one stage and her husband was in bed beside her, in pyjamas, and Father Niall was sitting at the end of the bed. This may well be true.

There is little corroboration for any version of the events that followed. We can only proceed carefully, constructing an account from the evidence of those who would come to Kilcoursey House that night, and from the physical and medical evidence which would later be retrieved.

· · · · ·

The Catholic parish priest of Clara, Father James Deignan, was the first person called to the house by Richard Flynn. That was around 1am. Flynn rang the priest at home and asked him to come to Kilcoursey House, and be prepared to anoint someone. Oddly enough, according to his own account, the priest didn't ask what had happened or who was ill. He didn't ask if it was Auntie May who was dying or one of the children or Richard Flynn's wife.

Father Deignan lived about a minute away. He knew Richard Flynn not only as a neighbour but as a minister of the eucharist at the Catholic church in Clara. When he arrived at Kilcoursey House he was met by Richard Flynn, who took him upstairs to a bedroom where a man was lying on the floor. Father Deignan gave the man the last rites. According to his own account he did not at that stage know who the man was, nor did he ask. He was unaware he was giving the last rites to a fellow priest. He did not know if the man was alive or dead at that stage.

Father Deignan's priestly duty done, he and Richard Flynn went downstairs. Having dealt with the dead or dying man's spiritual needs, it might be thought that the Flynns and the parish priest would as quickly deal with his medical needs. It was just after one o'clock. It would be another hour before a doctor would examine Niall Molloy, by which time he would undoubtedly be dead.

The account that follows, of what happened over the next hour, the explanation of the delay in getting medical help and the police, comes from Richard Flynn, his family and the parish priest, Father Deignan.

Flynn tried ringing the number of his own doctor, Daniel O'Sullivan of Kilbeggan, but could get no reply. Father Deignan decided to get a phone book and look up the phone numbers of some other doctors. But he didn't have his glasses and he couldn't read the numbers in the Flynn's phone book. He didn't ask Richard Flynn to read the numbers. Instead, he went back to his own house to get his glasses. When he reached home and got his glasses it didn't occur to him to save time by looking up doctors' numbers right away and ringing from his own phone. He thought that perhaps by now Richard Flynn might have got through to Dr O'Sullivan in Kilbeggan. He headed back to Kilcoursey House.

Richard Flynn hadn't got through. And it didn't occur to him at any stage to ring 999 and call for an ambulance. Nor did Father Deignan think of ringing 999. Later, giving evidence on oath, Father Deignan would say that he was unaware that 999 is the number for emergency services.

Twenty minutes had passed since Richard Flynn had called the parish priest. It was 1.20am when Father Deignan arrived back at Kilcoursey House with his glasses. Still no one called for medical help.

The three Flynn sisters, Maureen, Anita and Zandra, and Maureen's husband, Ralph Parkes, had just arrived home to Kilcoursey House in

Ralph's silver Porsche. When they were told what happened Ralph immediately rang David Flynn, son of Richard and Theresa, at his house in Tober, from where Parkes and the three Flynn sisters had just come. Parkes told David Flynn there had been an accident. David and Ann Flynn set off from Tober for Kilcoursey House.

Still, no one had managed to reach a doctor or to call the police. Still, no one thought to ring 999. There is no evidence independent of the Flynn family on whether Father Niall Molloy was alive or dead at this stage. They say he was dead. At some point the priest was moved a foot or so closer to the bedroom door, but no one would ever say who did that, or why, or when.

David and Ann Flynn arrived at Kilcoursey House at about 1.40am, having driven from their home in Tober. It was around that time that the parish priest, Father Deignan, drove Zandra Flynn to Kilbeggan, to the home of Dr Daniel O'Sullivan, the Flynn family doctor. Medical help was at last being summoned. Zandra Flynn told Dr O'Sullivan that Father Molloy was dead. Nothing was said about how the priest died.

Dr O'Sullivan had had a long, busy day, and tiredness had caused him to forget to transfer his phone from the surgery to his bedroom, as he routinely did. The surgery was locked and an alarm set and it couldn't be opened until the morning. Which is why Dr O'Sullivan hadn't responded to the phone calls from Kilcoursey House.

As he drove to Kilcoursey House, Dr O'Sullivan was assuming that Father Molloy had died of natural causes. It was 2am when the doctor arrived at the house. He recognised Father Molloy, and after examining him confirmed that the priest was dead. The body was warm and appeared to have been dead only a short time. Someone, perhaps fretting at the idea of the priest's body lying in someone else's bedroom, suggested that the body be taken from the house to a mortuary. Dr O'Sullivan said no, the body mustn't be moved. The police would have to be informed.

Theresa Flynn was lying on the bedroom floor, in hysterics. Her daughters Maureen and Anita were attending her. Dr O'Sullivan spent a long time trying to calm her. She had a bruise on her left cheek.

Theresa Flynn became very violent, and it took several people to restrain her. She was striking out, trying to hit those holding her down. Eventually, Dr O'Sullivan sedated her. Is he really dead? she asked. She became delirious and for a while she seemed to think that she had been in an accident with a horse.

Over the next forty-five minutes or so there was much toing and froing around the house, but still the police were not sent for. There would never be a full and reliable account of what happened in the house over that forty-five minutes, let alone the period during which Father Molloy was beaten up. It is known that Father Deignan spoke to the Flynn daughters in the kitchen, it is known that Father Deignan spent ten minutes talking to Richard Flynn. He refused to say what they spoke about and claimed that he spoke to Flynn in the course of his professional duties, which some took to mean that in his capacity as a priest he heard Richard Flynn's confession.

It is known that Dr Daniel O'Sullivan also talked to Richard Flynn. The two were alone. According to Dr O'Sullivan's account, Richard Flynn was calm, although there was a good deal of panic among other members of the family. Richard Flynn expressed regret that this 'awful thing' had happened. What was the awful thing? According to the doctor, Richard Flynn said that there had been an argument downstairs, and Father Molloy had later come into the Flynns' bedroom to discuss the matter further. There was a row over drink, said Richard Flynn, and suddenly Theresa Flynn and Father Niall Molloy physically attacked Richard Flynn. Flynn lost his temper and hit both of them, knocking them down. Father Molloy got up and Richard Flynn knocked him down again and the priest stayed down.

Flynn told the doctor that he splashed water on his wife and on Father Molloy. His wife eventually woke up. Father Molloy didn't.

Dr O'Sullivan finally decided to drive Theresa Flynn to Tullamore General Hospital. He feared she might be concussed. With sedation holding back her hysteria, she was helped downstairs. As Dr O'Sullivan was leaving the house he realised no one had sent for the police. He went to Father Deignan and told him he should fetch the gardaí. As the doctor helped Theresa Flynn into his car she called to someone to look after the horse.

It wasn't a pleasant drive to the hospital, with Theresa Flynn in distress and two of her daughters, Maureen and Anita, trying to calm her. Although it was almost 3am the roads were alive with traffic, cars streaming towards the doctor from some function in Tullamore, lights constantly blinding him. The doctor had had a long, tiring day and had then been roused from sleep, and throughout the twenty minute drive to Tullamore he was terrified he would have an accident. Theresa Flynn was admitted to Tullamore Hospital at 3am.

· · · · ·

Although Dr O'Sullivan had urged Father Deignan to fetch the police, when the doctor left Kilcoursey House at about 2.40am, about another half hour went by before the police were contacted. Sergeant Kevin Forde was roused from sleep, in his house attached to Clara garda station, at 3.15am. When he answered the persistent knocking at his front door he found the Catholic parish priest of Clara, Father James Deignan.

'There's a priest dead in the Flynns' bedroom at Kilcoursey House,' said the parish priest. The dead man had hit his head against a wall, he said. This was a terrible scandal in the parish, said the parish priest. He asked the police sergeant if there was a chance the whole thing could be kept quiet. Sergeant Forde had no intention of covering up anything. He said that the matter would have to be investigated.

Sergeant Forde called his superior officer, Detective Inspector Tom Monaghan, and told him about the death. The sergeant then set off for Kilcoursey House and arrived there at 3.30am. Dr O'Sullivan had arrived back from leaving Theresa Flynn to Tullamore General Hospital and took the sergeant upstairs and showed him Father Molloy's body. There was an orange towel over the priest's face. The sergeant lifted the towel and saw that the priest's upper lip was burst and there was a cut on the left jaw. 'He's been dead for a couple of hours,' the doctor said.

Sergeant Forde went downstairs and was taken into a room where Richard Flynn was sitting on a couch, appearing calm and unconcerned. Flynn had one arm spread along the back of the couch, a mug of coffee in the other hand. He was wearing pyjamas and dressing gown. 'Sit down, sergeant,' he said, 'and have a cup of coffee.'

Flynn apologised for bringing the sergeant out at this hour. He briefly mentioned the wedding. Then, indicating the body upstairs, he said, 'It's a messy old business.'

The sergeant began giving the necessary caution: 'You're not obliged to say anything . . .'

Richard Flynn waved a hand and said, 'I understand all that.' He continued, 'I'm very upset about my wife. I struck her with my left and I hit him at least twice with my right. That's all there is to it.' His hands were bruised.

Detective Inspector Tom Monaghan arrived at the house at 4.25am and was taken upstairs by Sergeant Forde to see the body. The detective noted a blood stain about nine inches wide, stretching from the body to a position near the bed. The drag mark was about eight feet in length.

When the detective and the sergeant went downstairs Richard Flynn again apologised for bringing the police out at this hour of the morning. David Flynn and his wife Ann were present. The detective asked to speak with Richard Flynn alone. He and Flynn went into a sitting room with Sergeant Forde.

Flynn sat down and said, 'I'm the culprit.' Again he apologised for bringing the police out in the middle of the night.

Detective Inspector Monaghan read the standard caution and Flynn said, 'I know you have to do that, I understand.'

What happened? Monaghan asked. Had he found his wife and Father Flynn in a compromising position?

'No, no, nothing like that,' said Richard Flynn. Father Molloy had been a close family friend for twenty-eight years, he said, and some time around midnight he and Theresa were in bed and Father Molloy was in the room. They were having a discussion and a stupid argument developed over who would go downstairs for another drink. He had refused to get a drink for the other two, although he was going down for a drink for himself.

At this point, Flynn said, his wife and his close family friend of twenty-eight years jumped up, rushed him and viciously attacked him. In self-defence, he hit his wife once and she fell down; he hit Father Molloy at least twice, probably three times. They were both unconscious and he tried to revive them. Father Molloy was having difficulty breathing. 'He had a heart condition.' Richard Flynn said he ran downstairs, rang Father Deignan, couldn't raise Dr O'Sullivan, and went back up. Father Molloy was dead and Theresa Flynn was having hysterics.

Detective Inspector Monaghan wrote all this down. Flynn's statement had taken about twenty minutes. He read his notes back to Richard Flynn, who agreed the notes were correct. The detective asked Flynn to sign the notes. No, Flynn said, he would make a full statement the next day. And, in the meantime, he'd like a photocopy of those notes.

At around 5.30am Richard Flynn had a conversation with another garda, Detective Noel Lynagh. The detective noticed bruises on Flynn's hands. Was that from hitting the priest? he asked. Richard Flynn said yes. 'I hit him under the chin,' he said, making an upwards striking motion.

At Tullamore General Hospital a doctor was examining Theresa Flynn. She was semi-conscious, on an intravenous drip, and unable to speak or keep her eyes open. Several times she tried to say something but no comprehensible words came out. She seemed to understand the doctor and when he mentioned the death of her friend she shed tears.

· · · · ·

As dawn broke, the police investigation got under way. Already, within half an hour of Sergeant Forde arriving at Kilcoursey, uniformed gardaí were taking up position, preserving the scene. Forensic detectives at the Technical Bureau in Dublin were notified and shortly after 8am the state pathologist, Professor John Harbison, was asked to come to Clara.

By now, word of the death had begun to spread. A priest friend of Father Molloy had been informed of the death and he in turn told someone else and at around 9am Susan Ryan was getting a call at her home in Glasnevin, Dublin, to tell her that her youngest brother, Niall Molloy, was dead. Of the eight in the Molloy family, four were now dead, two brothers and two sisters.

Susan Ryan's daughter, Suzannah Allen, who lived with her in Glasnevin, now phoned Kilcoursey House and asked for Theresa Flynn. She was told Theresa was in hospital. She spoke to Ann Flynn, David's wife. Father Molloy had been fine the night before, Ann said, when she and the other young people left the house to go for drinks. When they returned at 1.10am he was dead, and she thought it had happened about ten minutes earlier. Theresa was hysterical and Richard was in a state of shock, Ann Flynn said.

Suzannah Allen said that until she heard to the contrary, she would treat Father Niall's death as a heart attack.

The police went to see Theresa Flynn in hospital at around 11.30am. She was conscious and able to take visitors. Her account of what happened was scanty. There was no mention of an argument downstairs, or of Father Molloy coming to the bedroom to continue the discussion. She had no memory of a row about drinks or of suddenly, in concert with Father Molloy, attacking her husband. Theresa Flynn merely told the gardaí that she went to bed that night, fell asleep and woke up to find her husband chatting with Father Molloy in the bedroom. The next thing she remembered was seeing the priest lying on the floor. She felt for a pulse but there was none.

As that interview was finishing, Detective Inspector Tom Monaghan was arriving back at Kilcoursey House to take the formal statement which Richard Flynn had promised to make. He spoke to Ann Flynn, Richard's daughter-in-law, and she said she'd fetch Richard, he was out on the back lawn. The detective waited. After a while a bearded man came into the room. He introduced himself as Liam Lysaght, solicitor, Fitzwilliam Square, Dublin. He said Richard Flynn would not be making a statement.

Detective Inspector Monaghan had photocopies of the notes he had taken when he interviewed Richard Flynn during the night. He told the solicitor he had promised Richard Flynn a copy. The solicitor said he would accept the notes on Richard Flynn's behalf. Inspector Monaghan handed over the copy of the notes and left Kilcoursey House.

• • • • •

The preliminary police work had been done. The detailed investigation was about to begin. That afternoon, state pathologist Professor John Harbison arrived at Kilcoursey House. Four technical gardaí arrived. One was a photographer, one from the garda mapping section. Everything of relevance was photographed, the house was measured and details collected to enable a plan of the relevant scene to be drawn up. A fingerprint expert went over the Flynns' bedroom.

The fourth garda was Detective Garda Michael Keating of the Technical Bureau, whose expertise was in the examination of crime scenes. Dr Maureen Smith of the Department of Justice's Forensic Science Laboratory also arrived.

At around a quarter to two that afternoon Canon Patrick Murray from Athlone was ushered into the bedroom by Sergeant Forde, the local garda sergeant. Canon Murray had known Father Molloy since childhood. He formally identified the body.

Once the body and the area around it had been photographed, Professor Harbison went to work. He examined the priest's face, noted injuries to the left side of the upper lip and the left lower jaw. He measured the air temperature at 21.3 degrees centigrade. Rigor mortis, the stiffening of the body which follows about twelve hours after death, was present in the limbs and face. Professor Harbison recorded the body's rectal temperature at 31.5 degrees. It was about 2.15pm.

Professor Harbison and Detective Garda Keating wrapped the body in plastic sheeting and sealed it with adhesive tape, and the body was brought down to an ambulance and taken to Tullamore General Hospital.

· · · · ·

Because of the turn which events would take, the details of the investigation, what was found by Professor Harbison and by those examining the scene of the death (and what was not found) would prove important. The pathologist followed the priest's body to Tullamore Hospital and prepared for the gruelling task of autopsy. The police would take over Kilcoursey House for several days, in order to carry out a minute examination of the scene. The Flynns would stay at the home of David and Ann Flynn, in Tober, the old Flynn family home.

At Tullamore Hospital that afternoon, Professor John Harbison began the autopsy at 4.50pm. He opened the plastic sheeting wrapped around the body. An autopsy, although a routine event following a suspicious death, is a major and lengthy medical procedure. Professor Harbison would work on the priest's body for over five hours. Five gardaí watched as the pathologist worked. Among them were

Detective Garda Michael Keating, the scenes-of-crime specialist, and the garda photographer who photographed the autopsy.

Professor Harbison took scrapings from under the nails of both of Father Molloy's hands. He plucked samples of head hair, and undressed the body. As the pathologist gathered the physical evidence he passed it to the gardaí. Professor Harbison removed a wrist watch from the priest. It was still ticking. It's amazing how these things go, he remarked, the way watches keep on ticking even after being involved in violent activity. Professor Harbison had done a number of autopsies after an Air India 747 was blown out of the air off the Cork coast the previous month and many of the 329 victims had been recovered from the sea. The watches on all the victims were working. And this watch, Father Molloy's, was working too.

He removed a gold chain from the priest's neck, attached to which was a gold miraculous medal. The priest had £115 in notes on him. Professor Harbison plucked pubic hair and did a rectal swab.

The pathologist inspected and recorded a series of bruises on the priest's left jaw, around the mouth, on his nose and right ear and chin. He examined the hands and arms. There was no evidence of the kind of marks or bruising which would be expected on hands which had delivered punches. There were no defence marks, the bruises or cuts sustained when someone puts his hands up to block punches.

The external inspection was over. Now, Professor Harbison began the work which lay people consider grisly but which is a necessary part of an investigation of a suspicious death. Most of us experience a sense of revulsion at the thought of a body being opened up for examination. It smacks of disrespect for the dead, defilement of the corpse. In fact, it is a gesture of the deepest respect. The pathologist's work honours life by insisting that the ending of that life will be treated with the utmost seriousness. Enormous trouble is taken, every organ is examined in order to ensure that nothing will be missed, to ensure there will be as full an accounting of the circumstances of death as the pathologist's knowledge and skills will allow.

Professor Harbison began an internal examination of Father Niall Molloy's head. Here he found the subdural haemorrhage, the bleeding under the dura, the membrane covering the brain, which had left a clot about one-eighth of an inch thick. The brain was removed and retained in a chemical called formalin.

The face and neck were dissected, the trachea and larynx were opened and there was white froth inside. The chest was opened and the lungs were found to be grossly oedematous, hugely inflated and waterlogged (more precisely, fluid logged), a condition consistent with the results of head injury, a phenomenon known as 'cerebral lung'. The lungs were more than twice their normal weight.

The stomach, gastro-intestinal tract, liver, gallbladder, spleen, pancreas and kidneys were examined; samples of blood and urine and of stomach contents were taken.

The heart was removed and placed on scales. It weighed 400 grams, the upper limit of normal for a man of Father Molloy's stature. Acute heart failure was an alternative explanation for the pulmonary oedema (or waterlogging of the lungs), so a full examination of the heart was important. Professor Harbison examined every aspect of the heart, noting that the coronary arteries contained traces of atheroma (fatty deposits) but were generally open and unobstructed. The heart valves were normal, the aorta had minimal atheroma and the tissue surrounding the heart, the pericardium, was healthy. The myocardium was healthy in appearance but Professor Harbison took a sample for further study, noting an area of possible scar tissue.

In short, Father Molloy's heart showed the degeneration that might be expected in a man of fifty-two, but there was no evidence of heart failure. The sample of heart tissue was sent for further analysis, as were samples of the brain, liver, pancreas, lungs and kidneys.

It was about 10pm that evening when Professor Harbison concluded his examination of Father Molloy's body.

· · · · ·

The following day, the police returned to Kilcoursey House to carry out a detailed examination of the Flynns' bedroom. There was evidence of a struggle. There were tiny flecks and smears of blood on the edge and the outside of the bedroom door, on the outside and architrave of a closet door, on a wall, on some picture frames, on the architrave leading to the en suite bathroom, on a magazine on the bed, on the bedboard, on a magazine on top of the TV, on the TV screen, on a duvet and on the clothes of Niall Molloy and Richard and Theresa Flynn.

The wide dispersal of the blood suggested a struggle. Some of the blood flecks were watery and diluted. They might have come from bloody hands, washed and shaken. Most of the blood was in tiny quantities. On the white carpet, however, an eight-foot-long drag mark told the story of how Niall Molloy was dragged across the room as he lay dying.

There were two flecks of blood just below the knob of a closet door, close to the bedroom door, where Niall Molloy lay. The 'tails' on the blood flecks were widest at the bottom and thinnest at the top. This indicated that the blood had flown upward before it hit the door. The conclusion the police reached was that after Father Molloy was dragged across the room one of two things happened. He was violently flipped over on to his back, sending the blood upwards on to the door. Or, he was punched again, as he lay there, and the blood flew upwards from the blow.

Oddly enough, the police did not report finding in the bedroom the drinking glasses or the remnants of the nightcaps which the Flynns and Father Molloy were allegedly having. According to Richard Flynn, the fight with Father Molloy arose when they had been drinking and Flynn refused to fetch another drink for the priest.

The police reports of what was found in the bedrooms are thorough. Gardaí noted and collected two pieces of cotton wool found near the body, a tissue found on the floor, a button found in a flower box, a piece of a leaf found caught in Father Molloy's collar; they took Theresa Flynn's bra and roll-on corset from under her pillow, labelled them and took them away. They even found the pip from a peach, on the floor near the body, and labelled and seized it and reported the find. They noted the cigars found in the drawer of Richard Flynn's bedside locker. But there was no mention of any drinking glasses, of the remnants of any nightcap.

· · · · ·

After four days in hospital, Theresa Flynn was released. She went to the home of David and Ann Flynn, in Tober. She had slowly returned to normal; the only medication she received was Mogadon, a sedative. She still appeared to have amnesia. She was diagnosed as having Hysterical Dissociative Reaction. The amnesia which this entails is defined by one authority as: 'one of the commonest anxiety-stimulated and defensive dissociative reactions'. Put simply, medical opinion was that Theresa Flynn's mind had blocked out what it did not want to remember. 'Dissociative amnesia is, however, not a mere forgetting. It is an active process, a blotting out of awareness of unpleasant features.' The amnesia is selective and is 'limited to the particular element or experience that evoked it'. To defend itself from intolerable pain, the mind erases that which causes the pain.

Whatever Theresa Flynn saw happen that night in her bedroom was too much for her mind to accept and it erased the memory.

At 5pm on the afternoon on which Theresa Flynn was released from hospital the gardaí turned over Kilcoursey House to two of the Flynn daughters, Maureen Parkes and Zandra Flynn. The gardaí had finished their forensic examination of the house.

· · · · ·

The timing of Father Niall Molloy's death was just right for a nation grown used to sensational events. The Kerry Babies affair had enthralled the populace in 1984, and for four months at the beginning of 1985 every detail of the judicial inquiry into the events in Kerry had been retailed by the media. Now, coming at precisely the right time, here was a scandal that seemed a worthy successor to the Kerry business. A priest with a background in horsy circles had been found dead in a bedroom not his own, after a weekend of wedding festivities involving wealthy families. In rumour, the wedding became a high society affair, crawling with politicians.

The juxtaposition of the words 'bedroom' and 'priest' fuelled rumours of sexual entanglements. The business relationship between the priest and Theresa Flynn became the grounds for speculation about financial conflicts between the priest and the Flynns. The combination of sex and money added to the juiciness.

It was obvious what happened, according to the rumours. The priest was having an affair with Theresa Flynn. The fact that they were financial partners only enhanced the rumours. It was obvious. Flynn caught the two of them in bed. The fact that all this had no basis whatever in evidence didn't stem the rumours. The explanation of a fight over drink didn't impress many. There were too many gaps, and too many people willing to fill the gaps with rumour.

Father Niall Molloy observed his vows of celibacy. He and the Flynns were decades-long friends. The circumstances of the relationship between the priest and Theresa Flynn, and the circumstances of the evening of his death, had not the slightest hint of impropriety. It was entirely normal for a man, priest or not, staying overnight in the home of married friends he had known for decades and with whom he was at ease, to drop into their bedroom, perhaps for a nightcap, perhaps to thrash out some matter which had come up during the evening.

The speculation ravaged the grieving family of Father Molloy. His brother Billy was shattered by the priest's death. The circumstances of the death, and the jokes and the rumours which they provoked, added to the anguish. The grief at the priest's funeral was worsened by shock, puzzlement, anger. How could they be burying gentle Father Niall, only fifty-two, and how could he have died so violently in such strange circumstances? The family talked about how they might seek answers.

Perhaps there was a will. Perhaps there would be something in that which might enlighten them. Susan Ryan, the priest's sister from Glasnevin, spoke to Bill Maher, one of Father Molloy's nephews. Father Niall had dealings with a firm of solicitors in Athlone, Fair and Murtagh. Perhaps they could help.

Susan Ryan was convinced that something had been worrying her brother in his final weeks. She had last seen him a month before his death, when she had lunch with him in County Longford. After lunch they had walked and Niall didn't seem his usual self. Susan usually phoned Niall on Sundays for a chat and a week later she called and asked if everything was OK, saying she thought him in bad form the previous week. He said everything was all right. He knew that if he needed to he could talk to Susan.

She rang him again for their usual chat on Sunday 7 July, but there was no answer. Father Niall was at the Flynn wedding in Clara.

Now, on Friday 12 July, five days after Niall's death, Susan's daughter, Suzannah Allen, rang the firm of Fair and Murtagh in

Athlone. A Mr Egan said that he wanted to discuss an urgent matter with the family. They made an appointment for a meeting at his office in Athlone on the following Monday.

· · · · ·

That Sunday evening the Flynn family gathered with their solicitor, Liam Lysaght. Eight statements about the death of Father Molloy had been drawn up and would now be signed.

The first statement was from Theresa Flynn. It described in detail the events on the day of the wedding and the day afterwards. It was extremely short of detail on the death of the priest. She described falling asleep, waking to see Father Molloy sitting at the foot of the bed, Richard in pyjamas in bed beside her. 'My next memory is of waking up or regaining consciousness on the floor of the bedroom. Father Molloy was lying on the floor, near the door. I was dazed and thought he must have passed out.' She described trying to revive the priest. 'I heard an awful gurgling sound.' She didn't remember anything after that, the statement said.

The Flynn children (Maureen, David, Zandra and Anita) and their spouses (Ann Flynn and Ralph Parkes) then signed a series of six statements describing how they went for drinks at a pub in Clara, then back to David and Ann's house in Tober for sandwiches, how four of them returned to Kilcoursey House at about 1am to find Father Molloy dead and Theresa Flynn in hysterics.

The final statement was from Richard Flynn. In his shock on the night of the death he had talked freely. He then refused to sign the notes taken by Detective Inspector Monaghan. He offered a fuller statement the following day, then changed his mind and refused to give a statement. Now, his statement through his solicitor was a mere three paragraphs.

I refer to the notes taken by Inspector Monaghan and Sergeant Forde of my conversation with them on 8 July 1985; a copy of these notes has been made available to me and I have carefully read them.

They represent a correct description of what occurred and record accurately what I told Inspector Monaghan and Sergeant Forde.

I have nothing to add to what is contained in those notes.

And that was all Richard Flynn had to say to explain the death of his friend of twenty-eight years.

· · · · ·

The next morning, Father Molloy's sister Susan and her daughter Suzannah turned up at the solicitors' firm of Fair and Murtagh, in Athlone, for their meeting with Father Molloy's solicitor, a Mr Egan. According to their accounts of the meeting Mr Egan told them that Father Molloy and the Flynns had been involved in a number of deals, to do with the horse business, since 1972. Towards the end of the previous year, 1984, the three had come to see Mr Egan. 'They told him,' Susan Ryan later said, 'that Richard and his son, David, were in financial difficulties and needed to raise cash in a hurry. It was proposed that Father Niall and Mrs Theresa Flynn would buy some of the land at Kilcoursey from Richard Flynn for £35,000. They were to pay a deposit of £24,000, and subject to Land Commission approval the deal would be completed.'

Father Niall appeared to be having reservations about the deal, but Theresa Flynn said everything would be OK. If the deal went through they would have the land, if it didn't they would have their money back. Father Niall paid £11,000 as his share of the deposit.

The deal fell through when it was refused approval by the Land Commission. Subsequently, Father Niall called his solicitor on a number of occasions, worried about getting his money back and wanting to know what he could do about retrieving it. There is evidence to suggest that Niall Molloy was seeking to manoeuvre his way out of the partnership with Theresa Flynn. He sold a horse for £6,000, and instead of lodging the money in the joint account he lodged it in his personal account.

According to Susan Ryan and her daughter, Mr Egan said that soon after they rang him the previous Friday he received a call from Theresa Flynn. He told her Father Molloy's relations were coming to see him. 'She asked him if he had to tell us about the deal, and he told her he had.'

At around 4.30 that afternoon solicitor Liam Lysaght arrived at

Clara garda station with the eight statements signed by members of the Flynn family the previous evening.

At 7.50 that evening Detective Sergeant Thomas Dunne, from the Investigation Section of the Technical Bureau, went to the surgery of Dr Daniel O'Sullivan, at Main Street, Kilbeggan, where Richard and Theresa Flynn were waiting. Detective Dunne formally told the Flynns that he would ask Dr O'Sullivan to take blood samples from them, with their consent. He then gave them the standard caution that they were not obliged to give a blood sample, but if they did so the result could be given in evidence. They both consented. Richard Flynn remarked that he had nothing to hide.

· · · · ·

The next day, Detective Garda Michael Gillespie went to Tullamore General Hospital and spoke to the doctor who had treated Theresa Flynn. The doctor said that in his opinion Theresa had received 'a box in the face'. The garda asked for a copy of a medical report on Theresa Flynn. The doctor said he would provide one on condition he received the consent of Mrs Flynn.

· · · · ·

Three days later, on Friday 19 July, at 12.35pm, Detective Sergeant Dunne and Detective Inspector Tom Monaghan went to the home of David Flynn, in Tober, to interview Richard Flynn. By now, the information about the land deal involving Father Molloy and the Flynns had been brought to the attention of the police.

Richard and David Flynn insisted that the son should stay with his father.

Detective Dunne said they were investigating the death of Father Niall Molloy and they had reason to believe that Richard Flynn could help them with their enquiries. He gave Richard Flynn the standard caution about how he had the right to remain silent.

Richard Flynn said nothing. Detective Dunne then said he had reason to believe that Richard Flynn owed Father Niall Molloy a large sum of money and that the priest had expressed concern about getting this money back.

'Do you want to make a statement about this?'

Richard Flynn said he would make no statement without the presence of his solicitor, Liam Lysaght. The interview ended. The police visit to the house had lasted just five minutes.

Three days later Detective Garda Michael Gillespie, who had requested a medical report on Theresa Flynn's condition when she was admitted to Tullamore Hospital received a phone call from the doctor who had treated Mrs Flynn. The doctor said he had received instructions from Theresa Flynn's solicitor that no medical report was to be supplied to the gardaí.

On the afternoon of the following day, Tuesday 23 July, Detective Sergeant Thomas Dunne and Detective Inspector Tim Monaghan went to Kilcoursey House, where they had arranged to talk to Theresa Flynn. Richard Flynn admitted them to the house and led them to a room where Theresa waited with her solicitor, Liam Lysaght.

The police asked Theresa about what happened in her bedroom the night that Father Molloy died. She said she couldn't recall any details other than what was contained in the statement which her solicitor had given the police. The two gardaí turned to the matter of the business deal. Had she and Father Molloy agreed to buy land from Richard Flynn and had they paid him a deposit of £24,000? Yes, that deal had taken place. And had Father Molloy's share of that been £11,000? Yes.

And, said Theresa Flynn, when the deal fell through the money had been paid back to the priest. Richard Flynn hadn't paid it, but Theresa had, to stop Father Niall worrying. She had paid him the £11,000 about two months earlier. She had the money in a safe in the house, in cash, and she paid him.

Had she a receipt? No. And there were no bank transaction records to back up this story. But Theresa Flynn insisted she was telling the truth. It was her own money, it was in the safe, she handed it over and there was no record of the transaction.

Theresa Flynn also had an alternative version of why Father Molloy became involved in a deal to buy a part of Richard Flynn's land. It was all Father Niall's idea, Theresa Flynn said. He wanted to retire there and build a house on the land.

Solicitor Liam Lysaght told the police that Richard Flynn did not wish to be interviewed by the gardaí. And he wouldn't be making any further statement. The police left.

· · · · ·

By the beginning of August 1985 the forensic work had been done on the priest's organs and on material taken from Kilcoursey House. An analysis at the Forensic Science Laboratory showed that Father Molloy's blood contained 134.7 milligrams of alcohol per 100 millilitres. His urine contained 196.6 milligrams of alcohol per 100 millilitres. This was within the limits of social drinking and showed that Father Molloy was far from inebriated.

Professor John Harbison, the state pathologist, had called in a consultant neuropathologist to help him assess the injuries to the priest's brain. Professor Harbison carried out microscopic examinations of the brain, liver, pancreas and kidneys. To ensure he wasn't missing a thrombosis, he examined heart arteries, slicing through them at quarter-inch intervals. There was no thrombosis. No evidence of hypertension, no evidence of coronary infarct.

At the Forensic Science Laboratory, Dr Maureen Smith analysed the blood stains found in the Flynn bedroom. She found blood from Father Molloy on Richard Flynn's pyjama front. This was to be expected, if Flynn punched the priest. Father Molloy's blood was also on Theresa Flynn's nightdress and dressing gown, which was to be expected if she knelt beside the dying or dead priest.

The priest's blood was also found on the bedspread and duvet cover, on the magazine on the TV set and on the carpet. All of this was as might be expected.

Theresa Flynn's blood was found on the back of Richard's pyjama jacket. How her blood got there, if she was punched once in the face as she approached Richard Flynn, is not known. However, it is possible that a drop of blood flying away from her face landed on Richard's back.

Richard Flynn's blood was found on the duvet cover and on his own pyjama bottom. It is not clear where this blood came from. Flynn did not appear to be damaged, except for his fists, which were seen to be bruised and scratched. It is possible that the blood was from his damaged hands.

A small stain of Richard Flynn's blood was found on the back of Father Molloy's trousers. How it got there is not known.

There was evidence of a struggle. Richard Flynn's pyjama top was ripped under the left arm and the top button had been torn out. It was found in a flower box in the bedroom.

$$\cdot \quad \cdot \quad \cdot \quad \cdot \quad \cdot$$

While all this forensic investigation was under way, a strange thing was happening at the Merrion Road, Dublin, offices of the Combined Insurance Company of Ireland. At the beginning of the second week of August 1985, a month after Father Molloy's death, a handwritten letter arrived, scrawled on what seemed to be a page torn from a notebook. An address at the top of the page read: Kilcoursey, Clara, Offaly. The short note, dated 5-8-1985, said:

> Dear Sirs, I have a Policy on the life of Father Niall Molloy
> Policy No. 9257958 with your company. This man is now dead.
> I wish to make a claim on the policy — Please let me have the
> necessary forms. Yours faithfully, (Mrs) Theresa Flynn.

The company checked its files and, sure enough, policy No. 9257958 existed. It was a 'Little Giant' £16 accident policy taken out on the life of Niall Molloy. It had been initiated the previous November, six months before the priest's death. Father Molloy's address was given care of R. Flynn, Kilcoursey House, who was described as 'brother-in-law', and the priest's next of kin was given as Theresa Flynn, whose relationship to the priest was described as 'sister'.

The company sent to Theresa Flynn a request for a death certificate, a doctor's statement and details of letters of administration. There was no reply from Theresa Flynn.

$$\cdot \quad \cdot \quad \cdot \quad \cdot \quad \cdot$$

Richard Flynn was charged with manslaughter and assault. The case came before Mr Justice Frank Roe and a jury in the Circuit Criminal

Court in Dublin, on 12 June 1986, eleven months after the death of the priest. Flynn's solicitor, Liam Lysaght, engaged barrister Paddy MacEntee SC to act for the defence. The prosecution case was presented by Raymond Groarke BL. The trial lasted all of three and a half hours.

In most cases the prosecution takes the witnesses through statements which they have already made to the police, getting the witnesses to expand on their statements where necessary in the course of the examination. Then the defence cross-examines, again expanding the amount of information before the court, and the prosecution then re-examines on issues raised by the defence in cross-examination.

Usually, a prosecution lawyer taking a witness through a statement must ask broad questions, not specific questions intended to lead the witness to a particular conclusion. For instance, a lawyer would not ask, 'Was there a body in the room when you entered?' That would be a leading question. The witness must not be led into an answer. Such a question would be phrased, 'What did you see when you entered the room?'

The case began. Paddy MacEntee rose as each witness took the stand and cheerfully announced that the defence had no objection to the witness being led through his or her statement. After each witness was taken through his or her statement, MacEntee would more often than not rise again and just as cheerfully announce that the defence had no questions. The trial proceeded at an unsettling pace. The first nine witnesses rattled through in just ninety minutes.

When the state pathologist, Professor Harbison, took the stand, Paddy MacEntee didn't waive his right to question the witness. He noted the fact that Father Molloy's heart had shown signs of damage. In fact, Father Molloy was quite fit, his heart had suffered the degeneration of the average fifty-two-year-old male. But this left an opening for the defence. Paddy MacEntee questioned Professor Harbison just enough to bring a mention of heart degeneration into evidence. He asked Harbison if this could have been a contributory factor in the priest's death. Harbison could not do otherwise than say that it might. There was no way of ruling out the possibility that in the course of the priest's final moments, as he lay dying on the bedroom carpet, the air sacs of his lungs filling to the point of suffocation, his heart might have failed.

It was Harbison's opinion, however, that there was no evidence of a heart infarction, no evidence of thrombosis, just the normal degeneration of the heart. Harbison was convinced that Father Molloy had died as a result of pulmonary oedema following from his head injuries.

Paddy MacEntee did not elicit from Professor Harbison an opinion on whether any heart failure in Father Molloy's last moments might have been a major or minor factor in his death.

Police witnesses outlined to the court the bare facts of what they discovered at the scene of the death, as mentioned in their statements. They did not get to tell the court of their professional and experienced analysis of those findings. Once they had been led through their statements Paddy MacEntee announced that he had no questions and that was the end of that.

Richard Flynn did not have to give evidence, and therefore did not have to explain how the priest came to die in the Flynn bedroom. And since he was not giving evidence he could not be cross-examined. Theresa Flynn could not be compelled to testify in a case against her husband. No evidence could be admitted concerning the £24,000 land deal, nor could the court hear evidence from hospital sources about the condition of Theresa Flynn that night.

When the prosecution closed its case, Paddy MacEntee asked that the jury be removed from the court while he made an application. He wanted Judge Roe to direct the jury to find Richard Flynn not guilty. In most cases such an application is a routine one which is quickly rejected, at which point the trial continues with the defence presenting a case. Paddy MacEntee had, however, laid the groundwork for a serious application.

He proposed to give the court an interpretation of the evidence heard so far. He cast doubt on the ability of a jury of lay people to bring in a proper verdict in accordance with that evidence, and therefore justice would best be served by the judge directing the jury that the law required a not guilty verdict.

Given the fact that the evidence heard so far was limited, MacEntee had some latitude in constructing a sequence of events most favourable to Richard Flynn. He wasn't saying that the account he was about to give was what happened, only that it was a reasonable construction to put on the evidence which had been heard by the court.

The evidence heard by the court allowed the following interpretation: Father Niall Molloy, for whatever reason, attacked Richard Flynn, as Flynn had told the police. Richard Flynn had admitted to the police that he then struck the priest twice or three times.

The evidence allowed for the possibility, according to MacEntee, that Father Molloy had become extremely angry, that he rushed forward to attack Richard Flynn. At which point, due to a combination of anger and exertion, his heart failed.

Richard Flynn, defending himself, and unaware of the priest's fatal heart failure, delivered two or three blows. The priest fell to the floor, and his death was from natural causes.

MacEntee pointed out that Professor Harbison had agreed that the condition of Father Molloy's heart might have been a contributory factor in his death. It was not, however, MacEntee pointed out, established whether heart failure might have been a major or a minor factor in the death. Therefore, the court was free to draw the conclusion that it was a major factor. In fact, given the court's duty to give the accused the benefit of any reasonable doubt, the court was obliged to draw the conclusion that the condition of the priest's heart might have been a major factor in his death.

But how did this explain the medical evidence which showed the priest had suffered six blows to the face? MacEntee had an explanation for that. He pointed out that police had found traces of blood on a bedboard in the Flynn bedroom. MacEntee suggested that what happened was that Father Molloy, having suffered heart failure and received perhaps three blows from Richard Flynn (in self-defence), fell forward and hit his head against the bedpost, then against the bedboard, and then against the floor. This would account for the six blows.

At this stage, the prosecution case was closed, and the various witnesses who could have disputed this scenario could not be recalled. MacEntee was not putting forward any witnesses to support his scenario, he was merely basing it on the evidence already heard, therefore it could not be put to the test of cross-examination.

Detective Garda Michael Keating of the Garda Technical Bureau was standing at the back of the court as MacEntee spoke. Had the rules allowed him to put his expertise at the disposal of the court he could have told the court that the blood found on the bedboard had not been put there by the priest's head bouncing against the wood. Such a collision would have caused a characteristic starburst pattern of blood. The blood on the bedboard was a smear, as if someone with a bloody hand had touched it. Detective Garda Keating could have told the court that a thorough search of the room and the cataloguing of even the most minute traces of blood found did not support the pinball theory of Father Molloy's head bouncing from one object to another as he fell to the floor.

Professor Harbison, if asked to expand on his evidence, would have been able to say that there was no sign that Father Molloy's heart was any more damaged than that of the average fifty-two-year-old male, that there was no evidence that the condition of his heart had been a major contributory factor in the death, that his opinion was quite the contrary.

But the evidence had already been heard and Judge Roe had to make a decision. He said he had 'no hesitation' in giving the direction asked for by Paddy MacEntee. The jury was called back and the judge told them that 'Professor Harbison agreed that there was a possibility that Father Molloy died of a heart attack.' It was not pointed out to the jury that Professor Harbison had stated that there was no evidence of infarction or thrombosis, that it was his carefully considered opinion that head injuries leading to pulmonary oedema was the cause of death.

The judge continued, pointing out that the jury was 'not allowed to speculate that he died of head injuries caused by assault'. This was a curious interpretation of Professor Harbison's medical evidence. The pathologist had stated clearly that it was his opinion that the head injury was the primary cause of death. For the jury to accept that evidence would not be speculation.

The medical evidence had been turned on its head. The clear statement that head injuries caused the death was now speculation; the speculation that heart failure may have occurred in the priest's last moments became 'died of a heart attack'.

The jury was directed to find Richard Flynn not guilty and, having no choice in the matter, did so.

Judge Roe then proceeded to throw in some parting remarks. Perhaps he meant to be comforting. On the night in question, he said, 'All had a little more drink than perhaps they should have.' And that led to an unfortunate fracas. Clearly, the judge was declaring Father Molloy's death to be the result of an alcohol-induced fight. There was no evidence at all to support this. Any evidence that existed pointed in a contrary direction. Neither Richard nor Theresa Flynn had been tested for alcohol consumption. Analysis of Father Molloy's blood showed that he had taken a little more drink than was then permitted to car drivers. Professor Harbison had clearly stated that Father Molloy was not drunk.

In the body of the court, Billy Molloy, Niall Molloy's older brother, stood trembling with anger and disbelief. He had suffered over a year of grief, months of anticipating the court case. He had been sure that the truth of the events of that night would come out. He had prepared himself for the days of listening to the evidence, the painful listing of the medical findings when his dear brother's body had been cut open for autopsy, the rehashing of the events of Niall's death. He would put up with it all, and the jury would hear it all, and they would give their verdict and he would accept that.

Now, in not much more than three hours, it was all over. Not guilty. Some strange, incomprehensible legal manoeuvre and it was all over. The jury didn't arrive at a verdict; it was told what to do. The man who'd said 'I'm the culprit' was walking away from the court, declared innocent, and he could never be tried again. And the judge who had brought it all to a sudden end was sitting up there calling Father Niall Molloy a drunk.

There were reporters around Billy Molloy, asking the question that's always asked when no one can think of anything better: How do you feel?

His hands were shaking, his lips quivered. 'Sickened,' said Billy Molloy, 'sickened.' He'd lived for years in America, he said, and he was back home to live out his final years in his home country. And now he felt like throwing away his Irish passport and going back to America. There were tears in his eyes. 'Sickened,' he said.

Ian Maher, the dead priest's nephew, comforted Billy Molloy, steering the trembling man away from reporters and towards the door. Ian's brother Bill Maher was white faced. The two brothers were as shocked as Billy Molloy, but their anger was cooler. It couldn't end like this, it couldn't be left like this, there had to be something more.

· · · · ·

Father Molloy's family, still grieving, were caught up in a rage of anger and puzzlement. They had lost Father Niall, a man they loved and admired. His name had been tarnished by gossip. The only explanation they had of his death, a ludicrous argument over drink, a tale of the priest and Theresa Flynn suddenly attacking Richard Flynn, was simply unacceptable. It didn't make sense. Just thinking about it drove Ian Maher to distraction. He wouldn't have believed it possible that after a man was beaten to death, another man, with bruised hands, telling the police, 'I'm the culprit,' and giving an explanation about a sudden motiveless attack, could walk free. He couldn't believe that anyone could die violently, let alone a priest, and so few questions could be asked.

What about the eight-foot-long drag mark? No questions asked, no explanations. What about the long delay before help was sought, before a doctor was brought and the police were called? No questions asked, no explanations. What about the abrasion on Father Niall's left thigh, the evidence of a kick? What about the fact that there were no marks on the priest's hands of any fighting, no indication that he had hit anyone, no defence marks on the hands or arms? No questions asked, no explanations.

If Father Niall died of heart failure and fell, hitting his head repeatedly as he went down, and then died, how come Richard Flynn told Dr O'Sullivan, on the night of the death, that he knocked down Niall Molloy and that the priest got up and Flynn knocked him down again? If his heart failed he couldn't have got up.

What could have led to the violence? The family wondered about the £11,000 that Theresa Flynn owed to the priest. They didn't believe her story of having paid back the money. It was absurd that there would be no record of such a business transaction. In anguish, the family chewed over morsels of remarks made by the priest over the past year, looking for something that might have meant more than it seemed to at the time.

Father Molloy's family themselves became caught up in the

rumour machine which they had found so hurtful. Bereft of explanations, their speculation wandered. What if it wasn't Richard Flynn who hit the priest, what if there was someone else in the house that night? What if Richard Flynn was covering up, taking the rap for someone else? The family scrutinised every known detail of the comings and goings at Kilcoursey House that night.

They began leaking information about the case to the press, suggesting leads that might be followed. They lobbied politicians. Public feeling was with the family. Judge Roe's decision to take the case from the jury and declare Richard Flynn innocent had been greeted with widespread scepticism. The judge was quite entitled to reach that decision, but justice had not been seen to be done in such a way as to allay public fears about the case. Accepting that justice had been done meant accepting that Father Molloy had a heart attack just before Richard Flynn delivered three defensive blows, and that the priest's head had bounced like a pinball from one piece of furniture to the next until it hit the floor. The belief began to grow in political circles that the trial had not ventilated the facts of the case to public satisfaction.

There could be no new trial; Richard Flynn had been tried and found not guilty. The Molloy family lobbied for a public inquiry, but Minister for Justice Alan Dukes turned them down. There would be an inquest, he pointed out, and that would be a 'sworn public inquiry'.

Most inquests are nothing of the kind. They are limited to making findings on the identity of the deceased and on the direct medical cause of death. Usually, a confused lay jury sits in bafflement as medical experts rattle off strings of technical terms, whereupon the coroner suggests the jury might find that the deceased died in accordance with the medical evidence, and they so find.

Father Molloy's family hired a solicitor, Ben Rafferty, and he engaged Peter Charleton, a young barrister with a growing reputation and an interest in forensic pathology. If the inquest was all they would get, they would at least try to use the opportunity to the full. The lawyers came to the conclusion that the best that could be achieved was the overturning in the public mind of the trial result, and the substitution of an inquest verdict in line with Professor Harbison's evidence: that Niall Molloy died from a medical condition which resulted from his receiving head injuries that night in Kilcoursey House.

The inquest was scheduled for Friday 26 July, six weeks after the trial. A major drawback was that the lawyers were deprived of the material they needed to prepare a case. They had no right of access to the police investigation file. The copies of the Book of Evidence used at the trial had all been taken back by the office of the Director of Public Prosecutions.

The family lobbied for the release of the police file to their lawyers. Meanwhile, in the absence of hard evidence, they were drawn down a number of blind alleys. A doctor at Tullamore General Hospital suggested that Theresa Flynn had been admitted before 2am, not after 3am. The family seized on this as evidence that the story of what happened that night had been distorted. The doctor had no axe to grind; unlike almost everyone else involved he was not part of the establishment in the small town of Clara. If Theresa Flynn was admitted before 2am, this might mean . . .

And the speculation went on. It would later become clear that the doctor had simply made a mistake and Theresa Flynn had indeed been admitted to hospital at around 3am.

When Father Molloy's watch was handed back to the family they found that the glass was broken and the hands stopped at 10.40. The news was electrifying. It was like something out of Agatha Christie. Here, surely, was evidence of a fight much earlier, in which the watch had been broken and the priest had died. Had Father Niall died before 11am, and had there been a three-hour delay before a doctor was called?

The broken watch was a red herring. The watch could have been broken a day after or before the priest died. At 10.40 in the morning or the night. Professor Harbison had no memory of whether the watch had been broken when he carried out the autopsy, but it is unlikely that a pathologist of his experience would fail to note a broken watch. Gardaí who were present at the autopsy remembered Professor Harbison's vivid anecdote about the victims of the Air India 747 bombing, and about how their watches were still ticking and about how Father Molloy's watch was still ticking. It is clear that the glass on the watch was broken accidentally at some point after it was removed from Father Molloy's body.

The blind alleys of the time of Theresa Flynn's admission to hospital, and the broken watch, ate up much of the Molloy family's time and emotional energy in the weeks leading up to the inquest. They were also led into worthless speculation about a fight downstairs in the Flynn house, about remarks about a political row, all of which were of no help. But the family's lobbying paid off. Unease in official circles led to a conviction that the inquest should be seen to be as fair as possible. Just thirty-six hours before the inquest was due to open the Attorney General's office contacted the family's lawyers and told them they could have access to the police file on the case.

· · · · ·

On the stand, Richard Flynn was calm and self-assured. It was the first time he had publicly given any account of the events of that night in July 1985. He told essentially the same story he had told Inspector Monaghan in the small hours of the morning in Kilcoursey House. At the end of the evening, he and his wife and Father Niall Molloy were relaxing in the couple's bedroom, discussing holidays they intended taking in Normandy. His wife suggested he go down and get some more drinks. Richard Flynn told his wife that Father Niall had a drink, and if she wanted a drink she could get her own.

At that point, said Richard Flynn, and for no reason which he could discern, his wife and his old friend simultaneously took it into their heads to launch a physical attack on him. The priest 'viciously' attempted to punch Richard Flynn. Richard Flynn knocked his wife out with a single punch. He hit Niall Molloy twice. And he didn't remember anything that happened after that. He knew nothing about the priest being dragged across the carpet. He knew nothing.

Theresa Flynn was even less informative. She remembered nothing of a fight, nothing at all about what happened. She woke up and she saw Father Niall Molloy lying on her bedroom floor, dying. There was no one else in the room.

Barrister Peter Charleton, for the Molloy family, had the garda forensic witnesses establish that the pinball theory, of Father Molloy hitting his head against the bedpost and bedboard, didn't stand up.

Professor Harbison's opinion was made simple and transparent. There was no evidence of heart attack, there was no evidence of thrombosis, there was no evidence of hypertension in the liver. The heart might or might not have coincidentally suffered arhythmia and failed as the priest neared death, and might have contributed to the death, but heart failure was not the cause of death. The priest's heart was still beating as he lay on the bedroom floor, as the blood seeped out of him. Blood had collected on the carpet where he fell and where he lay after being dragged across the room. His heart had to have been beating for an eighth of an inch of blood to collect under the dura, the membrane that covers the brain. The injuries to the priest's head were the primary cause of death.

The Flynns' solicitor, Liam Lysaght, had engaged barrister James Connolly to represent the family. He brought in pathologist Dr Declan Gilsenan, in an attempt to find an alternative cause of death. Dr Gilsenan suggested heart failure, but that was undermined by Professor Harbison's evidence. Dr Gilsenan had noted one or possibly two spots on a lung section, which might have resulted from a fatty substance inhaled by the priest. He suggested the possibility that Father Molloy had inhaled vomit. Some of the vomit might have entered the lungs, resulting in pulmonary oedema.

It was a long shot. Professor Harbison disputed that the spots Dr Gilsenan saw on the lung section were necessarily derived from fatty substances. But if they were, they could have been blown into the priest's lungs when Theresa Flynn tried mouth-to-mouth resuscitation. There was no evidence of vomiting at the scene of the death, on clothes, or during the autopsy.

The coroner, Brian Mahon, scrupulously observed legal procedures but recognised the sensitivity of the case and allowed the lawyers great latitude. The inquest took place over two days, as opposed to the trial's three and a half hours. All of the evidence available was thoroughly discussed. The jury was out for just thirteen minutes before coming back with the verdict asked for by the Molloy family lawyers. Jury foreman Billy Bracken held the verdict on a piece of paper in his trembling hand as he read aloud that the jury found that Father Niall Molloy died as a result of head injuries.

It wasn't much of an accounting in the wake of a violent death, but for the Molloy family it was a rejection of the trial result which had smeared the reputation of their loved one and ascribed his death to a non-existent heart attack in the course of a drunken fight. Father Molloy's relatives were hugging, embracing, crying. Billy Molloy's hands shook as he left the courtroom, this time not with shock and anger, but with relief. The dreadful insult to Niall's name which he had felt in the wake of the criminal trial had been to some extent wiped away. Billy Molloy would himself die about a year later, still grieving his brother. Ian Maher told reporters simply that he was pleased with the verdict. His brother Bill dragged on a cigarette, the tension draining from his face.

The inquest jury verdict stood in stark opposition to the result of the trial. If no one was to be punished as a result of Father Molloy's death, that could be lived with; no one wanted revenge. It would have been better to have a clear, full and credible accounting of all that had happened, but little though it was, the inquest verdict was for the family of Niall Molloy a victory of sorts. If they still suffered the injury of the priest's death, they no longer had to suffer the insult of the fantastic explanation of the heart attack that left no trace and the pinball theory of the head injuries.

The mystery at the heart of the tragedy remained: why would a priest suddenly, for no reason, launch an attack on a friend of twenty-eight years, and why would the wife of that friend join the priest in such an attack?

In considering that mystery, Acting Coroner Brian Mahon, whose conduct of the sensitive inquest had been impeccable, summed up the feelings of observers of the inquest: 'I can only believe that something happened and this inquiry has not been told what that was.'

Unseen by the Molloy family, the jury foreman, Billy Bracken, made his way to his car. A passerby congratulated him on the verdict. He sucked in a breath and in a voice that was still far from steady he said, 'It had to be done.'

The massed ranks of the press photographers spotted Richard and Theresa Flynn leaving the court by the back way. As their solicitor led them to his car the cameras clicked and whirred like a flock of excited birds taking flight. The Flynns walked on, stone faced.

• • • • •

There were loose ends to be tied up. On the death of the priest's brother, Billy Molloy, the priest's eldest nephew, Ian Maher, was appointed to administer the estate. He began legal proceedings, suing Richard Flynn for damages for the loss to the family of Niall Molloy and the expenses incurred by the family in being represented at the inquest. He also sued Theresa Flynn for the money she allegedly owed Father Molloy for his share of the abortive land deal.

Theresa Flynn in turn sued the estate of Father Molloy for the £6,000 which the priest received for the sale of a horse, and which he had lodged in his personal account rather than in the joint account with Theresa.

As is always the case, the legal proceedings dragged on. Meanwhile, the case bobbed into and out of the news for various reasons. In April 1988 the Combined Insurance Company of Ireland revealed to Ian Maher that back in August 1985 it had received a letter of claim from a Theresa Flynn on account of an accident policy on Father Molloy. It wanted to know what was the relationship between the two, as she was identified on the policy application as the priest's sister. Maher was taken aback and told the insurance company that Theresa Flynn had no blood relationship whatsoever with his family.

The company had received no reply from Theresa Flynn when it wrote to her asking for a death certificate and other documents. Now, as the existence of the policy was exposed in the newspapers, Theresa Flynn denied that she had written the letter claiming the money owed on the policy. The *Sunday Tribune* brought a copy of the letter and a copy of Theresa Flynn's signature to a handwriting expert who gave an opinion that the letter of claim had not been written by Theresa Flynn.

The identity of the writer of the letter remained a mystery. How the writer knew of the existence of the policy, knew that Theresa Flynn was the beneficiary, and had the correct policy number, is equally a mystery.

Meanwhile, the Flynn fortunes were slipping. In November 1987 the Revenue Commissioners won a judgment against Richard Flynn for a total of £126,000. Over £33,000 of that was in tax owed by a business known as the Coffee Shop, in the Athlone Shopping Centre, which was run by Theresa Flynn. Other judgments were given, of

£32,000 and £60,000, relating to motor accessory shops owned by Richard Flynn.

The Flynns had sought to sell Kilcoursey House by auction. A number of Father Molloy's parishioners announced that they would attend the auction, where they would have something to say. The auctioneers were quoting a figure of between £250,000 and £300,000, which was about half what the Flynns were reported to have paid for the house a decade earlier. Locals in Clara were reported to be saying, sure, who would want to live in a house where a priest died in the bedroom? The house was advertised in the *Wall Street Journal*, the readers of which would have considerably more money to spend than the inhabitants of Clara, and considerably less qualms about living in a house with a history.

Ian Maher obtained an order of *lis pendens*, which requires that potential purchasers of a property be informed that there is litigation pending in relation to the owners of the property. The house was withdrawn from auction.

In April 1988 Ian Maher won his case against Richard Flynn in the Circuit Court in Tullamore, being awarded the relatively small Circuit Court damages. The money never mattered to Father Molloy's family, all that mattered was establishing responsibility for the priest's death. The Combined Insurance Company of Ireland awarded the £1,500 owing to the 'Little Giant' accidental death policy to the estate of Father Molloy. The cheque was given to his parish.

In August 1993 Theresa Flynn died, taking with her to the grave anything more she might have known about the events in Kilcoursey House.

· · · · ·

In the mid-1980s, when the office of the Director of Public Prosecution was in Stephen's Green, the authorities decided to enhance the security of the office. The DPP might well be a target for paramilitaries or criminals with a grudge. It was decided to set up a small lobby with a two-way mirror. The idea was that a visitor would go up in a lift and the lift doors would lead directly into the lobby. People inside the office would then be able to scrutinise the visitor. In the event of an unwelcome visitor making a threatening appearance in the lobby the door into the office could remain locked.

There was just one problem with this plan. When the mirror was installed it was hung the wrong way around. Visitors to the DPP's office found they could look into the office through the mirror, while staff anxious to scrutinise those ringing the bell saw nothing but their own reflection.

It was, perhaps, typical of the somewhat amateurish security efforts in which the state engaged from time to time. A few years later someone had little trouble breaking into the DPP's office and stealing a number of confidential files. It was believed that the theft was organised by a major Dublin criminal.

Among the files stolen was that relating to the death of Father Niall Molloy. Strenuous efforts were made on behalf of the state to retrieve the file. The file is believed to have contained two letters from Judge Frank Roe to the DPP, in one of which the judge explained his decision in the Father Molloy case.

The file was one of the matters with which reporter Veronica Guerin was concerned in her investigation of the business of major criminals, before she was shot dead in June 1996.

❼ Truths of the Heart

Ronald Reagan was coming to town and a whole lot of people got excited. Pleasure at the visit was largely confined to the establishment, and to the owners of such ventures as the Ronald Reagan Bar and Lounge, in Ballyporeen, Co. Tipperary. There, for £1, you could buy a small plastic bag of earth scooped up from the very area (or thereabouts) where Mr Reagan's ancestors had once allegedly lived. For some people the visit presented the opportunity to turn a buck.

For government ministers and business people the visit presented a business opportunity of another sort. The Irish economy needs US investment and tourism. Getting your photo snapped with the President of the USA mightn't be a great help in these matters but it could do little harm. It might, however, be damaging to those interests if a warm welcome was not seen to be extended.

For Ronald Reagan also, the trip had a business element, albeit political business. He seemed only mildly interested in his Irish ancestry, but it was 1984, an election year, and with a substantial Irish constituency in key US cities it would do no harm to be photographed with a pint of something in his hand, raising a glass on the oul sod. And Ronald Reagan, leader of the Free World, wanted to share with the Irish his thoughts on what he called 'truths of the heart'.

For the vast majority of Irish people the visit was a matter of indifference. Ronald Reagan was no JFK. To many he was a harmless old clown, a figure of fun. To others he was a harmless old clown who held an office worthy of respect. There would be elaborate preparations to accommodate the crowds wishing to see the distinguished visitor, but they would mostly prove unnecessary. The crowds who came to welcome the President were vastly smaller than those who welcomed JFK two decades earlier, and smaller even than the crowds that came on to the streets to see Richard Nixon when he came to Ireland in the early 1970s.

But there were others who were preparing a welcome for Ronald Reagan. Thousands of Irish people were opposed to the visit and they intended demonstrating their opposition. Some were ideologically opposed to everything President Reagan stood for. Some opposed his nuclear policies. Others specifically opposed the conduct of the Reagan regime in the third world. Awareness of that conduct is high in Ireland, partly because of the country's status as a former colony. Also, Ireland is not wholly dependent on Western-biased news agencies for its view of the third world. Many Irish Catholic missionaries, some quite radicalised and more just observant, bring back trusted and independent views of what is going on.

During his four-day visit, from Friday evening to Monday afternoon, President Reagan would land at Shannon airport; he would stay at Ashford Castle; he would visit Galway to accept an honorary doctorate; he would visit Ballyporeen, alleged home of his ancestors; and he would address the joint Houses of the Oireachtas at Leinster House. While in Dublin he would stay at Deerfield, the home of the US Ambassador, in the Phoenix Park. A total of 1,802 journalists, foreign and domestic, were accredited to cover the visit.

In the days leading up to President Reagan's arrival those supporting and opposing the visit argued the toss. Taoiseach Garret FitzGerald told the Dáil that the tourist industry could benefit and further American investment could be attracted by a positive response.

Student activist Joe Duffy addressed 300 UCG students and pointed out the irony that the government was supporting third world aid and at the same time inviting here the man trying to undermine the

Nicaraguan economy by illegally mining the waters around the country's ports.

Fine Gael's Peter Barry urged support for the visit, saying Ronald Reagan's concern for Ireland was 'real and long-standing'.

The South Tipperary Comhairle Dáil Ceanntar of Fianna Fáil unanimously passed a resolution of welcome. Senator Catherine McGuinness announced she would not attend President Reagan's scheduled address to the joint Houses of the Oireachtas. The Senate of the National University of Ireland voted to give President Reagan an honorary Doctorate of Laws. Several holders of doctorates announced that they were returning them. The Convocation of the National University of Ireland, the voice of the graduates, voted by 419 to 8 to disassociate itself from the giving of the honorary doctorate. A group of admirers of the President, led by solicitor Paddy Madigan, announced they were commissioning a bust of Mr Reagan and hoped to present it to him. The president of the Galway Trades Council turned down an invitation to attend the welcoming ceremonies.

The head of the Confederation of Irish Industry, Liam Connellan, warned that if the impression were conveyed that attitudes in Ireland were hostile to the US, this would have an impact on investment decisions.

The Irish Commission for Justice and Peace, a subsidiary of the Catholic Church's Episcopal Conference, issued a statement which said: 'Our natural courtesy to visitors should not be allowed to stifle the right to protest. To those who say that protest would injure our national interest we would answer that, on the contrary, what can hardly be questioned is the fundamental damage to the ethos and the freedom of our society which would result from a self-imposed censorship dictated by fears of displeasing outside interests.'

President Reagan's schedule had him arriving in Ireland at 8.30pm on Friday 1 June, and leaving at 3pm on Monday 4 June, a period of less than sixty-seven hours. The establishment wanted a smooth visit, the dissidents wanted to make their views known. The stage was set for a casual suspension of civil liberties that was breathtaking in its implications.

· · · · ·

Left-wing groups set up an organisation called the Reagan Reception Committee. Thirty other groups came together in a wider, less cohesive organisation called the Irish Campaign Against Reagan's Foreign Policy (ICARFP). The thirty groups were anti-nuclear, environmental and political. They included those opposed to US activities in the Philippines, Chile, El Salvador and Nicaragua. There were religious groups involved, as well as the Committee for Travellers' Rights, and the Irish Mennonite Movement.

There was no secrecy. All of the demonstrations planned were discussed openly in advance and were widely advertised. If there can be such a thing as a surfeit of democracy it was here, with everything being discussed endlessly before the slightest step was taken. All of the plans were for peaceful and orderly protest. Many of the groups under the ICARFP umbrella were non-violent not only in the negative sense of believing that violence would not achieve anything; they were positively non-violent, believing that a strategy of passive resistance in itself promotes an atmosphere in which change can be brought about.

The first demonstrations, designed to arouse support for future activity, were held weeks before the visit. CND organised a two-and-a-half-week walk, from Letterkenny in Donegal, to Ballyporeen in Tipperary, with a ten-foot-long mock Pershing missile being pushed in a pram. On 26 May, almost a week before President Reagan arrived, there was a march in Dublin, from the Garden of Remembrance in Parnell Square to the Department of Foreign Affairs at Stephen's Green. A range of protests was planned for the next ten days. They included marches, fasts, a Penal Mass on the hills outside Ballyporeen, a 'Climb For Peace' up the Galtymore Mountains.

Groups taking part in the 26 May march through Dublin received from ICARFP some notes on the behaviour expected. The mood of the dissidents can be gauged from those notes:

> It is essential in following the route that all instructions from the stewards and Gardaí are followed . . . The Gardaí have extended their fullest cooperation this afternoon, many giving up a weekend. Please make their work and the work of the stewards, who are all volunteers, as easy as possible.

The notes said that the ICARFP hoped 'to express through this non-violent and peaceful protest a message of hope and confidence in humanity'. The notes referred respectfully to 'Mr Reagan'. The march set the tone for the protest that would follow. Peaceful, with respect given to and sought from the authorities.

Sample chants were provided: 'Remember Romero, Keep Out of El Salvador,' was one. Another was, 'Great Powers Out of Poland and El Salvador.'

One of the ICARFP groups, Fast For Life, intended staging a seven-day fast beside the Bank of Ireland, at the Westmoreland Street side of College Green in Dublin. They went to Pearse Street garda station and met an inspector. They asked for permission to erect a shanty-shack, symbolic of the poor in the Third World, around which they would stage their fast. The inspector said they could do so, but only if they went around to the other side of the Bank of Ireland, to Foster Place, a little nook tucked well in off the street. That way, the shanty-shack would be out of sight of the presidential motorcade. The Fast For Life group agreed to this.

Four days before the visit the Conference of Major Religious Superiors, expressing 'revulsion' at President Reagan's foreign policy, affiliated to the ICARFP.

Dublin Corporation employed nine men to go around pulling down the hundreds of anti-Reagan posters which had appeared. 'We are just not having any of it,' said a Corporation spokesperson. 'We have the troops out.' The Corporation put up its own buntings and flags to celebrate the visit.

Women For Disarmament, another ICARFP group, planned to set up a 'peace camp' in the Phoenix Park. They sought advice from the Office of Public Works about the rules governing behaviour in the Park. They went to a solicitor several weeks before President Reagan's arrival. Again and again they discussed the legalities of their protest. Along with the solicitor they examined and discussed the Phoenix Park Act 1925 and the Phoenix Park Bye-Laws 1926. Women For Disarmament were taking pains to ensure that their protest would be held within the law.

· · · · ·

The women's protest started on Wednesday 30 May, two days before Ronald Reagan came. The Women For Disarmament met near the Papal Cross in the Phoenix Park. The idea then was to find a space within sight of Deerfield, the residence of the United States Ambassador, and to sit there. Just a few women arrived at first and they found a spot and sat there. And that was as strenuous as the protest got.

That same day the women held a press conference, presided over by Senator Mary Robinson, to announce their plans. The Office of Public Works told the newspapers that people 'who assemble in a simple and orderly way' in the Phoenix Park would be conforming with the bye-laws which govern the Park. Gardaí would be called only if there was evidence of serious infringement of the bye-laws.

The next day, some more women went to the Park. At one stage the women were told by officials of the Office of Public Works that they would have to take down a tent which concealed a bucket used as a toilet. The women did so. They were told they would have to take down placards from trees. They did so.

There was an agreement that there would be no drink brought to the camp. They didn't want to create a cider-party image.

After a while, four of the women got into a van and headed back into town. They were going to a base provided by Sisters for Justice, a group of nuns, where food and other essentials could be organised. At Dean Street the van was pulled up by detectives from the Special Branch. The women had been followed from the Park. They asked why they had been stopped and were told they had been acting suspiciously. One garda made some remark about Kevin Street, once the site of Provisional Sinn Féin's head office. After taking the women's names the gardaí let them go.

The Special Branch has two functions. One is to gather what is known as 'low-level intelligence', scraps of information about who is in what radical or dissident group, where they live, their habits, beliefs, family circumstances and associates. The second function of the Special Branch is to intimidate. They regularly watch and beset dissident groups, setting up their surveillance quite openly. They let the dissidents know they are being watched. New members may be stopped and questioned and may perhaps be frightened off.

In the Park that Thursday a couple of dozen Women For Disarmament had gathered in a field about lunchtime. They sat in a circle. As they sat there talking, an unmarked police car drove to within a few feet of them and stopped. Just maintaining a presence, letting the women know they were under close surveillance.

Ronald Reagan wasn't even in the country.

· · · · ·

The next day, Friday 1 June, President Ronald Reagan arrived at Shannon airport. All police leave had been cancelled. Over 7,000 gardaí, seventy per cent of the entire force, would be directly involved in providing security for the President. However, it quickly became clear that US Secret Service agents were in charge of security. Special temporary licences were issued to allow them to carry guns. Although they had no authority in Ireland they openly and unlawfully exercised the authority usually vested in the Garda Síochána. They issued prohibitions on movement, searched handbags, issued orders to gardaí and civilians alike, openly and unashamedly putting the gardaí in a subordinate position.

Just before President Reagan landed, a Cessna light aircraft flew in on precisely the same route, its pilot on a suicide mission in a manoeuvre designed to trigger any missiles that might be automatically targeting the President's route. The Irish Army set up Bofors RBS 70 ground-to-air missiles, also known as Sam missiles. 'Sam on the ground will be protecting Uncle Sam in the air,' an army officer said proudly.

Wherever President Reagan was to appear, rooftops were inspected, manholes were opened and sewers searched. Nets were set in the waters of Loch Corrib, so no enemy divers could swim underwater towards Ashford Castle. In the castle itself the US Secret Service vetoed the planned use of a second-floor luxury suite on the grounds that the President's window could be seen from nearby woods, where a sniper might find cover. The President would be accommodated downstairs. Thousands of pounds were spent refitting the new accommodations, installing gold taps and the like.

The President's specially prepared water was flown in so he wouldn't have to drink the local stuff.

Three employees of Telecom Éireann were banned from having any role in setting up or maintaining the extensive communications system used for the visit, having been designated 'security risks'. Two had left-wing leanings, the third had no record of political activity. The ban was enforced by the gardaí on the 'advice' of the US Secret Service, who apparently vetted anyone involved in any way with the visit.

President Reagan arrived at Shannon at 8.20pm on that Friday 1 June. Up in Dublin at around that time, near the College Green branch of the Bank of Ireland, the Fast For Life group was having problems. They had set up their shanty-shack with a sign saying that for millions in the Third World this was home. Some time that evening the police arrived. The shack was to be taken down, they said. The group said they had received permission from a garda inspector to stage their out-of-the-way protest. No matter, the shack had to come down. The group asked for time to discuss what they would do. The gardaí said they would be back at 9pm.

The gardaí returned at 8pm and said the superintendent wanted the shack taken down. The Fast For Life group had decided that they would not resist such a move but they would not themselves dismantle the shack. The group stood aside and watched the gardaí take down the shack. At the same moment, President Reagan was being welcomed at Shannon.

Up in the Phoenix Park about forty peace women were listening to a radio and when the President's arrival was announced they banged some pots and hissed in the direction of the US Ambassador's residence.

Five hundred protesters were kept a mile away from the airport as a carefully selected assemblage of 370 dignitaries welcomed President Reagan. The President leaned over and kissed one among the welcoming party, Marie Wiley, wife of a Fianna Fáil county councillor. 'Oh God, oh God,' she said, 'I'm bowled over! I never expected to be kissed by the most important man in the world!'

· · · · ·

Someone in authority had been worrying about the Women For Disarmament. By now, several dozen women had brought their backpacks and tents to the Phoenix Park. They were camped some hundreds of feet from where President Reagan would be sleeping. They were an embarrassment to the state. The problem was, they were very peaceful people who were a physical threat to no one. They weren't even noisy. They were breaking no law.

Someone went about examining the law in an effort to find a way of getting rid of the women. Someone had a look through the bye-laws governing the Phoenix Park.

The bye-laws are entirely unremarkable. They contain such provisions as 'No bicycle, tricycle or other vehicle shall be ridden or driven at any time on or across any footpath in the Park.' There is a provision outlawing 'cattle, sheep, pigs or goats' from being brought into the Park 'for the purpose of grazing therein'. Horses cannot be ridden 'on any newly-laid turf'. The bye-laws insist that 'No person shall train a whippet in the Park,' 'No person shall walk upon any flower-bed,' 'No person shall climb any tree in the Park.' You can't take a bird's egg or bathe or fish or walk on icy waters, discharge a firearm or disturb a grazing animal. 'No person shall take part in the game of pitch and toss' or engage in a musical performance or make a public address, nor shall they 'be trained or drilled to the use of arms, or practice gymnastics'.

Under Section 9 (3) of the Phoenix Park Act 1925, the Garda Commissioner has the right to make regulations for the conduct of traffic through the Park and for the preserving of order. Failure to obey such a regulation meant only a £5 fine, so it was hardly a draconian measure. But breaching a regulation was an offence under Section 7 (5) of the same Act, and the commission of an offence, albeit a trivial one, would give the police the right to arrest anyone who committed it, and to remove them from the Park. Trouble was, the women weren't committing any offence, they weren't breaching any regulations. They weren't training whippets, playing pitch and toss or being drilled in the use of firearms.

Ninety minutes before President Reagan's plane touched down at Shannon, the Garda Commissioner, Larry Wren, the country's most senior police officer, signed a new regulation.

I, Laurence Wren, in pursuance of the powers vested in me as Commissioner of the Garda Siochána, by Section 9 of the Phoenix Park Act, 1925, hereby prohibit, within a radius of one mile of the residence known as Deerfield, Phoenix Park, Dublin, over the period commencing at 6.52pm on the 1st June, 1984, and terminating at 3pm on 4th June, 1984, such period being a special occasion, the following:

(a) the erection of tents, temporary dwellings or shelters.

(b) the congregation of persons pursuing a common objective which in the opinion of members of the Garda Siochána may result in public disorder.

(c) the presence of persons acting in such a manner, which, in the opinion of members of the Garda Siochána, may cause public anxiety.

(d) the presence of persons carrying placards, symbols, signs, which in the opinion of members of the Garda Siochána, may result in a breach of the peace.

(e) the presence of persons, who, in the opinion of the Assistant Commissioner, Garda Siochána, or any of his assistants, are likely to interfere with the free movement of the President of the United States of America through the area.

Signed: L. Wren COMMISSIONER OF THE GARDA SIOCHÁNA
Dated this 1st day of June 1984.

Having signed this special temporary regulation, Commissioner Wren was on hand at Shannon to greet President Reagan as he arrived in Ireland. The Commissioner was wearing his full service medals. President Reagan was whisked away from Shannon airport in a helicopter to his accommodations in Ashford Castle in Cong, Co. Mayo, where St Cronan's Pipe Band greeted him with a rendition of 'Wrap The Green Flag Round Me, Boys'.

· · · · ·

Throughout that Friday the Women For Disarmament had been enjoying the third day of their protest in the Phoenix Park. There were a number of children with the women and it was a fine day and everyone had great fun keeping the children entertained, singing songs, making decorations.

They had a large placard that said:

Women for Peace Link arms together
Women all over the world Stand up and say NO!

The placard was illustrated with a graphic showing women linking arms around the world, a rainbow, a moon, some stars glittering and a dove of peace.

The gardaí came for the women that night, about an hour after midnight. The headlights of the police vans, cars and motorbikes lit up the gathering of women where they were sitting under a tree. A garda came forward and asked, 'Níl aon mná Éireannach anseo?'

It seems that the gardaí assumed that the women were foreigners, outside agitators from Greenham Common or further afield. There may have been an assumption that decent Irish women wouldn't involve themselves in this kind of protest lark. By asking in Irish if there were any Irish women here the police apparently intended to expose the women's foreignness. One of the women responded in Irish. About two-thirds of the women were from Dublin, others were from Donegal, Galway and the North. One was Italian, one American, one Scottish, each of whom had lived and worked in Dublin for some years. There were about three dozen women present. Their average age was twenty-five.

The women were lifted into vans and driven out of the Park and left outside the gates. They calmly regrouped and walked back into the Park, being followed all the way by the garda cars and motorbikes.

A couple of hours later, about 3am, the gardaí again removed the women. This time, to prevent the women going back into the Park, they drove them well away from the area, dumping them in small groups in various parts of the city. Women who appeared to the gardaí to be together were separated into different vans. They sang as they were driven to their dumping points. The women made their separate ways home in ones and twos. The wisdom of dumping women in deserted streets in the middle of the night would later be questioned. There would be no answers.

In the course of these evictions the gardaí made references to a 'regulation' or 'edict' signed by the Garda Commissioner which allowed the gardaí to carry out the evictions. The Women For Disarmament, having already gone into the legalities of their action with solicitor Heather Celmalis, were puzzled by this. They knew the law and were observing it; now the gardaí were talking about some new law.

On Saturday morning the women sought through their lawyers to find out what this 'edict' or 'regulation' might be. Heather Celmalis retained barrister Ruth-Anne Fitzgerald. The legal discussion revolved around whether it would be possible to obtain an injunction to prevent the gardaí from evicting the women from the Park.

· · · · ·

The women were back in the Phoenix Park at about noon on Saturday 2 June. In Galway, some of the country's leading academics were queuing up to honour President Reagan with a doctorate. A number of academics and intellectuals, bemused that a man who had openly and cheerfully broken international law by mining the waters around the ports of Nicaragua should be awarded, of all things, an Irish university Doctorate of Laws, held their own 'de-conferring' exercise at the same time. Peadar O'Donnell, the ninety-one-year-old writer and agitator, acted as honorary chancellor. Two UCG lecturers, Dr Pat Sheeran and Dr Des Johnson, walked around the centre of Galway city offering photocopied degrees for 10p each. 'Get your degree today,' they urged shoppers, 'tomorrow it will be worthless.'

As President Reagan's limousine made its way through Eyre Square one window rolled down a couple of inches and the tips of some fingers could be seen waving. This astounding sight appeared to be the President endeavouring to make personal contact with the people of Ireland. Two eggs were thrown at the limo, one of them missed. Gardaí later told reporters a young man was 'severely admonished' and released.

Back in Dublin, word had gone around about the eviction of the peace women from the Phoenix Park. In the afternoon their ranks were swollen to about eighty. Reporters visited the site and there were many visitors wishing the women well. Plain-clothes gardaí were seen taking the registration numbers of visitors' cars.

The women decorated the trees, sang and talked. In mid-afternoon there was a discussion about 'doing an action'. In the best democratic fashion the women sat around in a circle for two hours and tried to reach a consensus. The proposal was that they walk in a circle in front of the gate of the US Ambassador's residence. Some women had a proposal to coat the palms of their hands with red paint and make red handprints, symbolic of the blood of those killed by US-backed regimes around the world, on the white wall around the residence. The action would be a counterpoint to the official ceremony in Galway. Some women disagreed with the proposal and the discussion ended with everyone free to do what they wished.

The women crossed to the front of the residence and some put red handprints on the wall, others walked in a circle, some stood and watched. Someone chanted, 'Reagan has blood on his hands, Reagan has blood on his hands.' Some others sang, 'Give Peace a Chance'.

The gardaí moved in and began hauling the women away from the wall, carrying them back to the field, all the while straining not to get red paint on their uniforms. Some women just lay on the ground, others walked away. It was a minor incident, the gardaí preventing graffiti being put on a wall. Jane Morgan had disagreed with the action and decided not to take part. Now, watching it, she thought it very effective and regretted her decision.

Suddenly a car appeared, driving in among the protestors. Plain-clothes gardaí jumped out and arrested one of the women, pulled her into the car and drove off. The woman was Petra Breatnach. She was a supporter of the Release Nicky Kelly Committee, which had long protested the continuing imprisonment of a man wrongly convicted of a train robbery. (Kelly was to be released six weeks later, after four years in jail, and would subsequently receive a presidential pardon and monetary compensation.)

Breatnach was singled out from the other women and arrested under Section 30 of the Offences Against the State Act and taken to Cabra garda station.

• • • • •

The position on Saturday evening was that one woman had been lifted under the catch-all of Section 30, and the others had been told of some unspecified 'edict' forbidding their presence in the Park. Their lawyers had been unable to elicit any further information from the gardaí at the scene.

Barrister Ruth-Anne Fitzgerald rang Dublin Castle and was put on to a man who wouldn't give his name but was represented as being in over-all charge of arrangements for the Reagan visit. He said that, yes, a new bye-law had recently been introduced and, no, he couldn't tell her the terms of it.

The barrister contacted Cabra garda station. She spoke to a detective inspector who said he was in charge and that he was satisfied there had been a breach of the Commissioner's new bye-law. (In fact, the inspector didn't seem to know what he was talking about. There was no new bye-law, just a regulation made under the existing bye-laws.) She asked if he knew the terms of the Commissioner's bye-law and the inspector said he did. She asked him to tell her. He said that was not his job. The proper place for her to find out the details of the bye-law was in court.

The barrister asked again to be told what the new bye-law was, so that there would be no need for anyone to go to court. Her clients would obey the law, but they needed to know what it was. The inspector said it wasn't his function to explain the law. When was the bye-law introduced, Ruth-Anne Fitzgerald asked, what was its number, when was it published in the state bulletin *Iris Oifigúil*? It wasn't, said the inspector, his function to provide that information.

The position seemed to be that once the women broke the law they would be brought to court and only then told what the law was.

The lawyers, Fitzgerald and Celmalis, were still thinking in terms of obtaining an injunction to prevent the women being dumped in various parts of the city.

Fitzgerald rang the home of the Attorney General, Peter Sutherland. He wasn't there but rang back later, some time before 1am. Fitzgerald explained what was happening and asked Sutherland to find out from the Garda Commissioner what the terms of the new order or regulation were. Her clients, she said, were making every effort to ascertain the terms of the new order and were genuinely concerned to know what it was permissible to do in the Phoenix Park.

There are various procedures which must be followed when a new law is brought into force, procedures for the promulgation — or public stating — of the law. Fitzgerald told Sutherland that her clients would waive all that and accept a verbal promulgation of the regulation from him, over the phone, just so long as they learned the terms. The women, in short, were willing to obey the law once they found out what the law was. Sutherland, the Attorney General, chief law officer of the state, adviser to the cabinet on the making of law, said there was nothing he could do, he had no function in the matter.

Back in the Phoenix Park it was raining.

· · · · ·

The rain started late in the evening. There had been something over one hundred peace women in the Park earlier that day. As the evening wore on the numbers dwindled to perhaps sixty. The rain was unceasing, heavy and depressing.

The women spread industrial-strength plastic on the grass, held it down with wooden stakes, and settled down in sleeping bags and survival bags to try to get some sleep. The rain gathered on the plastic and ran down into the depressions formed by the sleeping bodies. Some woke to find the ends of their sleeping bags full of water.

President Reagan was spending the night well over a hundred miles away, in Ashford Castle, in Cong, Co. Mayo, one of the most luxurious hotels in the world. He was being guarded in Mayo by a thousand gardaí, as well as US Secret Service agents. Out on an island on Lough Corrib, a group of miserable detectives shivered in the dark. They were there to ensure that no one landed on the island and used it to launch an attack on the President. Installed on the island for a shift of fifteen hours, they were cold and tired and they lit a small fire for comfort. Suddenly the sky was alive with loud whirring as a helicopter swooped on the little island and over a loudspeaker a US Secret Service agent barked at the gardaí to put out the fire. The fire was extinguished and the cops continued to shiver in the cold and the dark.

At the women's camp in the Phoenix Park, people dropped by with dry clothes. One man arrived with packets of cigarettes and tea for about forty people. He said that he and his family were delighted with the protest.

By around 5am the numbers of women had dwindled further, to about forty. The women were waking up, finding themselves wet from the rain, and moving to shelter under the trees. Some set off home to find dry clothing. Others stayed on and tried to keep themselves warm and keep their spirits up. They staged a Miss Phoenix Park contest, which was won by a woman wearing a black plastic rubbish sack and two odd wellies. They played leap-frog. They staged a sack race, using survival bags.

At about 7am a number of garda vans assembled near the US Ambassador's residence. The women began to walk in a number of circles. At least one of the groups was chanting the name of Petra Breatnach, who had been snatched from their midst and arrested. Others sang.

The garda vans moved in across the grass, towards the women. More than one woman thought: 'This is like something in a movie.' About eight vans, a couple of hundred gardaí. Van doors opening, the police spilling on to the grass, fanning out, coming for the women.

The women's circles broke up and they began walking towards the gardaí. About ten of the women stood aside from all this. As far as everyone knew this was just another eviction. It had been agreed that some women would stand aside and look after the belongings left under the trees.

As the gardaí and the women came nearer to each other the women broke into groups of about five. Some were holding hands or linking arms. They were singing. There was a garda in a light blue uniform, an officer, saying something or trying to say something but he couldn't be clearly heard above the singing.

As soon as the gardaí grabbed a woman she slumped to the ground and lay there. There was no resistance to being arrested, just non-cooperation, bodies becoming dead-weight. Two of the women, having experienced rough policing at the Greenham Common peace camp, had cut their hair so that they could not be dragged by the hair. Some gardaí knew how to lift a protester, others were clumsy, like they'd just come out of Templemore.

The women were now lifted and carried to the police vans and thrown inside. At one van the gardaí made jeering remarks about locking up the women and throwing away the key, but similar remarks had been made the previous night and they weren't very convincing.

A young garda got into the back of another van. He was holding a piece of paper and said to the women, 'Right now, you've been arrested for disobedience of the Commissioner's edict. Just so that you know.' He fiddled with the piece of paper, obviously embarrassed, and left.

The women were taken to the Bridewell garda station, behind the Four Courts. Even as they were taken into the Bridewell the women didn't know where they were. They were carried from the vans and dumped inside. Jane Morgan was dumped in a corridor. Then she was lifted up and dumped on a desk. A man asked her name and address. She told him, he wrote it down. For some reason she thought he was a reporter. He asked her date of birth. She asked who he was and was told he was a detective sergeant. The detective was filling in a form and he asked loudly who was the arresting officer. A garda stepped forward and said, 'Me.' Jane Morgan had never seen him before.

The term 'arresting officer' was the first indication Jane Morgan had that she was under arrest.

The women were processed and put into cells. Some downstairs, some upstairs, about five in each cell. There were thirty women in custody in the Bridewell. Petra Breatnach was still being held at Cabra garda station. The arrests were not over yet.

· · · · ·

Word spread quickly. Someone heard about the arrests on a taxi radio. Within a few minutes a woman was knocking at the window of Heather Celmalis's home in Halston Street, not far from the Bridewell, to tell her that her clients had been arrested. Celmalis got dressed and set off for the Bridewell.

Three of the peace women, Mary Duffy, Elaine Bradley and Anne Barr, had left the Park some time during the night to change into dry clothes. They returned to the Park early that morning. Mary Duffy arrived back just before the mass arrest and saw the women being carried away. The other two arrived later and she told them what happened.

The three were preparing to gather up belongings. There were about eight cars parked in the vicinity, belonging to friends, husbands and relations of the arrested women and the men were helping with the packing. The three women were approached by gardaí and told that under Section 9 of the Phoenix Park Act the Garda Commissioner had signed an edict that made it illegal for 'people like you' to be within a mile of the Ambassador's residence.

The gardaí said that walking, camping, sitting or loitering was illegal. The women pointed out that there were a number of joggers puffing past. Was it illegal to jog? Why didn't the gardaí annoy those people?

'Don't give me any lip,' said a garda.

But, was jogging illegal? The gardaí said that jogging was not illegal. The three women began to jog.

They were arrested as they jogged, the gardaí jogging along behind them. The women refused to walk to the police vans and had to be carried.

'Ah, come on,' said a weary copper, 'could yez not walk to the van?'

As Heather Celmalis arrived at the Bridewell she saw Mary Duffy, Elaine Bradley and Anne Barr being dragged into the station. The latter two were being carried by their arms and legs. Mary Duffy was being dragged by the ankles. The gardaí apparently had some trouble trying to lift her. Mary Duffy is a thalidomide victim and has no arms. There were now thirty-three women detained in the Bridewell and one in Cabra.

Duffy was put in a cell alone. Some of the other women were upset by this isolation of their friend and complained about it. Duffy wasn't too upset, she was glad of the rest. She sang and was pleased to find that the empty cell gave off a terrific echo. She didn't know that she was going to be in the Bridewell for over thirty hours.

· · · · ·

Heather Celmalis tried to find out from the gardaí the reason for the arrest of her clients. The gardaí confirmed that the women had been arrested but couldn't or wouldn't give any further information. The mysterious 'edict' from the Garda Commissioner could not be shown or quoted. Celmalis left the station to consult with barrister Ruth-Anne Fitzgerald about seeking a decree of habeas corpus. When she returned at 1pm she was told her clients were now being formally charged.

· · · · ·

At this stage Ronald Reagan had just arrived in Ballyporeen, Tipperary, the alleged birthplace of his Irish ancestors. He was in the village for two hours. His entourage, police and reporters out-numbered the villagers by eight to one.

Ballyporeen is a village of two streets wherein dwell 350 souls, with 1,400 living in the surrounding parish. It's a dairy farming area, with many of the local young folk working in the Mitchelstown cheese factory. In the weeks leading up to the presidential visit there was a constant smell of paint from the village, as house after house was decorated.

The only connection between President Reagan and the tiny Tipperary village was a scrawl in a parish birth register which was interpreted to indicate that Michael, son of 'Thomas Regan' and Margaret Murphy, was baptised there on 3 September 1829. This was, perhaps, the Michael Regan who became Michael Reagan and married in London in 1852 and went to Illinois and had a son named John Edward, who had a son named Ronald.

Inspection of the scrawl showed clearly that the 'Regan' had been interfered with and had originally most likely been 'Ryan'. Father Redmond, the long dead parish priest who filled in the register, made his 'g' with an open loop and his 'y' with a closed loop and the 'g' in 'Regan' quite clearly has a closed loop. A squiggle which might or might not be interpreted as an 'e' has clearly been added. The tenuousness of the connection between the President and Ballyporeen didn't bother many. There had to be an ancestral homeland and Ballyporeen would do as well as any other.

The village had a Ronald Reagan Bar and Lounge, with a plastic sign above the door of the pub advertising this fact. Everyone knew the pub was really O'Farrell's and it had stood in that spot since 1922. The pub that stood there before it was burned down by the Black and Tans.

Local shops sold T-shirts that said, 'I've been to Ballyporeen, have you?' and car sun-visors that said, 'Ballyporeen welcomes Ronald Reagan.' In his grocery store, Fianna Fáil councillor Con Donovan was getting repeated requests for camera film, from the tourists already dropping by on their way through to somewhere else. Con was a member of the Ballyporeen welcoming committee. Perhaps ten or fifteen years ago he used to stock film in his store but he stopped because there was no demand for it. Now, he was looking up the phone number of the Kodak supplier.

It had been arranged that the President would visit the Ronald Reagan Bar and Lounge and pose for photographs with a pint of Smithwick's beer, pulled by the owner of the bar, John O'Farrell. The pub's ordinary beer was not acceptable, for security reasons, so a special barrel of Smithwick's beer had been flown in and installed with its own tap, under the supervision of the US Secret Service. John's wife Mary had written to several fashion designers suggesting that they loan her an outfit in which she would meet the President, in exchange for which they would get publicity. One designer, Vonnie Reynolds, supplied a suit, free of charge. Mrs O'Farrell arranged for her sisters and sisters-in-law to have a good position in the lounge when the President arrived.

Shortly before President Reagan appeared, a US Secret Service agent breezed in and barked, 'Get those women out of here!'

The women were ejected. 'I don't have any say here any more,' said Mary O'Farrell.

'I'm the landlord,' said John O'Farrell, 'but I don't have any control!'

Ronald Reagan arrived, John O'Farrell pulled the pint from the special barrel, Reagan hoisted it for the cameras. President Reagan walked down the street and waved to locals.

After the Reagan entourage roared away from the village an old man from Ballyporeen told a reporter: 'A little bit of us all died when the President departed.'

• • • • •

Up in Dublin, while President Reagan charmed Ballyporeen, the peace women were taken out of the cells and had the charge against them read aloud. It said that on being ordered by the gardaí 'in accordance with the provisions of Section 9 (3) of the Phoenix Park Act, 1925, to leave the Phoenix Park, you did fail to leave the said Park. Contrary to Section 7 (5) of the Phoenix Park Act 1925.'

Neither the women nor their lawyers knew what regulation of the Commissioner's they had allegedly broken. They had not seen the regulation written specifically for them, and it did not occur to them that a special law would be brought into force for only sixty-eight hours and eight minutes, bracketing the period of time that Ronald Reagan was scheduled to be on Irish soil. The precise legalities could wait until later. The first priority was to obtain bail for the prisoners. The lawyers asked that their clients be brought before a peace commissioner or district justice so that an application for bail could be made. On such a trivial charge bail was a certainty. The request was refused.

The routine that might have been expected was that the prisoners would be granted station bail, a procedure which allows people charged with lesser offences to post their own bail with the police. It clears the cells of people being held on trivial charges, who without doubt would be granted bail as soon as they are brought to court. Station bail is allowed at the discretion of the gardaí. Extraordinarily, the gardaí said they would grant station bail to just one of the thirty-three women in the Bridewell, Mary Duffy. The circumstances of Mary Duffy's arrest and detention were no different from the other women's. She is a strong woman who has learned to do with her feet most of what others do with their hands and she lives an independent life. She had no doubt that the garda decision was made because they were embarrassed to be locking up someone without arms. She refused to accept special treatment.

The other women were not offered station bail; they would have to wait until the gardaí were ready to bring them before a judge or a peace commissioner. Celmalis asked when that would happen. The gardaí couldn't or wouldn't say.

It was about this time that Ronald Reagan left Ballyporeen and flew to Áras an Uachtaráin, in the Phoenix Park, home of the President of Ireland, Patrick Hillery.

The Lord Mayor of Dublin, Michael Keating, had invited a small number of people to welcome the President. The usual torrent of hangers-on who might be expected at such a freebie were not present. 'I only invited those whom I knew would come,' Keating said.

. . . . .

There were four solicitors working for the women at various times: Isabel Ní Chuireain, Mairead Quigley, Breda Allen and Heather Celmalis. The four set about gathering statements from the prisoners for use in preparing a request for habeas corpus.

A couple of the women in the Bridewell had been locked up briefly before, after a peace demonstration in front of the embassy of the Soviet Union, but most had no experience of this kind of thing. Emotions ran to extremes. You were either high as a kite or in the depths of depression. You laughed or you cried. The cells were filthy, there were five and six people in cells meant for two or three. The toilets were blocked in some cells. They could only be flushed from outside the cells and were more often than not left unflushed. All the women were wearing clothes that had been soaked through in the rain. The smell of all this was appalling. The foul smell was one thing that lingered strongly in the memories of those in the Bridewell through that period.

The women did not on the whole have complaints about the personal behaviour of the gardaí in the station. While there may have been roughness (Mary Duffy was dragged downstairs by her ankles) and individual brusqueness, some of the women felt that the gardaí were embarrassed by their duties.

Among any group of thirty-three women the chances are that several will be menstruating. That was true of the women in the Bridewell. They asked for sanitary towels. They were told that the Bridewell provides 'only the basics'. Menstrual blood was smeared on the walls.

'You know what it's like to bleed in your knickers,' one of the prisoners appealed to a policewoman, who got three Tampax of her own and brought them to the cells. They weren't enough. It wasn't until barrister Ruth-Anne Fitzgerald found out what was happening and went to a local shop and came back with bags full of sanitary towels that the women were provided with what the Bridewell authorities do not consider 'basics'.

Mary Duffy was eventually put in a cell with some other women. The gardaí, as before, found it difficult and embarrassing to move a woman with no arms who would not cooperate. Duffy had been wearing a coat belonging to someone else when she was arrested and the gardaí searched it and took away nail scissors they found in a pocket. Very clever, mused Duffy, they must be afraid I'll cut my wrists.

In one cell there was a shortage of matches, so one cigarette was kept going at all times. Ventilation was lousy. Lighting wasn't much better. There was a small square of thick glass high up on the wall, another square of thick glass over the door, with a 60-watt bulb burning outside.

You got milk and sugar in your tea whether or not you liked it. Mashed potatoes and ham. Some of the women were vegetarians.

• • • • •

The prisoners knew from their lawyers that they could make a phone call, if it was practicable. It wasn't practicable, said the gardaí. Some prisoners convinced individual police officers to make phone calls for them, to relatives and friends, mostly to ask for dry clothing. Outside the Bridewell, the women who had not been arrested gathered to give support. A priest visited the Bridewell and said Mass in a corridor, the women kneeling in two rows, some delighted to get out of the cells, some sobbing.

Just before the Mass began one of the prisoners, Sister Frances, from the Sisters for Justice, asked the priest if he supported their actions. She said she felt she might be unable to attend otherwise. The priest replied that he had come into the jail especially to say Mass for the women and felt that this was indication enough of how he felt. But if it needed spelling out, yes, he did support the women's actions.

In the cells, as the hours passed, emotions swung this way and that. One woman, a student, was distraught. She had exams to sit the next day and didn't know if she would be free by then. Above all there was the feeling of powerlessness. Rage at times, tears of anger, frustration, anxiety, fear. As always, there was singing. Paper plates were torn into quarter-moon shapes and hung on strands of wool to decorate the cell. Plastic forks became brooms for paper witches.

Monica Barnes, Fine Gael TD, got a phone call and went to the Bridewell that evening. The gardaí first wanted the prisoners to select a spokeswoman to come out and meet Barnes. This search for ringleaders had been a feature of the garda activities in the Park. The women pointed out yet again that they were individuals, they had no hierarchy. The gardaí went around the cells flushing the toilets before Barnes was allowed in.

Barnes went from cell to cell and visited all the women. She was appalled at the conditions, with four and five to a cell, the place smelly. She found some women frightened, a high level of anxiety throughout, some worried about their families, not knowing what law they had broken, not knowing how long they could be held like this. She got the impression that the police weren't taking any pleasure from their job. It is apparent that some at least of the gardaí were quite sympathetic and humane in the carrying out of their orders. Mary Duffy would later describe some of the gardaí as 'civil'. Several of the women described one motorcycle garda as 'sweet'. Although there was evidence of gruffness on the part of some gardaí in the carrying out of an unpleasant exercise there was for the great part nothing personal in what they were doing. They were merely carrying out orders, removing from sight elements that the state wanted sidelined.

Some of the prisoners had visitors, others didn't. The gardaí would allow only one prisoner at a time to receive a visitor. Elaine Bradley's husband and two children were standing outside. They weren't allowed in.

A garda asked one of the kids, 'Is your mammy in there? Poor fella.' He gave the child ten pence. For a while afterwards, the child associated garda uniforms with nice people who give you money.

One man waited three hours in hopes of visiting his wife. A sergeant eventually told him he couldn't go in. 'You're a crowd of messers,' he told the man. Another man who had brought a change of clothing for his girlfriend was refused permission to bring it in.

Some of the prisoners became hysterical and banged on the metal doors. Upstairs, a woman called Sophie had been calling for her medication for what seemed a couple of hours. She was taking anti-biotics and the medication had been taken away. She became distraught and eventually the gardaí took her out into the corridor. She began having a seizure. The women in the cells, looking out through peep-holes the size of a 2p coin, shouted for Ludy to be let out of her cell to help Sophie; Ludy had medical training. They pleaded and screamed for fifteen minutes. They saw Sophie's back arch and her body drop. Some thought she was dead.

A garda said, 'Ah, she's just hysterical.'

They eventually allowed Ludy Methorsg out of the cell. She examined Sophie and said she needed hospital treatment. The gardaí wouldn't do anything on their own authority. They sent for the station sergeant, who agreed to allow the prisoner to be taken to hospital.

Having received a valium injection at Blanchardstown Hospital, Sophie was returned to the Bridewell forty-five minutes later, around 10pm. She was pale and shivering, wrapped in a blanket. Still considered a danger to Ronald Reagan, she was locked up for the night.

· · · · ·

Meanwhile, a cavalcade of cars carried Ronald Reagan and his entourage from the US Ambassador's residence to Dublin Castle, where a state banquet was being held in his honour. Few citizens turned out to welcome his passing car; thousands were preparing a protest.

At just after 8pm, as the car came on to Capel Street Bridge, a young man leaned across the barrier and shouted, 'Reagan out!' A plain-clothes garda jumped on him and threw him to the ground, smacking his head against the pavement. Another young man was

Jesse O'Dwyer is taken into court.

The garda station at Shercock.

Garda Seamus Galligan (left) and Sergeant Peter Diviney.

Garda Joseph Feely and Ban Garda Michelle Mannion

At Bailieborough courthouse, defence counsel Paddy McEntee (left) and Superintendent Pat Culhane, one of the gardaí who investigated the cover-up.

Father Niall Molloy.

Richard and Theresa Flynn.

Outside the inquest at Tullamore, state pathologist Dr John Harbison (left) meets Dr Declan Gilsenan, the pathologist opposing him on behalf of the Flynn family.

Attending the inquest, Inspector Tom Monaghan (left) and Sergeant Kevin Forde.

The day before Ronald Reagan arrived in Ireland, gardaí were mounting an upclose-and-personal 'low level intelligence' operation against the Phoenix Park women.

The threat to the Free World. Women for Disarmament gather in the Phoenix Park.

The Lynagh brothers carry Michael's coffin. Finbar Lynagh is front left, Colm Lynagh is front right. Jim Lynagh, with a bandage on his nose, is behind Finbar.

MARYANN STEPHENS

Karl Crawley, April 1982.

dragged by the neck and kicked. He shouted at his garda assailant to identify himself and was kicked again. From the garda point of view, these people had tried to interfere with the lawful progress of a distinguished visitor. What's more, some student activists were seen to be carrying leaflets.

The young man originally assaulted got to his feet and left the scene. There was no attempt at arrest. The second young man, a student activist, headed up towards the centre of the city with another student. At Middle Abbey Street they met *Irish Times* reporter Frank Kilfeather, who had witnessed the garda assault on the students at Capel Street Bridge. Kilfeather interviewed the two. As he did so a garda car arrived, gardaí got out and arrested the two students under Section 30 of the Offences Against The State Act, and took them away.

· · · · ·

Heather Celmalis and Ruth-Anne Fitzgerald, lawyers for the peace women, having taken statements from their clients in the Bridewell, began drawing up affidavits for a writ of *habeas corpus*. They also had to find a judge, not an easy task on the Sunday evening of a bank holiday weekend. They had a list of court registrars and they began phoning around.

In Dublin Castle the state's elite was gathering for a banquet to honour President Reagan, kicking off with Dublin Bay prawns and turtle soup, followed by roast prime fillet of beef in a Perigourdine sauce, washed down by a grand cru Chablis. The Catholic Church leader, Cardinal Tomás Ó Fiaich, had turned down an invitation to the banquet, as did the moderator of the Presbyterian Church.

The Attorney General, Peter Sutherland, who had disclaimed any responsibility in the matter of the arrest of the women, sat at Table J. At Table C the guests had the honour of the company of Garda Commissioner Larry Wren, who had signed the special law under which the women had been locked up.

There would later be complaints that Fine Gael hogged too many seats at the banquet, keeping out deserving Fianna Fáilers. Fine Gael handlers and minders and public relations specialists got seats, as well as relatives and cronies of Garret FitzGerald.

An anonymous spokesman for Fine Gael later explained the reasoning behind the seating arrangements: 'It is quite simple. We are in power, they are not.'

During the banquet, Taoiseach Garret FitzGerald delivered a carefully crafted speech. In order to maintain FitzGerald's liberal credentials the speech had to mention the oppressive regimes in Central America. But it was imperative that the Americans should not take offence at anything said. FitzGerald talked in vague terms of poverty and dignity and peace and democracy. The speech was so carefully worded that it managed to win approval from both US Secretary of State George Schultz and Catholic bishop Eamonn Casey, who had voiced opposition to President Reagan's policies.

In the streets outside, the Irish Campaign Against Reagan's Foreign Policy had organised a protest march. As the state's elite flattered President Reagan, 10,000 people marched in a circle through the streets around Dublin Castle. The protest was called Ring Around Reagan. Amid the protesters were a hundred women dressed in black plastic sacks, their mouths gagged and their hands tied, symbolising the locking up of the peace women. A poem written by one of the Bridewell prisoners, Sue Russell, was read to the demonstrators by Kate Shanahan.

At the end of the protest hundreds split off and marched down to the Bridewell. There they began a chant of, 'Let the women go!'

Inside the jail, after a night in the rain and about fifteen hours in filthy, smelly, cramped conditions, the women were exhausted. Some were grateful for the support but wished the marchers would keep the noise down. As the chant grew more aggressive some of the women became anxious. They disliked and feared aggression, even when directed against their jailers. Outside, the peace women who had not been arrested started singing, trying to calm the crowd. The demonstration eventually fizzled out.

About 200 students marched on Store Street garda station, where the two students arrested under Section 30 were being held. Seconds before the march arrived at the garda station the two were released.

The lawyers for the peace camp finally found a High Court judge, Donal Barrington, willing to hear a *habeas corpus* appeal. They went to his home in south County Dublin. Barrington gave them an order of *habeas corpus* but effective only from Tuesday morning. It was Sunday night. Barrington agreed that the state should have to bring the women before a court to explain their detention, but not for another thirty-six hours. The order was useless.

As the women prepared to spend a weary night in cramped, smelly, oppressive conditions, the banquet at Dublin Castle was ending. Arriving home from the celebration, Fine Gael cabinet minister Gemma Hussey got out her diary and wrote about the 'elegance' of the 'historic occasion', worried that she felt 'so plump', and recorded the words of praise she received from President Reagan when she was introduced to him. There was some unease among the establishment and Hussey noted a 'slight reserve and ruefulness on account of the mixed feelings in Ireland about it all'. It appears that cabinet members were quite aware of what was happening at ground level. Hussey noted in her diary that there were 'some quite big demonstrations' and concluded, 'I feel the gardaí over-reacted.'

Reservations aside, Hussey was pleased with how things had gone. 'All in all,' she summed up, 'despite the bloody security everywhere — which was obtrusive and annoying — it was good.' As she wrote those words and retired to bed the women in the Bridewell were trying to get some fitful sleep.

Ronald Reagan too had left the banquet. As he retired to the US Ambassador's residence in the Phoenix Park he was spared the trial of having to pass by a group of women sitting in the dark several hundred feet away, keeping a vigil for peace.

The lawyers returned to the Bridewell to explain the legal developments to the prisoners. They were there until 2am.

· · · · ·

Next morning, President Reagan's armour-plated Lincoln left the US Ambassador's residence on its way to Leinster House, where he would address the joint Houses of the Oireachtas. Down at the Bridewell supporters of the peace women gathered outside and sang 'Give Peace a Chance'. Some of the supporters chained themselves to the railings.

The singing was part protest, part for the encouragement of the prisoners, in their cells up above the street. One woman shouted up to the prisoners, 'Do you want us to be quiet? Do you want some time to think?' The noise was about to increase.

Hundreds of anti-Reagan demonstrators came marching down to the Bridewell to support the women. They chanted their slogans, not always to the satisfaction of the women.

'One, two, three four,
Open up the Bridewell door!
Five, six, seven, eight,
Organise to smash the state!'

One of the women appealed to the demonstrators. 'Please, we are making a non-violent protest. Sing if you want to, but don't chant.' After a while the numbers outside the Bridewell dwindled to relatives and friends of the prisoners.

· · · · ·

As President Reagan's cavalcade drove to Leinster House it passed crush-proof barriers bereft of a crush of citizenry. Onlookers were outnumbered ten to one by gardaí. The President's armour-plated limousine drove into a specially constructed tent attached to the front of Government Buildings, so no one could see him to shoot him as he got out of his car. He had to pass through an open space on the Merrion Street side of Leinster House on his way to the Dáil chamber, so a wooden barrier was built, sheltering him from any snipers that might be hidden in Merrion Square. The wooden screen was painted green and trees in black plastic containers were hired and placed at intervals along the barrier, for decorative purposes.

President Reagan was led to a dais by the Taoiseach, Garret FitzGerald, the Tánaiste, Dick Spring, and the leader of the opposition, Charlie Haughey.

The Ceann Comhairle, Tom Fitzpatrick, welcomed the President and noted the USA's commitment to 'the rights of the individual under law' and thanked him for the opportunity that Irish emigrants to the US had to 'breathe the air of freedom'.

As soon as the President began to speak Deputy Tomás MacGiolla stood up. 'Ceann Comhairle, on a point of order,' he began.

His parliamentary colleagues howled at him to 'Sit down! Sit down!' There was genuine embarrassment that dissent was so openly expressed.

Immediately, another deputy, Proinsias De Rossa, stood up. 'I wish also . . .', he said, and his voice was drowned in a torrent of abuse.

A third deputy, Tony Gregory, stood up and said, 'In solidarity . . .', and he too was showered with shouts of 'Out! Out! Out!'

The three deputies left the chamber.

Ronald Reagan had a remark prepared for the walkout and he stuck to the script, regardless of its appropriateness. 'There are countries in the world today where representatives would not have been able to speak as they have been here.'

It didn't seem to strike Mr Reagan that the three protesters had not been able to speak, they had been shouted down. And, anyway, to prevent any dissident voices being heard, all the microphones in the chamber except those in front of President Reagan and the Ceann Comhairle had been disabled.

President Reagan was ready with a remark because he wasn't surprised by the walkout. Some weeks earlier Taoiseach Garret FitzGerald had attended a meeting in Stockholm, organised by the Bilderberg Group. Bilderberg is an international outfit which links establishment figures in many countries, exchanging information and ideas. It was formed in 1954 with the intention of strengthening the relationship between the establishments in Europe and the US. Each year, several dozen rich people, politicians and academics are selected for invitation to a three-day secret meeting at which information is exchanged and matters of mutual interest are discussed on a strictly off-the-record basis.

At the meeting in Stockholm, Garret FitzGerald informed a US diplomat that when Ronald Reagan addressed the Dáil there was likely to be a walkout by left-wingers and President Reagan should be warned about this so it shouldn't surprise or upset him. FitzGerald went so far as to describe the layout of the Dáil chamber and pinpoint where the left-wingers would be seated.

About twenty members of the Oireachtas stayed away from the joint session. Fine Gael's Monica Barnes, opposed to President Reagan's foreign policy, and now disgusted by the fawning over the President while the protesters were locked up in filthy conditions, had absented herself from the Dáil during Mr Reagan's speech. TDs Brendan Howlin and Michael D. Higgins stayed away, as did Senator Mary Robinson. The vast majority of the TDs and Senators gave President Reagan a welcome of enthusiastic applause. (In her diary that night, Fine Gael cabinet minister Gemma Hussey would scold her left-wing colleagues for their protest. She wrote, 'it was undoubtedly an important speech.')

President Reagan began his undoubtedly important speech at noon. He was here to tell the politicians of what he called 'truths of the heart'.

He and his wife Nancy, he said, had been made 'as welcome as the flowers in May'. That wasn't true. Fewer turned out to welcome President Reagan than had turned out to protest at his visit. There were no welcoming crowds on the pavements to be controlled by the crowd-control barriers. As President Reagan spoke in the Dáil there were four thousand protesters outside in Molesworth Street. High above the crowd, on the top floor of an estate agent's office, a garda video camera was trained on the protesters, electronically recording the faces of those expressing dissent.

Joe Duffy, president of the Union of Students in Ireland, mocked the President's limited view of the country. All he saw, said Duffy, were 'the arses of his Secret Service agents through the windows of his car'.

Inside Leinster House, President Reagan told the politicians of 'your nation's historic regard for personal freedom'.

At that moment, just after noon, the prisoners in the Bridewell were being taken from their cells to a large underground room beneath the courts. Anne Barr, Lucia Bergmann, Elaine Bradley, Anne Browne, Mary Chance . . .

'Freedom,' Ronald Reagan told the assembled members of the

Oireachtas, 'is the flagship and flashfire of the future; its spark ignites the deepest and noblest aspirations of the human soul.'

Monica Corish left her cell, and Anne Claffey, Agnes Deegan, Mary Duffy, Orla Ní Éirli and Miriam Fitzsimons . . .

'The condition on which God hath given liberty to man is eternal vigilance,' Ronald Reagan quoted from John Philpot Curran and then told the Dáil, 'We must not hesitate to express our dream of freedom; we must not be reluctant to enunciate the crucial distinctions between right and wrong.'

Sister Frances, the nun from Sisters for Justice, left her cell, as did Marese Hegarty, Marion Howe, Aileen Jones, Mary Killian, Sheila McCarthy, Aileen McQuillan, Sofia Maher, Ludy Methorsg and Jane Morgan . . .

'Let us not take the counsel of our fears,' Ronald Reagan urged the Irish politicians, 'let us instead offer the world a politics of hope, a forward strategy for freedom.'

Petra Breatnach was brought from Cabra to join the women in the big room at the Bridewell. She had been detained for about forty-five hours already. Mary Kay Mullen was brought from her cell, Caroline O'Connor and Monica O'Connor, Catherine O'Reilly and Ruth O'Rourke . . .

'Those old verities,' said Ronald Reagan, 'those truths of the heart — human freedom under God — are on the march everywhere in the world. All across the world today — in the shipyards of Gdansk, the hills of Nicaragua, the rice paddies of Kampuchea, the mountains of Afghanistan — the cry again is liberty.'

In the cells of the Bridewell, Mary Phelan was being taken out, and Nina Quigley, Phillipa Robinson, Toni Ryan, Sue Russell, Scotlyn Sabean, and Catriona Ní Shiacuis.

'Thank you again for this great honour,' said Ronald Reagan, 'and God bless you all.' He then, at 12.50pm, went to lunch with President Hillery at the US Ambassador's residence in the Phoenix Park. There, as the brandied breast of chicken was served and the Californian chardonnay was poured, he spoke again of human liberty. President Hillery replied: 'Ireland shares with the United States a profound respect for the rights of the individual.'

The women were kept waiting for about two hours before being brought up to District Court No. 4 at 2.30pm. While they waited, some of them began singing and were told that if they didn't keep quiet they'd be done for contempt of court. Eventually, they were brought up in batches and formally charged with the crime which warranted a £5 fine. They were bedraggled and exhausted. They were remanded on £10 bail for two weeks. The mystery 'edict' which had incarcerated them had still not been produced.

They were released out into the street in batches of five, to where family and friends greeted them with hugs and kisses. As ever, there was singing.

'You can forbid almost anything
But you can't forbid me to sing.
You can't forbid my tears to flow
And you can't close my mouth when I sing.'

· · · · ·

While this was happening President Reagan had been taken to Dublin airport. RTE was broadcasting much of the visit live, including the arrival and departure. Pat Kenny was doing the RTE commentary on the departure. Kenny chatted to a friend from his college days who was now working in the Department of Foreign Affairs. One of the major talking points among reporters over the previous few days had been the extent to which the US Secret Service had taken over the security of the visit. Armed agents had been routinely giving orders to gardaí. Kenny had seen the US Secret Service agents clearing journalists from the concourse in Shannon, he had seen gardaí standing by as the Americans gave orders.

It isn't like that at all, said his friend from Foreign Affairs. The gardaí are in charge, the Americans are under garda orders.

Kenny and the TV crew set out to go to the commentary position. They were stopped by a US Secret Service agent. Kenny explained that there was twenty minutes to airtime, it would be highly embarrassing for everyone if TV screens remained blank during the President's departure. 'I have my orders,' said the agent.

Kenny's friend from Foreign Affairs saw what was happening and intervened. To no avail. The US Secret Service agent had his orders, and neither one of Ireland's best-known broadcasters nor an official from the Department of Foreign Affairs could deter the man from carrying out his duty. Kenny had a perfect right to brush aside the US agent, who had no authority whatever to give orders. But you don't brush aside armed men who take themselves so seriously.

The gardaí were sent for. No dice. The agent insisted that he had his orders from his superior out there on the tarmac, he wasn't obeying the Irish police.

A senior garda named Stephen Fanning was in the vicinity and was appealed to for help. He told the US agent to let Kenny and his crew pass through and do their work. 'I have my orders,' said the agent.

It was only when Fanning, who identified himself as the head of the Special Branch, ordered that the RTE people be let through 'on my authority' that the agent reluctantly conceded.

President Reagan flew out to London at 3.30pm, to meet his soul mate, Margaret Thatcher. Back at the District Court the women were still being processed. They were all released by 4pm.

When the women turned up at court on 19 June they found that the cases against them had been dropped, the police were offering no evidence. The police action had effectively interned the women during the period in which they might embarrass the state, and the state apparently now felt no need to go into court, where the women could be fined a maximum of £5, but where the state's actions would come under judicial scrutiny. There would be no due process.

· · · · ·

Although what happened to the Women For Disarmament was widely known, only the naive expected that the state would be made accountable for its actions. Politicians knew what had been done but almost all preferred to ignore the implications. Three weeks later one politician raised the matter in the Dáil. On 28 June, John Kelly TD, a conservative member of Fine Gael, the senior party in the coalition government, whose political sympathies lay closer to Ronald Reagan than to the peace women, could not stay silent. Kelly, a professor of constitutional law, raised the matter in a Dáil adjournment debate.

John Kelly spent much of his speech praising the gardaí and assuring the Dáil of what he called 'my bona fides' before he got to the point. He mentioned in passing the subordination of the Garda Siochána to the US Secret Service. 'What appeared to be a large portion of their normal peace-keeping and security-enforcing duties were appropriated, by what authority I am not clear, by a police force or a security force for which no one in this country was responsible.'

He was immediately warned off this issue by the Ceann Comhairle, Tom Fitzpatrick.

Kelly pointed out that 'the greatest principle of criminal procedure' is that an accused be brought before a judicial authority (a judge or peace commissioner) where it will be decided whether the accused will be granted bail or remanded in custody. Pointing out that the maximum penalty which could be imposed on the women, had they been found guilty, was a £5 fine, Kelly said, 'There is some explaining to be done, and I do not mean of the police, but more generally on the part of the state if we have a legal system which makes it possible for people to be held in custody for so long when the maximum charge on which they can be convicted is such a trivial one, carrying such a trivial fine.'

Kelly referred to suspicions that the object of the exercise 'was to keep those women on ice until such time as the President of America should have left this country'. He added that the Minister for Justice might care to disarm any suspicion that the law has been used here in order to keep out of sight some awkward people. Some people, he said, might consider such protestors a pain in the neck. 'In many ways they are a pain in the neck to me too but next time, Sir, it could be you or me. Unless we stand up for the people who are a nuisance it could be our turn next.'

When Kelly finished, Monica Barnes tried to raise the issue of the conditions in which the women had been kept in the Bridewell but was told by the Ceann Comhairle that she could not. Only the length of the detention could be discussed, not the conditions of detention.

The Minister for Justice, Michael Noonan, was supposed to reply to the debate. He announced that he had read in a newspaper that the women might take legal action. Although the matter was not *sub judice*, he said, it might become so in the future, so it would be 'highly undesirable' for him to comment. 'I am speaking in the shadow of a legal action.'

· · · · ·

Eight months later, in February 1985, the women and their lawyers got their first sight of the 'edict' which jailed them until Ronald Reagan left the country.

Twenty-eight of the women filed civil suits against the state. The matter slowly shuffled its way through the clogged arteries of the legal system. On 31 March 1987, almost three years after the mass arrests, the state settled out of court when Jane Morgan's civil suit was due to be heard. They agreed to pay her £1,000 damages and £900 special damages, plus costs. Twenty-seven other women also settled their claims, receiving £1,000 each and costs. It was a cheap way for the state to keep the matter out of court. The women, facing huge legal bills if they went to court and lost, decided to accept the settlement as vindication of their stance.

Immense powers had been brought into play to carry out mass arrests and to hold a group of people who were deemed an embarrassment to the state. A temporary edict aimed at a specific group of people was signed into law without democratic supervision or accountability. An obscure clause in an Act designed to regulate the mundane governance of a public park was stretched to its limit and dozens of people were rounded up and jailed on a trivial charge that carried a small fine.

The state, by dropping the charges, avoided due process and consequent scrutiny of its actions in a criminal court. By settling the civil suits it avoided scrutiny of its actions in a civil court. The Attorney General, Peter Sutherland, disclaimed any function in the matter. The Minister for Justice, Michael Noonan, avoided accountability in parliament by claiming he couldn't speak on a matter that was not *sub judice* but might be eventually.

Ronald Reagan went home and spoke many times about the truths of his heart and was re-elected. When he was caught trading missiles for hostages and funding Nicaraguan terrorists in defiance of Congress he lied about it, was caught lying about it, and was so popular that the media and his political opponents found it diplomatic not to call him on it. He went into happy and honoured retirement. As the decades pass, the Ronald Reagan Library will display to posterity the doctorate of laws conferred on him by Ireland's leading academics.

Taoiseach Garret FitzGerald retired in 1987 and published his memoirs in 1991. He described the Reagan visit and referred in passing to the protests, passing on to posterity his conclusion that 'the whole matter was handled in a very civilised way'.

Attorney General Peter Sutherland later became a European Commissioner, Director-General of GATT, and an executive of BP, before snagging a multi-million dollar position with Goldman Sachs, the international banking outfit. Minister for Justice Michael Noonan continues a successful political career and is now Minister for Health. Garda Commissioner Larry Wren, who signed the special regulation that existed for sixty-eight hours and eight minutes, received the thanks of a grateful state as he went into honoured retirement. John Kelly TD died in 1991. Monica Barnes TD lost her Dáil seat in 1992.

Proinsias De Rossa, who walked out of the Dáil chamber when President Reagan began speaking, later led his supporters out of the Workers' Party and formed Democratic Left. He subsequently became Minister for Social Welfare in a Fine Gael-led coalition. On the next occasion when demonstrators marched around Dublin Castle in protest at a state welcome for a visiting dignitary, May 1995, he would be sitting inside the Castle, sharing a table with the honoured guest, the Prince of Wales.

Senator Catherine McGuinness, who refused to attend President Reagan's Oireachtas address, was in 1994 appointed to chair the Forum for Peace and Reconciliation. Student activist Joe Duffy became Gay Byrne's representative on earth. Mary Robinson, who presided over the press conference announcing the women's peace camp, became President of Ireland six years later.

It doesn't matter very much that the law which was used to lock up the women remains in effect. The exact circumstances of the mass arrest are unlikely to be repeated. And the statute books are full of little laws which, if approached in the right frame of mind, could be used to lock people up when it suits the establishment. What does matter is the state's attitude to the freedom of the individual, to accountability of the police, and to those other 'truths of the heart' applauded by the politicians. And there is no reason to believe that has changed. When the circumstances are right, freedom is skin deep.

❽ Caught in the Crossfire

Michael Lynagh was standing outside Dunne's Stores in North Earl Street when Garda Liam Curtin came along. Lynagh was waving a Stanley knife and shouting obscenities. He wasn't shouting at anyone in particular, just letting rip. Several times he smashed his fist against the wall outside the shop. He appeared to be drunk. He began to wave the knife as though about to cut his wrists.

Garda Curtin quickly disarmed Lynagh, who began shouting about the RUC. There was a struggle.

A passer-by intervened and told the garda he had no right to arrest that man. Michael Lynagh made a break for it. Garda Curtin chased him and arrested him. Lynagh was charged with drunkenness, carrying an offensive weapon and resisting arrest.

Lynagh demanded that Garda Curtin return the knife. He said he wanted to do away with himself. The policeman decided that Lynagh needed his head examined. He took him to Store Street garda station, and subsequently to the Dublin District Court.

When Michael Lynagh was asked for his name he replied, 'Michael Ferguson.'

· · · · ·

There were twelve children in the Lynagh family of Tully, a village near Monaghan town. Although living in a border county, in an area where nationalist ideals run deep, the Lynagh family as a whole were not militant republicans, nor were they IRA supporters. One of the twelve offspring, James, became a committed member of the IRA from the early 1970s, when he was a teenager.

At the age of seventeen, Jim Lynagh was sentenced to five years in Long Kesh prison for possession of explosives. The possession charge was easy to make stick, as Lynagh had been practically sitting on a bomb in a car at Moy, Co. Tyrone, in October 1973, when it prematurely exploded. It was what is known as an own goal. He was badly injured. When he was released in October 1978 he was served with an order excluding him from the United Kingdom.

Jim Lynagh was a popular figure in his home area. The five-year sentence did his reputation no harm in County Monaghan, one of the three Ulster counties discarded by the unionists in the partition settlement in 1922 because they had too many catholics. Republican feelings are strong there and the year after Jim Lynagh was released from prison he was elected to Monaghan Urban District Council. He remained an active and increasingly experienced and senior member of the East Tyrone Brigade of the IRA. Lynagh would eventually become leader of an outfit that specialised in large-scale actions, involving up to a dozen gunmen. Most units of the IRA had reorganised into smaller cells, with one or two volunteers engaging in operations. This made the units more secure, less open to betrayal by informers. The tight-knit loyalty of Lynagh's followers allowed him to indulge his preference for larger operations, with greater firepower.

In April 1980 Jim Lynagh was arrested by gardaí and charged with membership of the IRA. After being held for four months in Portlaoise prison he was acquitted by the Special Criminal Court. Three months later he was again arrested by the gardaí, this time for the murder of UDR man Henry Livingstone, across the border in Tynan, Co. Armagh. Lynagh was the first person to be charged under the Criminal Law Jurisdiction Act, which allowed the arrest and trial of people in the South for crimes allegedly committed in the North. He was again acquitted.

It was shortly after this that the East Tyrone Brigade of the IRA carried out a notorious operation. On 21 January 1981, a dozen gunmen descended on two houses near the village of Tynan, in Armagh, just across the border from Monaghan. Two cars were stolen and their owners held at gunpoint. At about 9pm eight members of the IRA went to Tynan Abbey, an eighteenth-century mansion owned by the Stronge family, blew in the front door with explosives and started planting incendiary bombs.

The Stronge family was later described in a Provo statement as 'unionist aristocrats' and they certainly were that. Sir Norman Stronge was a former Speaker of the Northern Ireland parliament at Stormont. His son James was a retired member of the Grenadier Guards and an RUC reservist. They were in the solid upper-class unionist tradition, living in a big house on a 900-acre estate.

The two men were in the library of their home when the Provos came in. They were completely at the mercy of the intruders. There was no mercy, father and son were shot dead. The incendiary bombs exploded and the house was burned down. The IRA claimed that the killings were a reprisal for a series of unionist killings of nationalists. Sir Norman Stronge was eighty-six years of age.

The brutal, merciless and cold-blooded killings provoked widespread outrage. There was for years an affected belief among British Tory ministers and MPs that security cooperation with the state forces in the Republic had to be begged and pleaded for and extracted with great pains. In fact, since the early 1970s any ambiguities towards the IRA which might have existed within the Republic's establishment and its security forces had been eliminated. The dominant fear was that the Northern conflict might spill over into the South, and the IRA was pursued by the government and security forces in the South with determination.

Jim Lynagh had long been a target of the gardaí. Following the Stronge killings the police continued their efforts to put Lynagh away. They believed, as did the RUC, that Jim Lynagh had been the leader of the IRA group that killed the Stronges. They also believed that a Seamus Shannon, also from Monaghan, was a member of Lynagh's IRA unit.

Ten months later, in November 1981, Jim Lynagh was again arrested by the gardaí and charged with membership of the IRA. It was the old charge that Lynagh had beaten before and it is likely that he would have beaten it again. While out on bail to attend the wedding of his sister Mary to Seamus Shannon, Jim Lynagh went on the run. His IRA activities continued. The gardaí became more determined than ever to find Jim Lynagh.

$$\bullet \bullet \bullet \bullet \bullet$$

Gabriel Murphy was a bouncer at the Hillgrove Hotel in Monaghan. He had upset someone. On New Year's Eve 1981 they came for him with a gun. It was supposed to be a punishment shooting, Murphy was supposed to walk with a limp afterwards. He was shot in the leg and the wound was so severe that he died.

A younger brother of Jim Lynagh, Colm, aged seventeen, was charged with being one of those who attacked Gabriel Murphy. He denied it and his family protested his innocence, but in June 1982 Colm Lynagh was convicted of murder at the Special Criminal Court. Although Colm had not used a gun, the court judged that he had assisted in the attack and knew of the intention of the attackers, therefore he was guilty of the killing. He was sentenced to life in prison. The murder conviction was subsequently quashed.

$$\bullet \bullet \bullet \bullet \bullet$$

Michael Lynagh was twenty-seven when he was arrested by Garda Curtin in North Earl Street, in Dublin. He was two years older than his brother Jim. At the beginning of 1982 he and another brother, Finbar, had moved away from Monaghan, to Dublin. The house in Monaghan had become a target for police activity, as the efforts to re-arrest Jim Lynagh intensified. Members of the family were continually being stopped and questioned by gardaí.

Michael and Finbar had no involvement with illegal activities. Michael was an unemployed welder. For over two years, since the end of 1979, he had suffered from anxiety and depression. He had begun drinking heavily. In June 1980 things got so bad that he committed himself to a psychiatric hospital in Monaghan, St Davnet's. His father had worked at St Davnet's as a psychiatric nurse. Over the next eighteen months or so Michael voluntarily entered St Davnet's twice more for treatment. Michael received electric shock treatment and since last leaving the hospital, at Christmas 1981, he had been on medication to keep his depression at bay.

Michael had two minor brushes with the law. Once he was fined for urinating in a car park. The other mark on his record was an incident in a Monaghan hotel when a garda knocked over his drink. Michael believed the drink had been deliberately knocked over and a row followed. Michael was arrested and later fined.

In Dublin, Michael and Finbar shared a flat in Terenure. Finbar got work in a supermarket. Michael got occasional work, and when he wasn't working he would haunt the Manpower office in D'Olier Street in the mornings. In the afternoon he might visit the National Gallery or the National Museum. Although not involved in politics, he had friends and associates in Monaghan who were linked to Sinn Féin or the IRSP. Michael shared their republican views and lately he had started going to the National Library, where he studied material on Blueshirt activity in Monaghan during the 1930s. Michael was also attending a psychiatrist in Dublin.

Tuesday 9 March 1982 was a day of political high drama. Charlie Haughey, having been out of power for a few months, had failed to win a majority at the recent general election. However, by doing a deal with Independent TD Tony Gregory, committing government resources to Gregory's inner city constituency, Haughey had scraped through a Dáil vote and was now Taoiseach again.

That evening Michael and Finbar Lynagh were planning to move from their Terenure flat to a new flat on Belmont Avenue, Donnybrook. The new flat was next door to a flat occupied by Michael's sister Mary, and her husband Seamus Shannon. Seamus Shannon was the Monaghan man believed by gardaí to be involved in the IRA with Jim Lynagh.

On that 9 March, Michael Lynagh arrived at the old flat in Terenure along with a friend named Alan, who was giving Michael a lift, helping him move his gear to the new flat. They found three men searching the flat. The three were detectives and they arrested Michael and his friend.

The police used Section 30 of the Offences Against The State Act, 1939, which allows anyone to be picked up and held for forty-eight hours on suspicion of having committed, or being about to commit, a crime. Section 30, originally designed to enable the police to arrest someone behaving suspiciously in the vicinity of a crime (for instance, hurrying away from a suitcase in a period where bombs were being planted), had become a catch-all law. People were lifted wholesale in the wake of a crime, and when no crime had been committed they were lifted routinely as part of the everyday surveillance of republicans. People with expressed republican views were arrested under Section 30 as a matter of convenience, if they were in the vicinity of police activity, and the police didn't have any substantive reason to arrest them. They were held for a greater or lesser period, sometimes they were questioned, sometimes they were just left in a cell, then they were released.

Although the killing in the North was at its greatest in 1972, that year only 229 people were arrested under Section 30 in the South. By 1979 the routine use of Section 30 had lifted that figure to 1,431. When Michael Lynagh was arrested under Section 30 that 9 March, his was one of 2,308 Section 30 arrests carried out in 1982.

· · · · ·

Michael was taken to Rathmines garda station and interrogated. Sometimes there were three or four detectives asking questions, sometimes there were six.

'Where's your brother Jim?' 'What are you doing up in Dublin?' 'How long have you been in Dublin?' 'We want the names and addresses of your brothers, sisters, your friends and associates.'

'How much do you get from the Social Welfare?'

Michael was particularly offended by that last question. He had no problem answering questions about his movements but, with a stubborn logic that makes no sense except if you're under pressure and you're trying to hold on to some kind of dignity, he refused to tell them how much he was getting on the dole. He refused on the grounds that they must have access to that information and they could get it for themselves.

'You're a different kettle of fish to your brother Jim,' said one detective. The cops came in and went out, the questions became repetitive.

Michael's friend Alan, who was being questioned in another room, was a Protestant.

One of the questions to Michael was, 'What are you doing driving around town with a left-footer?'

The questions kept coming back to the shooting of a garda in Tallaght. They also ranged over membership of the IRA, the INLA, the Gaelic language, Michael's views on industry, agriculture, poverty, the Middle East, the police, the legal system, the British Army, the RUC, what life was like in north Monaghan and in south Armagh, about emigration, abortion and de Valera. Amid the questioning came the remark, 'Nobody is afraid of you Northerners any more. What will happen to you is what's happening in other countries — you'll be driven out the road some night and won't be heard of no more.'

Out at the front desk of the garda station two of Michael's sisters were asking to see him. No, they were told, no visitors.

· · · · ·

Two hours after Michael was arrested at the Terenure flat, his brother Finbar arrived at the new flat in Donnybrook. There was some kind of commotion going on next door, in the flat of his sister Mary and her husband. Finbar called in to see what was going on.

There were half a dozen detectives there. They were arresting Mary's husband, Seamus Shannon, the suspected associate of IRA gunman Jim Lynagh. They arrested Finbar as well, under Section 30. He was male, he was in the vicinity of a man believed to be in the IRA, so he was lifted.

Carmel Lynagh, another sister, home from her job as a nurse in London, was visiting Mary and Seamus Shannon. As Seamus and Finbar were being taken away she pleaded with the detectives to tell her why the men were being arrested.

The detective who appeared to be in charge, and who was arresting two people supposedly because he had reason to believe they had broken the law, replied, 'He'll probably be back in forty-eight hours.'

An hour later, with no sign of Michael Lynagh, Carmel and Mary Lynagh came to the conclusion that he too had been arrested. They went to Donnybrook garda station where they were politely received by an elderly garda. He made a phone call and then told them that Michael and his friend Alan were being held at Rathmines and Finbar Lynagh and Seamus Shannon were being held at Crumlin.

The women went by taxi to Rathmines and the garda on duty confirmed that Michael and his friend Alan were being held. When the sisters asked if they could see the men the garda went back and consulted a garda who was sitting at a desk. He came back and said no, they couldn't visit.

Carmel explained that Michael had suffered a depressive illness and was only a short time out of hospital and needed medication. No, she was told, no visitors.

Carmel was insistent. She explained that she was a nurse and that Michael needed the medication. If they would just let her see him for a few seconds he could tell her where the medication was and she could fetch it.

A garda looked up and said, 'Get out of here and go home. The people dealing with this will be back at nine o'clock in the morning.'

The women took a taxi to Crumlin garda station and had no problem in being admitted to see Finbar and Seamus for a few minutes. Carmel then phoned St Davnet's Hospital but was unable to reach Michael's psychiatrist, Dr John Owens. The phone was answered by someone who seemed annoyed at being disturbed at that late hour and hung up twice. After a third phone call Carmel was told she should ring in the morning.

Inside Rathmines garda station, Michael was still being questioned. It went on until about 1am. He was then put in a cell until approximately 10.30 next morning, at which time the questions began again. Questions about the shooting of the garda in Tallaght, a bomb which injured a garda forensic expert, and the shooting in a Dublin pub of IRSP man Harry Flynn. Michael knew nothing about any of this.

About half an hour after the questioning resumed, Carmel Lynagh finally got in touch with Dr John Owens, Michael's psychiatrist at St Davnet's. She told him about Michael's arrest and Dr Owens promptly rang Rathmines garda station.

Finally, the women were allowed in to see Michael and his friend Alan. The two appeared badly shaken, especially Michael. He repeatedly asked Carmel if she was OK and asked her not to worry their parents with this thing. He told Carmel where his medication was and she brought it to the station along with cigarettes and newspapers. As a nurse, Carmel was of the opinion that Michael was on the verge of a breakdown.

The four arrested men were released later that day. The incident was a routine one. Neither brother had a finger laid on them by the gardaí, there was nothing unusual or harsh about the questioning. They received what many a hardened republican would consider a mild interrogation. The Lynagh brothers were not, however, hardened republicans. They were just related to one.

The experience left marks on both brothers. They talked over the arrests and the questioning and decided that in such a situation the best response was to answer all questions as politely as possible and hope that this would convince their interrogators that they had nothing to hide.

· · · · ·

The harassment continued, with several police visits to the new flat in Donnybrook. During one raid every flat in the house was searched, disturbing and frightening the other tenants and causing trouble for the brothers. The two Lynagh brothers began to suspect that they were being followed by the Special Branch.

There were indications that some at least of the suspicions were justified. But it's entirely possible that the brothers were experiencing fear and paranoia that hyped every incident, however innocent, into a suspicion, and hardened every suspicion into a certainty. What is clear is that the arrests and interrogations had left Michael and Finbar Lynagh frightened and shaken. And the older of the two was a man with serious psychiatric problems.

· · · · ·

Almost six weeks later, on Sunday 18 April, Michael was sitting in the flat reading a book, at about one o'clock in the morning, when five detectives arrived and began searching the flat. They arrested Michael under Section 30 of the Offences Against The State Act. They wanted to know where Finbar was. They asked Michael if he had any guns.

Ten minutes later Finbar arrived home. He too was arrested under Section 30. He appeared stunned by what was happening, so much so that one of the detectives remarked that he seemed like a junkie. Finbar was made roll up his sleeve to show that his arm didn't have needle tracks. The two brothers were brought to the Bridewell garda station in separate police cars.

Michael, sandwiched between two gardaí, had a silent ride to the police station. In the other car, a policeman was warming to the theme that Finbar looked like a junkie. Finbar was told he looked like he was doped to the eyeballs. A detective told him he was as mad as a hatter. But, then, weren't all the Lynaghs mad?

He was asked if he knew where Jim Lynagh was. Finbar didn't reply.

'We have him, the dirty bastard!' About ten hours earlier police surrounded a house at Newbliss, Co. Monaghan. When Jim Lynagh emerged from the house he saw the gardaí and made a run for it. The police opened fire. Jim Lynagh wasn't hit, but he halted and was arrested. He wasn't carrying a gun, but he had twelve rounds of ammunition on him.

Jim Lynagh was taken to Monaghan garda station and held there for two days. He would subsequently be found guilty of possession of ammunition and would be sentenced to five years in jail. During the two days he was held in Monaghan garda station he wasn't questioned. Up in Dublin, his brothers weren't being so lucky.

'We have him, the dirty bastard!' The detective wanted a reaction from Finbar. 'Do you hear me?' He flashed a torch in Finbar's eyes, rapped him on the arm. 'Do you hear me?'

At the Bridewell, Michael told the sergeant in charge that he was on medication. He had taken the tablets with him from the flat when he was arrested. He said he didn't feel well and he wanted to see his GP, Dr Hoban of Morehampton Road. He asked the sergeant what were his constitutional rights. The sergeant replied that he'd been arrested under Section 30 of the Offences Against The State Act, 1939, and that was that.

Michael was taken through the Bridewell to a cell, and as he looked at the bars, the walls and gates it occurred to him that this was just like the kind of prison you see in a movie. He was scared. He was taken down a maze of corridors and he was looking at steel doors and bars and he could hear the echo of his footsteps. He was put in a cell. About an hour later a garda told him that Dr Hoban couldn't be contacted.

During the night, over what seemed a period of hours, both Michael and Finbar were questioned separately about Jim Lynagh. Michael was confused and frightened and sure that something terrible had happened or was about to happen. There were relays of detectives, sometimes they shouted, the interrogation was intense. When the questioning stopped Michael was taken to a cell and left there for the night.

Next morning, after a breakfast of a slice of bread and a plastic beaker of tea, the interrogation continued. Finbar was fingerprinted and had a swab test. After a couple of hours he was told to strip. His clothes were taken away. He was shown other clothes and recognised them as Michael's. It is probable that the gardaí had brought those clothes from the flat. Finbar refused to wear them, saying they were Michael's and his brother would need them. He returned naked to his cell.

Finbar didn't want to use the urine-stained blanket or mattress in the cell, so he lay naked for five hours on the wire mesh of the bed.

Several detectives came to the cell during this time. One walked around Finbar, looking him up and down, making remarks about Finbar being naked. 'Are you a homo?' one asked. Would Finbar like someone to be moved into the cell with him? asked the detective.

'At least he has balls,' said one detective to another. 'It's more than his brother has.' In the 1973 explosion at Moy, the insides of Jim Lynagh's legs had been badly injured, but his genitals were not damaged. However, such remarks appear to have been an in-joke among the detectives hunting Jim Lynagh.

About an hour after breakfast Michael Lynagh too was told to strip in his cell. He recoiled from this and lay on the bed and curled himself up into a foetal position, wrapping his arms around his legs. Detectives began pulling at his arms and legs. Eventually, the detectives forcibly removed his boots, socks and jeans. After a few minutes his jeans were thrown back in to him. Having begun the stripping process and having been half-successful, the detectives let Michael keep his clothes. It may have been that his distress caused them to have pity on him.

Later, Michael was taken to another interrogation room, where he met a senior officer. Another detective took a swab test, rubbing Michael's hands with cotton wool and liquid. The detective also combed Michael's hair with a comb that had cotton wool attached. The detective doing the swab had a holstered gun on his hip, a big gun with a brown handle. As the detective repeatedly pulled his jacket back from the gun Michael wasn't sure if the detective wanted to have the gun ready for trouble, or if he was just showing off. Michael felt sick.

The senior officer pointed to a pile of clothes which he said had been brought from the flat. Michael was to strip and to change into these, his clothes were needed for forensic tests. Michael examined the clothes, then sat down. He just sat there. The senior garda asked Michael what he was doing.

'I was thinking,' said Michael.

The senior garda told Michael he had one minute to think.

The detective who had arrested Michael was in the room and offered to strip him. The senior garda said no.

Michael's head sank down to his chest. He was tired. He had decided that he wasn't going to strip himself or answer any more questions, but he wouldn't fight them any more, he wouldn't resist any more when they stripped him.

· · · · ·

The two brothers would spend another night and most of the next day in the Bridewell. They received routine visits from a doctor and solicitor. On the first morning Michael had asked for his medication. A detective told him he'd get a tablet when he started talking. They gave him a tablet two hours later.

At one point Michael had been lying on his bed in the cell when one of the teams of detectives that periodically visited the cell lifted him up 'to get a look at you'.

Michael felt weak and fell on the floor.

One of the detectives threw a toilet roll at him and told him, 'You've shit yourself.'

The brothers' exit from the Bridewell was as traumatic as their entry. Before Michael was released he was told he was going to be charged with refusing to strip, refusing to account for his movements, and membership of the IRA. Fifteen minutes later he was released. He bloody-mindedly refused to sign for his property on the grounds that it was his and he didn't see why he should sign anything to get it back.

There was only one set of keys to the flat and Michael asked for them as Finbar was still in custody. The gardaí said they had no keys. Michael refused to leave the station. He was dragged out, trying to hold on to the door, being pulled by the arms and hair. At about eleven that night in Donnybrook, two detectives returned two bags of clothes which they had taken from the flat. And the keys.

Finbar who had still refused to wear Michael's clothes and had insisted that clothes of his own be brought, was now wearing the urine-stained blanket in the cell. This was what he wore when he left the Bridewell. One detective threatened to take the blanket away and throw him out on the street, naked. Then, he was told, he'd be arrested and sent to Dundrum Mental Hospital. Another detective offered Finbar a lift home, which he refused.

As Finbar left the Bridewell dressed only in the blanket, he saw four detectives standing by a minibus outside. Saying they would take him home in the minibus, they grabbed him and there was a struggle. Another detective ran up and shouted, 'Stop it, stop it!'

Finbar was released and went into a pub where he rang a friend who came and collected him.

The next day the brothers decided to seek help in stopping the harassment. They went to Amnesty International but were told that local branches of the organisation don't deal with events in their home country. They went to the Irish Council for Civil Liberties and made statements. They went to the *Sunday Tribune* and made a statement. They went to the offices of the IRSP paper, *The Starry*

Plough, in Gardiner Street, but were told that the paper wouldn't be coming out for a while. They went up to the Sinn Féin office in Blessington Street to make a statement to the Provo newspaper, *An Phoblacht*, but the two supposed IRA men didn't know that the *Phoblacht* office was in Parnell Square. A woman from the Sinn Féin office offered to take them to the offices of *An Phoblacht*.

As the three walked across Dorset Street and into North Frederick Street a couple of detectives jumped out of a car. Michael was grabbed by the lapels and thrown against a wall. Finbar was also pushed against the wall. A detective began searching Michael's pockets.

When Michael objected the detective said, 'I can do what I like. I'm not looking for money, I'm looking for guns.'

There was the usual crowd of shoppers in the area and the police eventually seemed embarrassed, got into their car and drove off.

The brothers continued telling their story to anyone who would listen. They visited the office of solicitor Pat McCartan, but he wasn't in. A secretary took their names, but they never returned. They made a statement to a *Sunday World* reporter but nothing appeared in the paper. It seems the notebook with the statement was lost. The *Irish Times* carried Finbar's account of his exit from the Bridewell in a blanket. Nothing appeared anywhere else.

· · · · ·

It had been four months since Michael Lynagh had last left St Davnet's, the psychiatric hospital in Monaghan. That Christmas he had seemed in good form, to be coming out of himself. However, his depressive illness was severe and he remained unstable. He had in the past attempted suicide several times, or had lightly cut his wrists in apparent suicide attempts. He failed to establish a relationship with the psychiatrist he was seeing in Dublin and on 28 August he returned to Dr John Owens in St Davnet's. Dr Owens prepared a course of therapy.

In early September 1982 Michael Lynagh went on a bender. When he left the Donnybrook flat on the evening of Saturday 4 September, he seemed in a good mood, no depression. He spent the evening drinking with a friend named Anthony Ballantine and stayed Saturday night at Ballantine's flat. The drinking resumed on Sunday morning and continued that evening. Michael spent Sunday night at Ballantine's flat. He now had a job, and on Monday morning he left the flat, apparently setting off for work.

It was around 3pm that afternoon when Garda Liam Curtin, from Store Street garda station, on patrol in Dublin city centre, spotted Michael Lynagh outside Dunne's Stores in North Earl Street. Michael hadn't gone to work, he'd been drinking again. The garda, seeing that Michael was a danger to himself and perhaps to others, had no option but to arrest him. Michael's fear of the police, his fear of what would happen to him if they found out that he was Michael Lynagh, Jim Lynagh's brother, his fear of the detectives coming again, led him to give his name as Michael Ferguson. Wanting to conceal his Monaghan origins, but yet account for his northern accent, he gave a Belfast address.

By the time Garda Curtin got Michael Lynagh before the District Court he suspected that Michael had problems that went beyond his drunkenness. He asked the court to remand Michael Ferguson to Mountjoy prison for a week, for psychiatric assessment. Justice Delap agreed, and Michael was remanded to Mountjoy.

Solicitor Pat McCartan (later to become a Democratic Left TD) was appointed by the District Court to represent Michael. At 12.30pm next day, Tuesday 7 September, McCartan visited Michael in a cell in the Bridewell, after the remand. There, Michael revealed his real name and said he had given an alias because of his fear of attracting further attention from the police. He told McCartan he was attending psychiatrists in Monaghan and Dublin. He was, he said, suffering from mood swings, from elation to despondency. He said he didn't know how to convey his medical history to the prison authorities without revealing his identity.

As well as his fear of attracting the attention of the detectives, he was afraid that he might lose his job. McCartan advised him to give his correct name.

Michael said he had been drinking heavily and had become more depressed. He had bought the Stanley knife to take his life. He had a superficial cut on one wrist. He seemed very upset, agitated, disjointed, physically and mentally unwell.

McCartan would only later discover that Michael and Finbar Lynagh had called to his office some weeks earlier, on the day they went around Dublin telling people their story.

· · · · ·

When Michael hadn't returned to the Donnybrook flat by Tuesday, Finbar Lynagh began to worry. He went to Michael's workplace and was told that Michael hadn't come in on Monday or Tuesday. He went to Anthony Ballantine's flat but found nobody there. When Michael didn't come home the next day, Wednesday, Finbar again called to Michael's workplace, with the same result. He went to Anthony Ballantine's flat again and was told that Michael had left there for work on Monday morning and hadn't been back since.

That day, in Mountjoy, Michael was examined by Dr Barry Teeling, who found him physically fit. There was a superficial cut on one wrist. It looked to Dr Teeling like a pin had been drawn across the wrist. Michael told Dr Teeling that he had been in a psychiatric hospital. He didn't remember why he had been put in jail. Dr Teeling found nothing unusual in all this. It was, he knew, such a common thing in prisons, people slashing their wrists, self-mutilation. And many people don't remember why they've been put in jail, or don't choose to remember.

The next day, Thursday, Michael was interviewed by a psychiatrist, Dr Charles Smith. Michael seemed perplexed, confused, uncertain. He told the doctor of his psychiatric history and seemed keen to resume treatment. He welcomed a suggestion that he be sent to Dundrum Mental Hospital for examination. Dr Smith noticed a superficial cut on Michael's wrist. He decided that he would make arrangements next day to have Michael transferred to Dundrum.

At some stage, Michael gave his real name and Finbar's address. That evening, when Finbar came home to his flat in Donnybrook he found a letter waiting, from Joan O'Brien, a probation and welfare officer at Mountjoy prison. It said that Michael Lynagh was on remand at Mountjoy and was anxious to have clean clothing for his court appearance on 14 September. And he was anxious to see Finbar.

Concerned about Michael being in prison for some unknown reason, but relieved that his brother's whereabouts had finally been revealed, Finbar decided to visit Michael at lunchtime next day. Afternoon visiting began at 2pm.

The next day, Friday, prison officer Martin Gannon brought Michael his lunch at 1.25pm. Michael ate most of the food, chicken and chips. He then took a sheet from the bed and tied it to the bars of the window. He looped the other end of the sheet around his neck.

At 2.10pm, prison officer Martin Gannon was counting the prisoners in their cells. He looked into Michael's cell and saw him hanging by the neck from the cell window. Gannon rushed into the cell and pushed the body upwards to take the weight off. Other prison officers came to his assistance and helped get Michael down.

About five minutes or so later, around 2.15pm, Finbar Lynagh arrived at the prison. He was kept waiting for forty-five minutes. He asked why there was such a delay and a prison officer told him that Michael was ill and couldn't have visitors. After a while there was a phone call and Finbar was told he could go in. He was taken to an office.

There were three people in the office, one a uniformed garda, Sergeant John Leahy. The others, Assistant Governor Quigley and Dr Barry Teeling, were casually dressed. If Finbar was introduced to them he didn't catch the names and he had no idea what all this was about. They started asking Finbar questions. What was Michael's health like? Had he attended St Davnet's? Had Michael ever used the name Michael Ferguson? Did he have a flat in Belfast? Had Michael had psychiatric problems?

Finbar's instinct was not to answer questions about his brother's health until he knew who these strangers were and why they were asking questions. Suddenly he realised that they were talking about Michael in the past tense. Finbar became agitated. What was going on, where was Michael, what was this about?

One of the men said that a Michael Ferguson had hanged himself in his cell an hour earlier. Michael Ferguson might be Michael Lynagh. Dr Barry Teeling introduced himself to Finbar and said he would take him to Michael's cell.

Sergeant Leahy went along with Finbar and the doctor. Michael was lying on a bed in the cell. His mouth was almost but not quite closed. Both eyes were bulging, the right one barely open, the left closed. Finbar, in shock, took it all in. Michael's chest seemed very enlarged. On his left wrist there was a straight and narrow line of dark red blood, almost brown. There was no sign of any flow from the cut.

Dr Teeling was talking. Finbar found himself staring at the doctor's flowing hand as it pointed one thing out and then another. There, on the table beside the bed, the remains of the chicken and chips Michael had for lunch. A knife and fork lay on the plate. There, the hand moved on, the mark where Michael had tried to cut his wrist. The doctor's hand swung up, pointing at the window from which Michael had hung himself.

'What did he hang himself with?' asked Finbar.

The doctor's hand pointed to a white sheet on the bed. The doctor said, 'You can see he's still warm,' and put his hand on Michael's forehead.

Finbar stood there for a minute, then turned and left the cell. There was a priest standing outside. He shook Finbar's hand and said he was sorry. 'He had a lot of harassment,' Finbar said. 'They wouldn't leave him alone. I could tell you why, Father.'

· · · · ·

It was an unmarked garda car and the occupants were keeping an eye on those arriving in Monaghan for the funeral of Michael Lynagh. One member of the family had been seen talking to a reporter and some friends of the family in a bar. After a while the staff refused to serve them. They had orders from the manager. The manager had been approached by the police.

Now, the unmarked car drove past some mourners. One of the gardaí looked directly at a member of the family. He smiled. He reached down and grabbed the bottom of his tie and pulled it up over his head like it was a noose and his face went into a strangled expression. Then the unmarked car drove off.

· · · · ·

Seamus Shannon, Michael Lynagh's brother-in-law, was later arrested by the gardaí and held on the grounds of RUC suspicion of his involvement in the killings of Norman and James Stronge. He was extradited into RUC custody in July 1984 and in December 1985 at Belfast Crown Court he was acquitted of the killings.

About eighteen months later, on the evening of Friday 8 May 1987, three men entered the home of Mrs Josephine Mackle, who lived in a rural area about three miles from the village of Loughgall, Co. Armagh. They were from the East Tyrone Brigade of the IRA and they told Mrs Mackle they wanted the loan of a JCB digger for about an hour. Two of the men took the digger and loaded the bucket with 400 pounds of explosive and set out for Loughgall, with the bucket raised up high.

The third joined five more IRA men in a blue Hiace van which had been hijacked the previous evening, and also set off for Loughgall. One of these six in the blue van was Jim Lynagh, brother of Michael, Finbar and Colm, and leader of the East Tyrone Brigade.

The East Tyrone Brigade of the IRA had remained as active as ever. Attacks on RUC stations were a central part of the strategy. The aim was to destroy the RUC stations and then intimidate local builders to prevent them re-building the stations. This, it was believed, would drive the RUC out of whole areas, as had been done by the IRA when attacking the RIC in the 1921 War of Independence. The previous August a bomb in a mechanical digger had been used to demolish the Birches RUC station, near Portadown, and the bomb at Loughgall was to be a repeat of that operation.

The RUC station at Loughgall opened only for a few hours each day. It closed at 7pm. By arriving after that time it appears that on this occasion the aim of the Provos was not to kill RUC officers but to destroy the station. This wasn't out of kindness or squeamishness. The weapons which the eight Provos were carrying had been used in several killings or attempted killings of members of the Ulster Defence Regiment.

On this evening, however, there were three RUC men inside the station, and five members of the SAS. And outside, hidden in five scattered locations, were another nineteen SAS soldiers, in civilian clothing.

The RUC had for weeks known about the plan to blow up the police station at Loughgall. They found out almost certainly from an informer. Several hundred police and troops were deployed in Operation Judy, designed to kill the members of the IRA unit carrying out the bombing. About two dozen SAS men were stationed in the village, most of them in the RUC station. They fired an estimated 1,200 bullets at the eight IRA men.

Jim Lynagh was wearing a flak jacket, and as soon as the shooting started he dived back into the van. The van driver was already dead and the flak jacket was no protection against the general purpose machine guns that riddled the van. All eight IRA men died, the heaviest single loss sustained by the organisation during the modern conflict.

The SAS saw another van approach the village. They laced that too with bullets, killing Anthony Hughes and severely wounding his brother Oliver, neither of whom had anything to do with the IRA.

Two days later, a huge crowd turned out to attend the funeral of Jim Lynagh as his body was brought back across the border to Monaghan.

· · · · ·

At the inquest into the death of Michael Lynagh, the coroner, Dr P.J. Bofin, invited the jury to add a rider to its verdict, asking that the prison authorities take whatever measures were considered necessary to prevent a repeat of such a suicide. The jury did so.

At the time that Michael Lynagh, depressed and fearful, killed himself, there was a prisoner in the jail who had then served four months of a three-year sentence for burglary. Four months after Michael Lynagh's death, the prisoner tied a sheet to the bars of his cell window and hanged himself.

Over the next seven years, seven prisoners in Mountjoy killed themselves, mostly by hanging themselves from the window. Only then did the Minister for Justice appoint an Advisory Group to examine the rate of suicide in prisons. A month later another prisoner hanged himself in his cell. Two more prisoners hanged themselves from their cell windows before the Advisory Group issued its report in 1991.

The report noted that the suicide rate in Irish prisons in recent years was double that in England and Wales, and that the number of suicides in Mountjoy was 'a matter for special concern'.

Two years later, in 1993, a visiting committee from the Council of Europe, assessing places of detention, noted that only half of the Prison Deaths Advisory Group's 57 recommendations had been implemented and 'it appears that no action has yet been taken on some of the more important measures proposed by the Advisory Group.'

⁹The Confession of Christy Lynch

Christy Lynch had a key, but he knocked on the door. No answer. He opened the door and went in and up the stairs. There was music coming from the bedroom, a radio playing. He had work to do but he didn't want the woman in the flat to come out and suddenly happen upon someone — give her the fright of her life. He knocked on the door. No reply. He opened the door, put his head in. Vera Cooney was dozing in bed. She sat up with a start.

'Sorry, I didn't mean to frighten you. I'm doing a job for Mr Martin — papering and decorating.'

Christy Lynch was a soldier, a gunner with the 2nd Field Artillery Regiment stationed in McKee Barracks. He left national school just before turning fourteen and had a year at technical school. Then he went to work in the dispatch department of the *Irish Independent*. Then a series of jobs — Taylor-Keith, Hely Thom, Dublin Corporation, a few more. He got married in 1972 and joined the army the following year. In 1974 his daughter Debbie was born. In 1976 he was twenty-six and he and his family were living in a flat in Portmahon House, Rialto.

The flat was owned by Stuart Martin of Brent Ltd, an electrical company. Christy did nixers for Mr Martin, odd jobs, decorating and the like, at the flats at Portmahon House. Early in September 1976 Stuart Martin asked Christy to do some wallpapering, painting and plastering at another house owned by Brent Ltd, 77 Strand Road, Sandymount. He would pay Christy £80.

Around this time Christy Lynch was going through a bad patch. He was gambling a lot, on the horses and dogs. He regularly lost part of his wages and then gambled most of the rest of the money — sure he could win it all back — and losing that too. It was causing trouble at home and Christy was beginning to catch on to himself.

On 2 or 3 September Stuart Martin drove Christy out to Strand Road. On the way out he stopped and got an extra key cut. Christy would need the key as most days the house would be empty. The house was two storey, Victorian style, in two flats. The bottom flat was empty. The top flat was occupied by Vera Cooney.

· · · · ·

The job began on Sunday 5 September 1976. That was the morning that Vera Cooney was lying on in bed when Christy arrived. Christy worked away until about 5.30pm. He was about to pack up and go home when Vera Cooney came out of her room wearing a long housecoat. She asked Christy if he'd like a cup of tea. They drank tea and had a chat. Christy thought she was a nice person, a bit lonely maybe, full of chat.

Vera Cooney was fifty-one. She worked for the Dublin Gas Company and had done so for twenty-eight years. Neighbours would say later that she didn't mix much, didn't often speak to people, but when she did she was friendly. Some thought she was a bit nervous of living alone. They said she put a 'Guard Dog' sign on the gate, although she had no dog.

Stuart Martin of Brent Ltd, who owned the house, was Vera Cooney's brother-in-law. Vera looked after the house and in return had the upstairs flat rent-free. She had lived there for ten years.

After that first day's work Christy Lynch went off to the Glen of Immal with his unit, for training. He didn't go back to 77 Strand Road until Wednesday 15 September. The house was empty that day, Vera

Cooney was at work, and Christy worked there all day without seeing anyone.

This is Christy Lynch's account of Saturday 18 September. He was a bit late getting to work at McKee barracks. He had been at the dogs in Harold's Cross the night before and had, as usual, lost. He and his wife Marie had argued about his gambling. He worked until about noon, changed into civilian clothes and walked up into the city centre. Christy had always liked walking, didn't usually take buses. Walking helped him think.

He visited a coin fair in the Gresham Hotel, just for ten minutes or so. He had an old coin and he had made enquiries about it previously and had a letter from a museum saying it might be valuable. Someone at the coin fair told him to go around to 'the man with the funny name in Cathedral Street'. Christy went around to the coin and medal shop run by Emil Szaver and found that the coin was worthless. He walked on out to 77 Strand Road. This was about 1pm. There was no one in the house. Christy turned on the radio in Vera Cooney's room. There was news of something boring, something about cows, something about a fire. Christy turned the radio off. He was in a bad mood, feeling guilty about how his gambling was causing rows at home. His mind was wandering. He wasn't in the mood for working. There was an electrical cable hanging down, running across Vera Cooney's door. It was dangerous, he thought, and he took it down. That was as much work as he wanted to do that day. He pulled a few bits of wallpaper off the wall, picked up some screws that had fallen, cleaned up and left. It was about 2pm.

As he walked away from the house he saw two young men pushing a red Renault.

He walked back to Rialto and went into McAuley's pub for a pint. He walked some more, down by the canal. He sat down, sorting things out in his head about the gambling, the messing. He loved his job, loved the army life, had a fine marriage and a lovely two-year-old daughter — gambling wasn't fun any more, it was a problem. He knew the arguments with Marie were his fault. He went home. Marie was up visiting her mother. He put on the kettle and went across to the Mascot, bought a pack of cigarettes and two birthday cards.

His father's birthday was next day — one card from himself and

251

Marie, one from little Debbie. After a cup of tea he went up to see his father, who was in bad health. That evening he also met Eugene Delamere, aged eighteen, a friend who had helped him on a couple of previous nixers. He'd be doing the stairs at 77 Strand Road next day, would Eugene give him a hand with the ladder? They agreed to meet at 11am next day.

Christy got home that night before 9pm. His wife was there. He had wanted to get home in time for a television programme he liked, 'Starsky and Hutch'.

· · · · ·

There was a message on the patrol car radio. Report of a body found. Strand Road, Sandymount, number 77. Garda Martin Hynes was driving, Garda John Dineen took the call. It was shortly after noon on Sunday 19 September. The house was on a corner on the sea front, with the ESB station out there just across the water. There was an ambulance there when the two gardaí arrived. The two ambulance men from the fire brigade were inside the house, with Christy Lynch and Eugene Delamere.

Garda Dineen spoke to Lynch. Lynch told him that he and Delamere had come here to do some wallpapering and found the body. 'It was an awful thing to come across,' he said. Garda Hynes asked Lynch to come upstairs and look at the body. Lynch was reluctant at first but went up anyway. He appeared shocked and was very pale. He asked if he could get some fresh air.

Christy Lynch had left home that morning at about 11 o'clock to meet Eugene Delamere and go to Strand Road. They got there at around noon. Christy opened the door and Eugene went in first, a step or two ahead, in and up the stairs. Eugene stopped. There was something at the top of the stairs, legs and hands. Lynch, looking past Delamere, could see the body, something covering the head. They went on up, Lynch first. There was a quilt or bedspread of some kind covering the head. Lynch bent down and pulled it away. There was a knife sticking out of Vera Cooney's chest. Both men turned and ran down the stairs.

Delamere got to the door first and opened it. Lynch called him back. They should tell someone, call the police. There was a phone in the hall and Lynch rang 999. He couldn't get through. He handed the phone to Delamere. 'You hold the phone, ring 999 again, dial again. I'm going up to see is there anything I can do.'

Lynch went back up the stairs. Vera Cooney was dead, no question.

Down in the hallway, Eugene Delamere dialled 999, then dropped the phone in panic. He thought there might be a madman in the house. Lynch came down and called for the police and ambulance.

When the ambulance came up Gilford Road and around into Strand Road, Eugene Delamere was standing on the corner, waving, this way, over here. Christy Lynch was standing at the gate. The gardaí arrived then and after a while there were quite a few of them. Lynch and Delamere were asked to come down to Irishtown garda station and make statements about finding the body. They got a lift from a Sergeant Sweeney. When they got to the station Sergeant Sweeney got them water, two or three cups each.

. . . . .

There was a lot going on that week and the media paid little attention to the discovery of the body. The *Irish Press* and *The Irish Times* carried short mentions of the murder on Monday 20 September. The *Independent* made the most of it. Front page, above the fold, large type: 'Gruesome Bedroom Murder'. The opening paragraph read: 'The brutal murder of a forty-year-old blonde spinster in her Sandymount, Dublin, home yesterday morning is baffling gardaí.' Wrong and wrong. She was fifty-one, the murder was the day before yesterday and gardaí weren't baffled at all. The case was a cinch.

. . . . .

Vera Cooney died hard. She was strangled first and there were scratches on her neck where she apparently tried to pull at the thing that was choking her. The strangling didn't kill her. She was still alive

253

and she was stabbed three times in the chest. It was the knife that killed her. The third thrust was so powerful that the state pathologist, Dr John Harbison, had to straddle the body on his knees and use pliers to extract the knife. Medical evidence could only establish that she had died some time between 9am and 9pm on Saturday, the day before her body was found by Christy Lynch and Eugene Delamere.

No fingerprints were found in Vera Cooney's flat, apart from her own. There was a considerable sum of money left untouched in the flat. Nothing had been stolen or interfered with. A bathroom window was open, but it was a difficult way to get in. Three people had keys to the house: Vera Cooney, Stuart Martin and Christy Lynch.

After spending some time at the garda station Christy Lynch and Eugene Delamere were asked to come back at 4pm and make their statements. Lynch knew his wife would be visiting her mother, and anyway it was his father's birthday, so he went to his parents' home. He told them what had happened.

He went back to Irishtown garda station at 4pm. Christy Lynch had never been involved in a police inquiry before. He had no police record and couldn't remember ever being in a police station. He was asked to give his fingerprints and did so. He knew they did that for elimination purposes. The police gave him tea. There were sandwiches, but he was too upset to eat. He made a formal statement about finding the body. The statement was read back to him and he signed it.

Over four years later the Chief Justice of the Supreme Court, Tom O'Higgins, would say that at that stage, 'One would have expected in such circumstances that [Lynch] would have been thanked for his cooperation and encouraged to go home to his wife and family.'

Garda evidence would later be that at that stage and for a long time afterwards there wasn't the slightest suspicion that Christy Lynch had been involved in the death of Vera Cooney.

'Is that OK now?' asked Christy Lynch. 'Can I go?'

'There might be a few more things we'll have to go over,' said a garda.

In theory, Christy Lynch could have walked right out the door and there wasn't a thing the police could do to stop him. But you'd want to know the law very well to feel confident about doing that — and you'd be less than a good citizen if you didn't do everything possible to help the police in their enquiries. Christy Lynch didn't know much about the law. And, besides, he was a good citizen, a soldier of the state, a member of the security forces that ministers get dewy-eyed about when they talk of those who hold the fabric of society together.

Christy Lynch stayed. You want help, game ball, anything I can do.

Eugene Delamere's statement was taken and he too stayed on or was kept in the station for several more hours. He began falling asleep. He was awakened by shouting. It was coming from somewhere in the station.

He recognised Christy Lynch's voice, and Christy was shouting, 'I didn't do it!'

· · · · ·

Marie Lynch left her flat in Portmahon House, Rialto, and went to a phone box. She had no phone at home. It was about 10pm that Sunday night. She had returned from her mother's house at about 6pm. An hour later, Christy's brother Brendan called round and told her about Christy finding a body and being down at the police station in Irishtown. Brendan had visited his parents earlier that day and they had told him. At about 5.30pm his mother had asked him to ring the station and find out when Christy was coming home. He did so and was told it would be some time later. He gave Marie the number of the station.

Marie rang the number from the phone box. Yes, Christy Lynch was there.

'Could I speak to him?'

'Hold on a minute.' There was a pause. 'Yes, you can, hold on.'

At the station, Christy Lynch was told his wife wanted to speak to him. He was taken to a phone and picked it up.

'Hello? Marie?' The phone went dead.

Back in the phone box. 'I'm sorry, Mrs Lynch, you may not speak to your husband, he's being questioned.'

'Is he coming home? Could you let me know for definite?'

'I couldn't say.'

'Will you send someone out and tell me if Christy isn't coming home?'

Marie Lynch stayed up until 3am. No sign of Christy. In court, the gardaí would deny that any such calls were made. They had the station log book to confirm this. No such calls. None from Marie, none from Brendan. Not even the one that Brendan Lynch made from Sundrive Road garda station. He had gone there some time that night, when he couldn't get through to Irishtown garda station. He asked if the garda there would please ring Irishtown garda station for him. The garda was an obliging sort. Sure, no bother. The garda rang. And he would later swear on oath in court that he rang. There was no record of the call.

· · · · ·

It was cold. This new room hadn't had the heating on. The gardaí had just got the keys to it and one of them was bringing Christy Lynch in. Interrogation rooms have no pictures or calendars to distract a suspect's attention. There should be no phone in the room. The suspect should feel isolated, uncomfortable; the physical and psychological environment should be dominated by the police.

The articles of furniture should be placed so the subject cannot lean or rest upon them.

(*Criminal Investigation Techniques, Schultz*)

Although the police are limited in the amount of time they can hold a suspect, the suspect may not know this and may believe he can be held indefinitely.

Christy had been in this room and that, this garda coming, that one going, sit down there a minute, come on out here. Anywhere he went there was a garda with him. He went to the toilet, there was a garda.

Now, in the cold room, he had just come in, he was pulling his coat around him. The garda who had brought him in turned around and said, 'Why did you do it?'

Christy looked at him. 'What?'

'Forget it,' said the garda.

Various gardaí would swear in court that Christy Lynch stayed in the station voluntarily, that he underwent of his own free will all that followed. At no stage, they would swear, did Christy Lynch ask to go home.

When interrogating suspects, the police employ tried and trusted techniques. They:

display an air of confidence in the suspect's guilt and from outward appearance maintain only an interest in confirming certain details. The guilt of the subject is to be posited as a fact. The interrogator should direct his comments towards the reasons why the subject committed the act, rather than court failure by asking the subject whether he did it.

> (*Miranda judgment, US Supreme Court, describing*
> *established interrogation techniques*)

According to one authority, the police interrogator must:

rely on an oppressive atmosphere of dogged persistence. He must interrogate steadily and without relent, leaving the subject no prospect of surcease. He must dominate his subject and overwhelm him with his inexorable will to obtain the truth. He should interrogate for a spell of several hours, pausing only for the subject's necessities in acknowledgment of the need to avoid a charge of duress that can be technically substantiated but with no respite from the atmosphere of domination. It is possible in this way to induce the subject to talk without resorting to duress or coercion.

> (*Fundamentals of Criminal Investigation, O'Hara*)

The events of that night and the next morning are described here from Christy Lynch's point of view, as taken from various transcripts, summaries, press reports and interviews. All allegations have been denied on oath by the gardaí concerned. The garda account was that Christy Lynch had made his initial statement about finding the body and they were asking him questions about it, just chatting.

It is midnight, perhaps. Christy Lynch doesn't have a watch. He has lost track of time. Before this is over he will see dark outside the window and see light outside the window and make a guess. It is, he thinks, about midnight. It is eight hours since he came to the station, twelve hours since he found the body.

'Why did you do it, Christy?'

Lynch was tentative about asking for this to stop:

'Can I go now, are you finished?'

'Just a few more minutes, Christy.' Then, again. 'Why did you do it, Christy?'

At 1.30am the 'special boys' arrived. They weren't boys by many a year, but they were rather special. Two detectives with exemplary records in dealing with serious crime. Both had been and would later be involved in some of the most controversial cases of the past twenty years.

According to Christy Lynch's evidence, the two detectives sat him down, one on each side of him and told him they wanted a statement admitting to the murder.

The detectives denied this in court.

'We are the special boys,' said the older of the two, according to Christy, 'we're experienced at getting confessions. We've handled dozens of murders and know a murderer just by looking at him.' The detectives denied saying this.

Christy said in court that he was called a murdering bastard, that one of the detectives said his fingerprints had been found on the knife. 'Did you touch the knife when you found the body?' Christy saw this as a ploy, an offer of a way to get himself off the hook, to say he touched the knife when he found the body so it would look like he had reason to fear his fingerprints were on the knife and he was trying to explain them away. He knew he hadn't touched the knife. He said so.

The detectives denied that any of this happened. It is now 3am. The special boys leave and are replaced by a friendly detective inspector, an amiable chap, a father figure, in Christy's description, and he even looks a bit like Christy's father. It is eleven hours since Christy came to the station, fifteen hours since he found the body.

According to Christy's evidence the conversation went like this.

'If you tell me, Christy, I'll help you. If you confess to me about this I'll personally try and get you down for two or three years. If not — we will prove you guilty anyway and get you ten or fifteen years.'

'I didn't do it. I never harmed anybody in my life.'

'If I walk out that door now I will be finished with you. There's nothing I can do for you to help you.'

Christy asked were his fingerprints on the knife, like the special boys had said.

'Well, I couldn't say at this stage.'

Christy had mentioned earlier that his father was ill.

According to Christy Lynch, the detective inspector now said, 'A long drawn-out trial would kill your father. And if you admit to being guilty the trial will be over in a couple of days. There will be no notice in the paper and it won't affect your father at all.'

Later. 'Is there any chance of getting out of here?'

'No, you won't be able to leave for a while yet.'

The detective inspector denied in court that any of this happened.

It is now 4am. It is twelve hours since Christy came to the station, sixteen hours since he found the body. The detective inspector leaves. The special boys come back. The questioning continues. It goes on until 6am, then there is a twenty-minute break. Then the special boys return and the questioning continues until 8.30am.

In court, Lynch's lawyer, Diarmuid O'Donovan, would say to the older of the special boys, 'I suggest to you there was a concerted conspiracy between you and [the other detective] to get a confession out of the accused.' The special boy replied, 'That is not correct.'

'Were ribald remarks made about the accused man's sexual powers?'

'Nothing like that was said at all.'

'Did you hit him during the interview?'

'I certainly did not.'

The other special boy also denied that Christy Lynch was verbally or physically abused.

Why didn't Christy Lynch ask for a solicitor? It's the kind of thing everybody is supposed to know you can do. The onus is on citizens to learn their legal and constitutional rights from some source or other and be sufficiently confident of those rights to insist on them — rather than the onus being on the state to ensure that the rights of people in police stations are protected. In court, later, Judge Butler seemed to think that everyone should know their rights.

'Do you watch television?' he asked Christy Lynch.

'I do, my lord.'

'Do you look at it? Do you look at "Z Cars", "Task Force"?'

'No.'

'Or even "Kojak"?'

'I look at "Starsky and Hutch".'

If Judge Butler watched 'Kojak' or 'Starsky and Hutch' he might know that in the USA the police are required to inform suspects of their rights, and not assume that they've picked up sufficient knowledge of the constitution from watching TV cop shows.

· · · · ·

It is 10am on Monday 20 September. It is sixteen hours since Christy Lynch came to Irishtown garda station. It is twenty hours since he found Vera Cooney's body. He has not slept. He has not been out of sight of a garda in all this time. He has not been in contact with any relatives, friends or solicitors. According to him he is being held against his will and has been constantly subjected to demands that he confess to the murder. According to the gardaí he is here voluntarily, can leave at any time, but doesn't choose to do so. He is merely being asked to expand on his original statement. The senior of the special boys will say that they talked about his family, army life, things in general.

At 10am the special boys have left Irishtown garda station. When they were leaving, according to Christy, one of them said, 'We will be back tonight, and tomorrow night, and the next night, until we get a confession out of you.'

This was also denied in court by the gardaí.

It's 10am, a long night over. Christy Lynch has been in custody, alone with the police, for sixteen hours. It's a new day. People will be looking for him. Christy Lynch is taken from Irishtown garda station and driven to Donnybrook garda station. The questioning continues.

· · · · ·

Another two hours. One garda, another garda. Admit it for your own good. You just picked up the knife and stabbed her, isn't that right? No, says another garda, he strangled her first.

Strangled? Christy was puzzled. He had seen the knife. He didn't know Vera Cooney had been strangled.

It is now twelve noon, Monday 20 September. It is twenty hours since Christy Lynch came to make a statement. It is twenty-four hours since he found the body.

Another two hours coming up. It was around then, noon on Monday, that Marie Lynch arrived at Donnybrook garda station with two-year-old Debbie. She asked if she could see Christy. Not now, he's being questioned. Would you like something to eat? No, thanks. They brought some cakes for Debbie.

'Your wife is outside, Christy. You won't see anyone until you admit to murdering Miss Cooney.'

Christy is thinking: *I can say yes, I can say I did it. It will all come out, if it goes to court, they'll know I didn't do it, I'll tell them all about this and they'll know I just said it to stop all this.*

'Anyway, Christy, your wife doesn't want to see you until you confess.'

Jesus, what are they after telling Marie? What does she think happened, to make her not want to see me?

'Admit to it, Christy.'

Back tonight. And tomorrow night. And the next night.

'Why did you do it, Christy?'

Think.

'Come on, Christy.'

Two or three years. Ten or fifteen years.

'Christy . . .'

No.

At some point during this two hours of questioning, from noon to 2pm, Christy Lynch was left alone for ten minutes. There was a copy of the *Irish Independent* in the room. The front page carried prominently a story on the murder. The story was inaccurate. It got Vera Cooney's age wrong and got the day of the murder wrong. It said the body was found in the bedroom — the body was found on the landing. It said that no knife was found — the knife was all too prominent in Vera Cooney's chest. It said it was a three-storey house. It said that two workmen had been unable to gain entry and called the police who opened the door with a master key. It said Vera

Cooney was dressed as if ready to go to Sunday Mass — she died on Saturday, and the evidence was that she was getting ready for bed. None of this mattered. What mattered was a sentence which read: 'There were stab wounds in the woman's chest and a cord was fastened around her neck.'

Being constantly told that there is no way out, that this will not end unless he agrees to tell the truth — and when telling the truth is equated with signing his name to a statement — the suspect begins to consider the possibility of just getting it over with. Do what they say. This relentless psychological battering will end. Afterwards he can explain all about what went on and why he signed. Anyone would understand if they knew what he was going through.

It is 2pm, shortly after Christy Lynch has read the story in the *Independent*. 'I killed Vera Cooney,' he says. 'I did it with a bit of a cable. I stabbed her with a knife from the kitchen table.'

Vera Cooney wasn't strangled with a cord or a cable. She was strangled with a scarf.

It is shortly after 2pm. Christy agrees to make a confession. The detective inspector suggests he get some sleep. Twenty-two hours after he went to Irishtown garda station, twenty-six hours after he found the body, Christy Lynch sleeps.

. . . . .

The Central Criminal Court, 27 May 1977, eight months after the murder of Vera Cooney. The trial had lasted five days. The jury was out for four hours. They came back at 10pm and found Christopher Anthony Lynch guilty of the murder of Veronica Frances Cooney. Judge Butler sentenced Lynch to penal servitude for life.

In the body of the court Marie Lynch screamed. She had to be helped from the court by Brendan Lynch, Christy's brother. Christy Lynch was taken to Mountjoy prison. In December the Court of Criminal Appeal set aside his conviction and ordered a new trial. Christy was released a couple of days before Christmas.

The new trial took place in April 1978 and lasted thirteen days, over a three-week period. Just as in the first trial, there were lengthy legal arguments about the admissibility of Lynch's confession. These statements were the only evidence against him. Judge D'Arcy admitted them, Lynch was again found guilty and again sentenced to penal servitude for life.

The statements were many and varied. Once Christy agreed to talk he talked and talked. Some parts of the confession, he said in court, came from what he had been told by gardaí, other parts from what he had seen at the house, still more from the story in the *Independent*.

'How many times did you stab her?'

'Once.'

'No, you stabbed her three times.'

'Well, if that's what happened, it must have happened.'

He talked of strangling Vera Cooney with a cord or a cable or something . . .

'No, this is what was used,' holding up a scarf.

'Well . . .'

This is Christy Lynch's version. The gardaí denied in court that it happened like that. They said he made a straightforward, unprompted, voluntary confession.

Mountjoy was cold. What you do is take two metal bowls and fill them with hot water. Put one on top of the bed — that warms the bed a bit. Put the other under the table, the heat from that takes the chill off your feet. Pull a blanket around you and eat your food. It's so cold you don't blow on your food to cool it, you blow on it to heat it up.

After a while, he was sent to Arbour Hill. That was much easier. It wasn't cold, for a start. Marie had become pregnant again while Christy was between trials. She never brought Debbie up to Mountjoy, but then the kid began fretting for her father, so when Christy was convicted a second time Marie started bringing Debbie to see her dad in prison. The army had been good through all this. Officers appeared as character witnesses; Marie got £12 a week from the army on top of her Prisoner's Wife's Allowance. There was a collection at Christmas.

Christy kept thinking this had to end, there had to be some kind of justice. His barrister, Diarmuid O'Donovan, had resolved to take the case as far as possible, regardless of Christy's ability to pay fees. Eventually, the Supreme Court was scheduled to take the case. Meanwhile, Christy got on with life in jail. Marie, Debbie and the new child, Paul, born in 1978, got on with living outside.

Christy held up well; maybe it was the army discipline. More than once, when doing hard time was getting to a prisoner, a prison officer would suggest he go down and have a chat with Christy. A prison officer at Arbour Hill told Christy's parents that a lot of prisoners say they're innocent, but Christy was the first one he had really believed was innocent.

Christy's father was dying of cancer. Once a month Christy was allowed out under escort to visit him. The dying man told Christy, 'I'll live to see you cleared.'

That year, 1978, turned into 1979, and that turned into 1980. Christy's new son, Paul, was one and then two years old and Christy hadn't seen him. Debbie was five and then six. Christy was missing important years.

Nine days before Christmas 1980. Christy was working in the print shop. He had first done a year and a half at carpentry in Arbour Hill, then changed to the printing. When he was in his teens he had worked for Smurfit's printers in Clonskeagh.

About 4.15pm, ten minutes or so before he was due to knock off, a prison officer named McCann, a sound man, called Christy, and told him to come back to his cell.

'Get your things together.' McCann was smiling.

'Why?'

'You're cleared, you're acquitted. The Supreme Court gave its decision today.'

Christy Lynch's father died six months later.

．．．．．

Chief Justice O'Higgins (sitting with Justices Walsh and Kenny) said in his ruling: 'The fact that for almost twenty-two hours the appellant was subjected to sustained questioning, that he had never had the opportunity of communicating with his family or friends, and that he never was permitted to rest or sleep until he made an admission of guilt, all amount to such circumstances of harassment and oppression as to make it unjust and unfair to admit in evidence anything he said.' And since there was no evidence against him apart from his own statements, Christy Lynch's conviction was quashed and he was ordered to be released.

Chief Justice O'Higgins noted an important point concerning the function of the courts in protecting the rights of citizens. Quoting Chief Justice Earl Warren of the US Supreme Court, he said: 'A ruling admitting evidence in a criminal trial, we recognise, has the necessary effect of legitimising the conduct which produced the evidence.' To permit the use of evidence improperly obtained would make the courts party to that invasion of rights.

So far, it's the kind of decision that might have gardaí slamming their desks and muttering through gritted teeth about pansy judges who don't know what it's like in the real world. He did it, didn't he? He admitted it. OK, so the gardaí kept him awake for a while, big deal. Go ahead and call it oppression and harassment, but he spilled the beans, there was no other way. What about poor Vera Cooney, quiet, inoffensive and horribly dead? What about her rights? No one cares about the victims. Constitutional rights, technicalities, how many angels can dance on the head of a pin? And a self-confessed murderer walks free. He did it, didn't he? Everything points to that.

Everything except the evidence.

. . . . .

There were two strands to the police investigation. One, becoming increasingly the dominant one in serious cases, was the effort to get a confession out of a handy suspect, Christy Lynch. The other was the routine police work, the taking of statements and the gathering of as much evidence about the crime as possible. Once the confession was obtained, the other evidence became superfluous. But it contained important facts.

Christy Lynch was wrong when he thought he saw two young men pushing a red Renault outside 77 Strand Road at about 2.30pm that Saturday when he left the house. He mentioned it in his initial statement. He couldn't have known that this would be significant, he couldn't know that the ordinary coppers plodding on their patient way would find the two people with the red Renault. They were not two men, they were a man and a woman. And they confirmed that they had been pushing the car there at that time. This seemed to corroborate Christy's confession. He had indeed left the house at that time. He could not have seen the car from the house, there being no window on the Gilford Road side.

Except — his confession was that he left the house at 2.30pm having already murdered Vera Cooney. And the police investigation had turned up three unconnected and disinterested witnesses who saw Vera Cooney alive at 4pm.

So, it is established beyond a reasonable doubt that Christy Lynch left the house at 2.30pm and that Vera Cooney was alive at 4pm. Did he go back? There is not the slightest evidence of that — not even in the confession. And if he did go back to the house, and if his confession was reliable, why would it not say he went back after 4pm and committed the murder?

If Christy Lynch strangled Vera Cooney with a scarf, why did he first say he did it with a cable, with a cord, and only mention the scarf after further interrogation?

The confession says that Christy is in the flat reading a book or poking around the bookshelves — the implication being he's looking for money — when he turns around and Vera Cooney is standing there. He grabs a scarf and strangles her.

But, if she has just come in, how come she is wearing slippers, carrying her pyjamas, obviously preparing for bed? Given that Vera Cooney was seen alive after 4pm, and that the estimate of the time of death stretched as far as 9pm, the evidence tends to suggest that she was murdered much later in the day than the 2.30pm when it is known Christy Lynch left the house.

The confession just doesn't square with the available facts. These discrepancies were pointed out by Justices O'Higgins and Walsh. The discrepancies were there during the two trials, but they were outweighed by the graphic confession. Confronted by a confession apparently freely given, a jury tends to dismiss awkward facts that don't fit. Who could believe that an innocent man would admit to murder?

Christy Lynch went back to the army. When he came out of jail he got his back pay. He and Marie then had to repay the money she received from the state and from the army. In prison, he had had no option but to drop his gambling habits. Instead, he picked up the habits of rolling cigarettes and doing crosswords.

The Lynch case became a landmark in defining some of the limits to which the police can go in the interrogation of suspects. There were lessons to be learned by the courts, by the politicians and by the gardaí, about the dangers of uncorroborated confessions signed after lengthy interrogation. They weren't learned.

Four years after the dreadful death of Vera Cooney, four years during which Christy Lynch was locked up, during which the confession of Christy Lynch ensured that no other leads would be followed, the chances of the police picking up the threads of the investigation were non-existent and the case remains unsolved.

⑩ A Day in Court: Elvis Lives

There was serious stuff going on here. A bank was trying to put the clamps on a businessman from Killiney who owed them £29,973.69p. His business was going belly-up and he was selling his house and leaving for Spain, pronto ('I want a quick sale,' he told the estate agent) and the bank wanted to make sure that when he went he left at least £29,973 behind. And 69p.

And then a barrister, one hand resting on her thick volume of *Bromley's Family Law*, wanted the court to issue an order under Article 40.4 of the Constitution, which is the *habeas corpus* clause. She wanted someone to be directed to produce a child before the court.

Serious stuff, so serious that the court clerk stuck a cardboard 'In Camera' sign on the door of Court No. 3 and the court was cleared. Lord knows what painful issues were being dealt with, and what danger the child might be in.

Like clowns at a funeral, the Elvis Presley fanatics rose and shuffled out of the courtroom and stood in the Round Hall, patiently waiting for the child's fate to be decided so that the court could deal with their own bitter little row.

The Presley fans were fighting over which is the 'official' Elvis fan club. There were eight of them in court and nine reporters. It was August 1991, summer, the height of the silly season.

This was the vacation sitting, which meant that apart from the room upstairs wherein a massively long judgment in a tedious business case was being laboriously read out, only Courtroom No. 3 was functioning. There were no wigs or gowns; Judge Barr wore a blue suit and he had a red rose in his buttonhole.

And after several years of slagging one another, the Elvis buffs were having their day in court.

Elvis Presley died in 1977 but not so that you'd notice. There was something about the guy that causes certain adults to worship him, to imitate him, to stand around and talk about him as though he hadn't overdosed on cheeseburgers and dodgy chemical substances. Presley was a simple man with a limited view of the world around him. After an early period of innovation, bringing rhythm and blues to a white audience, Presley became trapped in a commercial machine that relentlessly churned out lucrative product which exploited his celebrity, not his musical talent. He was paraded through a stream of crap movies and recorded countless mediocre songs. Although making occasional attempts to retrieve his music career, Presley mostly went along with the commercial flow, content to rake in the millions and enjoy a simple if vulgar lifestyle. The money-machine ground to a halt when, in the words of an investigator from the Medical Examiner's office, 'Mr Presley underwent his terminal event while sitting on the commode.' His stodgy, stuffed, clogged system imploded as he strained once too often to achieve a bowel movement.

One might have imagined that this pathetic end might have burst the bubble of the Presley legend. Instead, it powered a Presley obsession which has generated far larger amounts of money than the living Presley could coin. Throughout the world Elvis Presley fan clubs bring together disciples in whose lives The King still looms large. On the wilder shores of Presleydom there are those who believe that the man faked his death so as to slip away from the limelight and that he is to this day enjoying a carefree life in some backwater, smirking at the success of his stratagem. Most fans, however, accept that their hero is gone to the great jukebox in the sky. Through their collective activities they seek to commemorate the man and his music, to spread the message and to re-create a sense of The King's presence. Some of the disciples dress like Presley, mould their hair in styles he made famous. They collect Elvis memorabilia and make pilgrimages to his home, Graceland, in Memphis. They grow sideburns and wear shades and gyrate to the sound of his records. They wear blue suede shoes and some of them even wear imitations of the sequined jump suits of Presley's Las Vegas period. From time to time they hold events at which numbers of Presley imitators take the stage and vie to create the most convincing impression of their loved one. It is reported that when he was alive Presley was eating in a local steakhouse when he found that an Elvis Presley Impersonation Contest was about to take place. Unrecognised in his corner booth, Presley decided, on the spur of the moment, urged on by the steakhouse owner, to take part in the contest. He came third.

In Ireland, some of Elvis's fans had come to a parting of the ways. Now, pay attention. This can be as hard to figure out as a row between Serbs and Croats.

Once upon a time (1974 to 1987 approx.) there was the TCB Fan Club, which was the Taking Care of Business Fan Club. Apparently, Elvis Presley used to say, 'Taking care of business' a lot. It was a catch phrase of his, like Bruce Forsyth's 'Didn't he do well!' or Frank Carson's 'It's the way I tell 'em!' Elvis would say, 'Taking care of business' and his flunkies would chortle.

In 1985 there was a split in TCB, and at a meeting attended by thirty-seven people the Memories of Elvis Appreciation Society of Ireland was set up. MOEASI thrived and TCB flagged.

MOEASI's secretary and head honcho is a man named George Twamley, a thin man with a fuzzy beard. Mr Twamley lives in St Kevin's Gardens, Dartry, in a house he calls 'Graceland'.

TCB collapsed in 1987, leaving MOEASI cock of the walk. For reasons unspecified, a Mr John Kavanagh had been drummed out of MOEASI. Mr Kavanagh, from Bluebell, is a man with black hair swept back over his head, just like Elvis used to have. Mr Kavanagh is a Presley imitator, regularly taking to the stage to re-create The King's movements while an Elvis record plays in the background and Mr Kavanagh silently mimes the words. Mr Kavanagh remained a member of TCB after leaving MOEASI. Then, TCB collapsed.

In July 1987, at a meeting attended by thirty people, the Elvis For Everyone Fan Club (EFEFC) was set up, with Mr John Kavanagh as secretary and main man. Where MOEASI and TCB had vied in their reverence for the dead King, the rivals were now MOEASI and EFEFC.

As the years went by MOEASI (the Twamley outfit) registered itself as The Irish Elvis Presley Fan Club Limited (or TIEPFC Ltd). It began to call itself and be called by others 'The Official Elvis Presley Fan Club'.

EFEFC (the Kavanagh outfit), however, had now registered itself as The Official Elvis Presley Fan Club of Ireland, Elvis For Everyone Limited (or TOEPFCIEFE Ltd).

TIEPFC Ltd (Twamley) was holding a function in the Clarence Hotel, Dublin, the following Sunday and it was worried that the public might confuse it with TOEPFCIEFE Ltd (Kavanagh), which was holding a function in another Dublin hotel on the Saturday. So, TIEPFC Ltd sued TOEPFCIEFE Ltd and asked the court that the latter be told to stop calling itself the Elvis Presley fan club and in particular to stop calling itself 'official'.

Each side came to court clutching documents explaining how much money each had raised for charity. Mr Twamley said on affidavit that his club was 'the leading and best-known Elvis Presley Fan Club in Ireland, and enjoys extensive goodwill'.

Mr Kavanagh said on affidavit: 'At all times I acted in the best interests of the music of Elvis Presley.'

Judge Barr listened patiently to all this and gave a provisional judgment, to hold the line until such time as the two Elvis clubs might get around to mounting a full-scale legal battle. The judgment concluded that TOEPFCIEFE Ltd should stop calling itself 'official', although it could still call itself an Elvis Presley Fan Club. Mr Kavanagh gave an undertaking to that effect.

So, TOEPFCIEFE Ltd had to drop the O (for Official) and henceforth be TEPFCIEFE Ltd, so that it be less likely that we might confuse it with TIEPFC Ltd.

The two clubs had to pay for their own lawyers. We taxpayers paid for the judge and the clerk and the court staff and the use of the hall.

Three and a half years later, a TIEPFC Ltd member makes headlines. On the stage of Johnnie Fox's pub, in Glencullen, in the Dublin mountains, it is New Year's Day 1995, and John Reid, an Elvis impersonator and leading member of TIEPFC Ltd, is singing 'Blue Suede Shoes'. John is technical manager at the UCI cinema complex in Tallaght, he's aged thirty-six and he's wearing a blue Elvis costume he made himself, with hundreds of sequins stuck on to it. John is Elvis crazy, has an Elvis hairstyle, has made the pilgrimage to Graceland (the old Elvis home, not George Twamley's) and performs in tribute to The King.

John is gyrating in an appropriate manner and he hits a dramatic note in the song and sinks to his knees. He doesn't get up. He collapses. There is an American marine in the audience and he jumps onstage and massages John's heart. A doctor and a nurse come forward to help. An ambulance is sent for, John is rushed to hospital. He survives for a week on a life support machine. On 8 January he dies. The date is the sixtieth anniversary of Elvis Presley's birth.

Some of John's organs are donated so that others might live. He is by all accounts a decent man and it would have pleased him that in death he could help others.

George Twamley of TIEPFC Ltd says everyone is shattered. Another member of the club, Tom Mahony, says that John dying on what would have been Elvis's sixtieth birthday 'was a nice thing in the end, because he really lived for Elvis'.

At John's funeral another Elvis fan sings The King's favourite gospel song, 'How Great Thou Art'. A friend of John, Patricia Nolan, is quoted: 'It was an absolutely huge funeral. You'd swear to God it was Elvis himself.'

⑪ Sweet Money

The barrister was honoured to be asked. It was a dirty job, cleaning up one of the nastiest little financial scandals to afflict modern Irish capitalism, but someone had to do it. And who better than Ciaran Foley, Senior Counsel.

The Greencore Scandal was the starting pistol that saw the country stumble through an unprecedented period of successive scandals, financial and moral, that left the populace perplexed, entertained and angered. In the atmosphere of the times, it became urgent that the government be seen to be doing something to clear the air. So, an investigator was found. Ciaran Foley, SC, High Court Inspector. As the scandals unfolded, unconnected but delivering a succession of hammer blows to the establishment's credibility, hardly an area of public life would be left untouched by controversy. Before the dust settled Ciaran Foley himself would end up on a witness stand, explaining how hard he had worked, and how tough the job was and how honoured he had been to be asked to do it. And why he thought it necessary to sue a number of people because of what they said about him.

· · · · ·

It started with a cosy arrangement between Chris Comerford and the Gladebrook Four. Comerford was the chief executive of Siúicre Éireann, the state-owned sugar company. Comerford was raised on a 200 acre farm in Kilkenny, one of eight children. He became a scientist specialising in sugar beet, quickly rising to management, becoming chief executive in 1984. He married and had four children. As the end of the 1980s approached there was talk of privatisation, and Comerford set about stripping down the sugar company in order to make it profitable, closing plants in Tuam and Thurles. The company was being prepared to be the first of the semi-state companies to be floated on the stock market.

Siúicre Éireann had deep roots in the areas where its factories had employed successive generations. The factory closures, doing immense damage to small communities, were controversial, but Comerford had powerful backing. For the politicians, the business world and the huge financial institutions, ideologically committed to a policy of privatisation, Siúicre Éireann was the cutting edge of the chisel carving out a brave new world free from state interference.

Siúicre Éireann was established in 1933. As the state sugar company it played a large role in the agricultural sector and the name Siúicre Éireann became one of the most recognisable in the state, at both the production and consumer ends. For generations it put a packet of sugar in every larder in the land. The state held the entire share-holding of Siúicre Éireann until 1991, when the privatisation was to take place. It was in the run-up to privatisation that the roots of the Greencore Scandal lay.

There was a sugar distribution company called SDH, of which Siúicre Éireann owned 51 per cent. The other 49 per cent was owned by various investors. SDH, although a separate company, was in effect an arm of Siúicre Éireann, as its entire business consisted of marketing and distributing the sugar company's output. The top management of SDH comprised Charles Lyons, Thomas Keleghan, Charles Garavan and Michael Tully. These were the men who became what we will call the Gladebrook Four.

The four realised that there were sweet possibilities in the changing circumstances that surrounded the impending privatisation of Siúicre Éireann. They decided in 1988 that they should organise a management buy-out of the 49 per cent of SDH shares not owned by Siúicre Éireann. They worked out that this would cost them £3.2m. At this level of society a term regularly mentioned is 'tax efficient'. This means arranging your affairs so that you pay as little tax as you can get away with. The four, Lyons, Keleghan, Garavan and Tully, decided that for the purposes of this little adventure their tax exposure would best be limited by constituting themselves as a separate company, with the tranquil name of Gladebrook Ltd.

The bad news was that, wealthy as the four might be, they were £1,000,000 short of the £3.2m they needed to buy the 49 per cent of SDH shares. The good news was that they figured out a way to raise the £1,000,000. They would borrow it from a subsidiary of SDH, their own company. Before they could do that, they needed the OK of the board of Siúicre Éireann, the majority shareholder in SDH. They went to Chris Comerford, the Siúicre Éireann chief executive, and told him of their proposal.

Luckily for the four, Chris Comerford had a high opinion of their abilities. He presented the loan proposal to the Siúicre Éireann board and said that he was sure the Gladebrook Four would 'contribute strongly to the future success of Siúicre Éireann'. Within Siúicre Éireann, great trust was placed in the judgment of the chief executive, and there was a limited review process. The £1,000,000 loan was approved, on terms which the report of a future inquiry would term 'exceptionally generous'. Gladebrook Ltd now had in place the £3.2m necessary to buy the 49 per cent of SDH that Siúicre Éireann didn't own.

Chris Comerford's high opinion of the Gladebrook Four was reciprocated. Lyons, Keleghan, Garavan and Tully were big fans of Comerford. So much so that when, in July 1988, three months before Comerford steered the Gladebrook loan through the Siúicre Éireann board, beef baron Larry Goodman approached Comerford with a job offer, the Gladebrook people were aghast. Without Chris at the helm of Siúicre Éireann they were not at all sure that the company could be guided through the rough waters leading to privatisation. They persuaded Comerford to stay on at Siúicre Éireann and arranged to 'top up' his salary to the tune of £40,000 a year. Thus, a privately-owned company doing business with a state-owned company, was shelling out forty grand a year to 'top up' the salary of the chief executive of the state-owned company. This was done, said the Gladebrook Four, because when Comerford was head hunted by beef baron Larry Goodman the Four 'saw it as critical that he should remain in his position' in Siúicre Éireann. They arranged to channel the forty grand to Comerford through Delante Ltd, a company registered in Jersey. This arrangement was kept secret from the board of Siúicre Éireann.

Comerford would later claim that as an added incentive for him to turn down the Goodman approach he was offered a share in the management buy-out of SDH, an offer that meant he would become a partner of the Gladebrook Four. This claim was denied. It would become central to the events that followed.

The complex deal that was unfolding required share transfers, meetings that had to be held prior to certain dates, the minuting of decisions. Minutes were in one case drawn up two years after a meeting supposedly took place. Minutes were drawn up showing that the Gladebrook Four attended a meeting in Carlow on 5 December. The meeting was actually held eleven days later, at the International Airport Hotel in Dublin. Chris Comerford attended that meeting, but the minutes didn't mention him.

Among the morsels which future investigation would reveal would be copies of faxes from one party to another, concerning an important meeting. The faxes included minutes of the meeting. The faxes were sent two days before the meeting was held.

· · · · ·

The next stage in the drama involved Siúicre Éireann buying up the 49 per cent of SDH which it didn't own, the 49 per cent which had been bought by Gladebrook Ltd. Privatisation was coming and Siúicre Éireann wanted to wrap up SDH before being floated on the market. Why didn't Siúicre Éireann simply buy the 49 per cent in the first place, before it was bought by Gladebrook? Why not cut out the middle man? There were a number of reasons. One major reason was the controversy arising from the shutting down of sugar factories.

The workforce was in a militant mood and might strike. Back in 1987 SDH had come in handy in undermining a strike at Siúicre Éireann. Being a subsidiary of Siúicre Éireann it was not drawn into the dispute and was able to import sugar and keep Siúicre Éireann's customers supplied. If SDH had been wholly owned by Siúicre Éireann it would have attracted pickets. During the stripping down of the sugar company, with the possibility of industrial unrest in the face of the dumping of workers, it was thought prudent to keep SDH at arm's length.

Now, with the stripping done and the company ready for privatisation, Siúicre Éireann wanted to buy up the 49 per cent of SDH it didn't own. Once that happened several people were going to get rich very quickly. It was around then that the Gladebrook Four became the Gladebrook Five.

The fifth entity in Gladebrook Ltd was a company named Talmino. Talmino was a Jersey-based company, its ownership steeped in secrecy and controversy. Talmino was to get 22 per cent of Gladebrook Ltd. It would be Chris Comerford's claim that he was offered Talmino as a way of bringing him into the management buy-out. This would be denied.

In the midst of all these manoeuvres a meeting was held at the Arbutus Lodge Hotel, in Cork, one of the country's more prestigious establishments. At this meeting there was to be a discussion of the share-out of the profits that Gladebrook Ltd was going to make. The Gladebrook Four, Lyons, Keleghan, Garavan and Tully, were there. So was John Murphy, a solicitor who was acting for the four. And Chris Comerford, chief executive of Siúicre Éireann.

At the meeting, one of the original Gladebrook Four, Michael Tully, became upset, claiming he wasn't getting a big enough cut. He complained, 'I'm only half a man, here. Everybody else is a full man.' This was believed to be a reference to the fact that the other three members of the Gladebrook Four were each getting shares of over 20 per cent of Gladebrook, while Tully was getting only 10 per cent. Mr Tully became so upset over this that he began crying. His cut was eventually agreed at 12 per cent.

There was a problem at the heart of the deal. Talmino was getting 22 per cent of Gladebrook, but who owned Talmino? Chris

Comerford would claim that the Talmino cut had the Comerford name on it, that solicitor John Murphy was to make the arrangements. Murphy would claim that Talmino belonged to him, to Keleghan and Lyons. This conflict would rumble along out of sight but it would eventually erupt and tear the entrepreneurs apart.

By and by, in 1990, the sweet deal came to fruition. Siúicre Éireann bought Gladebrook Ltd, thereby buying the 49 per cent of SDH it didn't already own. Chris Comerford, as chief executive of Siúicre Éireann, was buying Gladebrook. And Chris Comerford, as the claimed owner of Talmino, the part-owner of Gladebrook, was selling Gladebrook. The price agreed was £9.5m. This was £6.3m more than the Gladebrook Four had paid for the shares the previous year.

The Talmino share of the proceeds, in the form of a loan note, was worth £2.1 million. Its ownership was still a matter of dispute.

Siúicre Éireann was privatised in April 1991 and became Greencore. Chris Comerford became chief executive of the new company. It had made £20,000,000 profit in the previous year. Politicians lined up to laud this example of a moribund semi-state company blossoming in the sunlight of the marketplace. Freed from the constraints of semi-state slavery, Chris Comerford's salary bounced up to the heights of £135,000.

Underneath the surface, the unresolved arguments about money were raging. Chris Comerford and Charles Lyons both began litigation. The dispute about who owned Talmino and its 22 per cent of the profits was boiling. Me, said Comerford; me, said Murphy. There was now a danger that if litigation went ahead the participants in the sweet deal might end up explaining all this from a witness stand at the Four Courts. A meeting was set up to try to reach agreement. Three rooms were booked at the Shelbourne Hotel. Chris Comerford attended, as well as Garavan, Lyons and solicitor John Murphy. There were various lawyers present to facilitate negotiations.

The crucial element at issue was the £2.1m Talmino loan note. Who was entitled to it, Chris Comerford or John Murphy and his Gladebrook clients?

Murphy and Garavan took a break from the meeting at one point and sat on the stairs in the Shelbourne. 'The problem that Chris has,' said Garavan, 'he has got to be seen to win.'

'As long as I get £1,000,000,' said Murphy, 'that's my side of it dealt with. I don't care whether it comes from the note, or where it comes from.'

A bewildering range of transactions was discussed as the parties edged towards provisional agreement. Solicitor John Murphy would get £1,000,000 from Garavan. Comerford would get the Talmino loan note. Comerford would pay Garavan £150,000 out of his proceeds from Talmino. Garavan would pass this to Murphy. Charles Lyons was to be paid £104,000. A quarter of a million pound loan would be released and 'consultancy payments' of tens of thousands of pounds would be arranged. All the parties would cease and desist in legal actions against one another. Chris Comerford would strike out his legal claim that he owned Talmino.

They were very close to agreement, then the whole intricate solution to the interminably complicated deal fell apart.

· · · · ·

Reporter Sam Smyth is an amiable chap. As well as a sense of humour, he has a good instinct for news and a nose that twitches when he is in the vicinity of something that doesn't quite add up. A source suggested he should have a look at this Talmino business, an obscure legal row over who owned what. Chris Comerford had lodged an affidavit at the High Court. Smyth went nosing around. This was only days after the abortive negotiations at the Shelbourne Hotel. Had agreement been reached at that meeting and had Comerford withdrawn his legal claims, the whole thing might have been buried in private documents and the public might never have known.

Instead, two weeks after the Shelbourne meeting, the *Sunday Independent* published a front-page lead story by Sam Smyth. Smyth would be the first to admit that the story was not a great read. The lawyers had been at it.

In recent years, litigants, with one-time Taoiseach Albert Reynolds prominent among them, have created an atmosphere of fear in journalism. It isn't enough that you do not deliberately libel someone; a journalist must ensure that nothing written might be open to an interpretation never intended but which might be construed as libellous. Writings which might be harsh, insulting or hurtful, but not libellous, might nevertheless be judged libellous in court. With lawyers claiming huge fees, the gamble increases. To defend a libel suit where damages may be ten or twenty thousand pounds, a newspaper might have to risk £60,000 in legal costs. Often, the figures are vastly greater. Juries, taking their cue from reading about million-pound settlements in Britain, have steadily raised awards. Lawyers' costs in turn shot up.

Increasingly, newspapers have tended to settle cases, even where they know that there has been no libel and where they reckon they have a reasonable chance of successfully defending the action. Juries and judges are unpredictable and the price to be paid if the case is lost is too high. Journalists dealing with touchy subjects, therefore, write with a care bordering on paranoia. Lawyers are employed to scrutinise every sentence. Sam Smyth's story on how Chris Comerford was taking legal action to lay claim to Talmino was carefully vetted. So bare and lean was the eventual story that many readers could make little sense of it. At the time, it seemed an odd story to run as a front-page lead. In retrospect, it was one of the great scoops of its day. The following year, Sam Smyth received the Journalist of the Year award for his story.

Enough people understood the carefully worded story for it to ruin a whole lot of Sunday breakfasts. As soon as he read the *Sunday Independent* that morning the chairman of Greencore, Bernie Cahill, called a board meeting for the following Tuesday. The *Sunday Independent* story was the first inkling Cahill had that his chief executive, Chris Comerford, was claiming beneficial ownership in Talmino, a company which had benefited from transactions with Siúicre Éireann.

On Monday, Chris Comerford hurried to confer with his lawyers about what he could and should say at the next day's emergency board meeting. Someone pointed out that Comerford had a problem. He was claiming a beneficial interest in Talmino but he had not disclosed such an interest when Siúicre Éireann was being privatised and became Greencore. This was contrary to stock exchange regulations. At the board meeting next day Comerford claimed that the beneficial interest in Talmino was not his but held in trust by him for his adult children. It was true that his litigation had claimed that Talmino was his, but a trust was supposed to have been set up for his adult children and that hadn't been done by the person designated. The board was, however, insisting on Comerford's resignation.

Comerford wasn't going easily. Negotiations stretched over several days and in a final ten-hour session, ending at 3 o'clock in the morning, a deal was agreed. Comerford would go but he would receive a generous severance package. He would receive, in installments, a sum equivalent to two years and three months of his gross salary of £135,000 a year. He would receive all his outstanding holiday pay, expenses and bonuses. He would get to keep his share options and would be paid his full pension entitlement and gratuity on reaching the age of sixty. And he would get to keep and own his company car. The package was estimated to be worth around £1,000,000.

There were some raised eyebrows when news of this settlement came out. Greencore subsequently reneged on the deal and refused to pay the money. Comerford sued them. They counter-sued for negligence and breach of fiduciary duty.

Similarly, company secretary Michael Tully resigned on agreement of a healthy severance package. It was subsequently frozen and he too sued.

As the scandal erupted, newspapers rushed to snap some shots of Chris Comerford. As it happened, his daughter was getting married. Photographers descended on the church, snapping away. This greatly disturbed Comerford. Much later, in a newspaper interview, he would complain about this. The official photographer hadn't been able to get into the church, Comerford claimed, and missed a shot of Comerford escorting his daughter up the aisle. 'That I won't forget. It was unfair. It was her day. If they wanted a photograph of me that was fine, but this was her day. She shouldn't have been brought into it.'

Very sad. But odd. It wasn't the photographers who brought Comerford's daughter into the affair, it was Comerford. It was he who claimed that the Talmino shareholding belonged to his adult children. If his adult children were to be beneficiaries of a controversial transaction involving millions of pounds Comerford couldn't reasonably complain about any of them having their picture taken.

The Greencore Scandal was spilling out in front of a bemused public. In the months to come it would seem like Sam Smyth, in tugging at the loose end that was the Talmino dispute, had started the unravelling of whole stretches of the fabric of Irish public life. Within days came news of the Telecom scandal, in which Telecom had purchased a site it would never use and from which a number of people made millions. People started asking about money made from the sale of Carysfort College. A letter was published in which prominent stockbroker Dermot Desmond claimed a £2,000,000 fee for 'intervention at the highest levels', seeking political favours on behalf of a client. Confidential Aer Lingus documents found their way to Celtic Helicopters, owned by then Taoiseach Charlie Haughey's son.

Nothing connected the various controversies, but their coincidence in time, within a period of months, would give the country an atmosphere of sleaze. Bishop Casey's son turned up in America; the business sector contributed to the fun when multimillionaire Ben Dunne was caught freaking out on cocaine in Florida. Allegations emerged of a 'golden circle' of wealthy people. An example suggested was a number of people who were given an opportunity to get in on a sure-fire property deal, at very generous prices, which involved threatening the tenancy of many of the elderly residents of Mespil Flats, in Dublin.

To deal with the first of these scandals, the government, eager to distance itself from the growing smell of greed and questionable practices, decided to set up an inquiry. Greencore had already hired accountants Arthur Andersen to look into the affair. Now the government set up its own inquiry under the Companies' Act, hiring accountant Maurice Curran to look into the beneficial ownership of the various companies involved in the affair. Furthermore, as if eager to show it had nothing to hide, the government set up another inquiry under a different section of the Companies' Act, this time appointing two inspectors, through the High Court, to investigate the Greencore affair.

For this, which would become known as the Inspectors' Inquiry, the government decided it must appoint a barrister and an accountant, to ensure that the team could negotiate the tricky legal and financial maze that was the Gladebrook deal. It all happened very fast. The *Sunday Independent* story broke on 1 September, Chris Comerford got the boot from Greencore on 3 September, by 12 September Maurice Curran had been appointed and by 16 September the personnel for the Inspectors' Inquiry had been appointed.

The accountant chosen was Aidan Barry, the barrister was Senior Counsel Ciaran Foley. Foley, called to the bar in 1973, an SC since 1986, had dealt with a lot of company law and was eminently qualified for investigating financial intricacies. He felt honoured to be asked. In the first days of their inquiry the inspectors set about hiring assistants and acquiring facilities. They had meetings with the Attorney General's office and the Department of Industry and Commerce; they met lawyers and accountants who had special knowledge of the Greencore affair. They worked out the likely structure and course of their investigations and applied for and got permission to extend the scope of the inquiry. The inspectors decided they needed their own offices and their own security. They needed access to forensic expertise through the Department of Justice.

The inquiry was expected to take four weeks, with a report from the inspectors on 14 October.

It wasn't until 23 September, a week after the inspectors' appointment, that the Department of Finance let the inspectors know that they were setting up a committee of civil servants to meet the inspectors and discuss the 'cost element of the assignment'. The inquiry was a week under way before the first move was made to establish how much it would cost.

Three days later Foley and Barry wrote to the Department of Justice, setting out their costs. They requested an initial retainer, or brief fee, of £10,000 each per month 'or part thereof'. On top of that Foley and Barry would each charge £1,750 per day, and this would be on the basis of a seven-day week. There would also be costs for the hiring of offices, support staff, accountants, stenographers, secretaries, security etc. They would propose hiring partner-level accountants at £125 an hour and senior accountants at £75 an hour. Two secretaries had been hired at £300 a week. Office accommodation, including rent, rates, service charges and security, would cost £1,358 a week.

It was 2 October, over two weeks after the inquiry began, before Foley and Barry met with the committee of civil servants charged with negotiating their fees. One of the things worrying the civil servants was the likely public reaction if it became known that Foley and Barry were paid such a level of fees. The Hamilton inquiry into allegations of slick handiwork in the beef industry was under way at the time and the legal fees being charged at that tribunal were a source of controversy. The daily fees of £1,890 for senior counsel for the state had astonished and angered the public. The Beef Tribunal looked like it might never end and the costs were heading up into the stratosphere. The last thing the state needed was another row about costs.

Before the 2 October meeting, the civil servants made discreet enquiries in legal circles about barrister Ciaran Foley. What kind of fees might he command? They were told he would be in the £1,300 to £1,500 per day range. Even this was more than the civil servants thought appropriate. In court, barristers getting a top rate are expected to think on their feet and have immediate command of a full range of professional and personal knowledge. The investigation of Greencore didn't require that kind of work. The civil servants also believed that it was an honour for a barrister to be chosen for such an inquiry. (And Ciaran Foley, indeed, considered himself honoured to be asked.) Professionals, including lawyers, often generously put their talents to use in public service without requesting the top rate. So, at the 2 October meeting, the civil servants had some hope of negotiating the fees downwards. There were five civil servants at the meeting (two from Justice, two from Industry and Commerce and one from the office of the Attorney General), plus Ciaran Foley and Aidan Barry. The meeting started at 10.15am and lasted ninety minutes.

Foley and Barry were told that £10,000 was in excess of the brief fees paid to state barristers at the Beef Tribunal. If any brief fee was appropriate, the civil servants felt, it would not exceed £6,000. And they weren't convinced a brief fee was appropriate. Brief fees are paid to barristers to cover the period leading to a court appearance, at which time they receive a daily rate. Foley and Barry's daily rate would apply from the moment of appointment, back on 16 September. And the notion of a recurring brief fee, an extra £10,000 a month, on top of the daily rate, was unprecedented.

Denis Crowley, a civil servant from the Department of Justice, said they hadn't expected a claim for a daily rate in excess of £1,500. Foley and Barry calculated they were worth £175 an hour, working out at £1,750 a day, and they wouldn't budge. A barrister caught up in lengthy proceedings loses touch with solicitors, and therefore loses future business, argued Foley.

Colm Gallagher, a civil servant from the Department of Industry and Commerce, said there was a worry about the cost going public if it was raised at the Dáil's Public Accounts Committee. There had been rates of £800 to £1,000 a day agreed for work of this kind in the past. Foley and Barry wouldn't budge.

Their only concession was that they would drop the demand for a recurring, monthly retainer. They would agree to just a one-off brief fee of £10,000 each on top of the daily £1,750. Colm Gallagher said he could understand a barrister looking for a brief fee, that's the way barristers work. But Aidan Barry wasn't a barrister, he was an accountant. Paying a brief fee to an accountant was 'novel', said Gallagher. Foley and Barry thought otherwise. You couldn't make fish of one and fowl of the other, went the argument. Both of them wanted the £10,000 brief fee. The meeting ended with the civil servants saying they would go back to their ministers. Foley and Barry believed that agreement in principle had been reached, pending ministerial confirmation.

The matter still hadn't been fixed up five days later, when the inspectors gave the High Court their interim report. The inquiry was going to take somewhat longer than had at first been thought. They got an extension of time until 18 December to bring in a full report.

Two days after the meeting with the civil servants, Minister for Industry and Commerce Dessie O'Malley rang Aidan Barry. O'Malley said he didn't want to see a 'gravy train' getting up steam. It was a somewhat abrasive conversation, with O'Malley asking for a copy of the inspectors' interim report and Barry informing him that only the High Court had the power to give the report to whomever it deemed should see it. 'Don't get legalistic with me,' said O'Malley, according to a memo of the conversation written by Aidan Barry.

O'Malley questioned the hiring of support staff, accountants charging up to £125 an hour. Why couldn't Aidan Barry carry out the accountancy tasks himself, he wanted to know. 'I appointed you and not your partners.'

Barry explained that the task was complex and he wanted it accomplished in 'as short a time-frame as possible'.

O'Malley rang again four days later, more angry this time. Three times he said he didn't want the state liable for high fees. He said that in future civil servants would be employed to carry out such investigations. 'Neither you or any members of your profession will ever be retained again by me or my successors,' he said.

Aidan Barry pointed out that there were thirty-three companies to be inquired into and while he and Ciaran Foley wanted to complete the task as quickly as possible they didn't want to miss anything.

Meanwhile, a civil servant noted in a letter to the inspectors that the question of fees was one that was still 'pending agreement'. Foley and Barry were outraged. As far as they were concerned the fees had been agreed, pending ministerial confirmation. On 14 October they wrote to the Attorney General that the civil servants were refusing 'to determine a reasonable market rate' for the backup staff necessary to conduct the inquiry. The inspectors were without 'proper and adequate resources'. They would 'not be subjected to unjustified and unwarranted attack in the impugning of their professional integrity in the course and conduct of this investigation as Officers of the Court'.

The civil servants found themselves in the middle, between the inspectors and the politicians. As far as they were concerned, Foley and Barry had held all the cards when negotiating fees. Usually in such negotiations there were others waiting in the wings who might underprice demands being made. Here, with Foley and Barry a month into the inquiry, the civil servants had been dealing with what they thought of as a monopoly supplier already chosen. And the pressure didn't stop there. The inspectors threatened to go to the High Court 'on the issue of the availability of resources'.

The civil servants were, in the words of one of them, 'sensing a climate' among politicians. There had been unfounded allegations that politicians were trying to cover up the Greencore scandal and no minister wanted anything to happen which might appear to support that notion. Allegations in court that politicians were starving the inquiry of funds would create dangerous controversy. Foley and Barry wrote to the Attorney General that it would be 'unseemly' if they were to go to the High Court 'on the issue of availability of resources to properly conduct a meaningful investigation'.

After consultation between several members of the cabinet it was agreed on 17 October that the fees sought by Foley and Barry would be paid.

Had the inquiry lasted the four weeks allotted to it, Ciaran Foley would have earned £59,000, and Aidan Barry the same. But the inspectors were coming up against stubborn, nit-picking resistance by those being investigated. The inquiry dragged on into December 1991. The politicians were becoming more uneasy. On top of their £10,000 retainer, the two inspectors were between them earning £24,500 for every week the inquiry lasted. At a cabinet meeting in late November, when the inquiry was already six weeks beyond its original deadline of 14 October, ministers expressed concern at the escalating costs. A week later Dessie O'Malley was back on the phone to Aidan Barry, on two days in succession. O'Malley continued to rage about the cost and said that his views were shared by the other fourteen people around the cabinet table. The inspectors defended their work and said the inquiry was very complicated.

And it was. There is no doubt that the two men were working hard, trying to make sense of a very complex matter. They had found themselves, in words which Mr Foley would later use in the Circuit Court, 'aghast at the illegality — alleged — apparent illegality' they found in their examination of the sweet deals which led to the privatisation of Siúicre Éireann. They were feeling the pressure of an intense workload, on an assignment which they were determined would be scrupulously carried out. And they were feeling the pressure of the politicians' increasing unease with the soaring costs.

Meanwhile, the Arthur Andersen report commissioned by Greencore was completed on 23 October. The Curran inquiry into the affair was completed and the report published on 4 December.

The inspectors, Ciaran Foley and Aidan Barry, decided that despite the hard work their deadline of 18 December could not be met. They went to the High Court and asked for another extension.

Brian McCracken SC, a lawyer representing Dessie O'Malley, the Minister for Industry and Commerce, opposed the granting of the extension. 'The fees being sought by the inspectors are excessive and warrant review,' said McCracken. The 18 December deadline should be enforced. 'We don't know what stage they are at, there is no internal report at this stage, we don't know what remains.'

Mr Justice Kevin Lynch said he believed the inspectors were 'reaching a stage where finality is around the next bend'. The lawyer for the inspectors, Dan Herbert, asked for an extension of the deadline to the end of January. 'What does the end of January really mean?' asked the judge.

'Some date in February,' said Mr Herbert.

Judge Lynch granted the extension, saying he wanted an 'almost certain understanding' that the final report would be ready on 11 February 1992. He said the inspectors had worked 'as hard as could reasonably be expected of them' and had 'carried out their duties in an extremely conscientious manner'. He said that he would alter an old expression: 'I am not going to spoil the ship for a halfpenny worth of time.'

On 18 December, according to his time sheets, Ciaran Foley worked only four hours, an unusually short day for him. That was the day that the final report would have been due at the High Court, had the inspectors not gained a time extension. Foley left the office at 1.30pm. Some time in the small hours of the following day Foley was driving on Monkstown Road, near his home, when he was stopped by a garda. He was taken to a garda station, where he refused to supply a urine or blood specimen.

Just over a year earlier, on 6 December 1990, Foley had been stopped in the same area when Garda Noel Heaslip saw Foley's black Mercedes crashing a red light, stopping and starting for no apparent reason and weaving in a right-hand lane. The garda asked Foley to step out of the car. Foley seemed quite indignant. When the garda mentioned the red light Foley said the lights were broken. He was asked to blow into a breathalyser. He held the gadget to his mouth and blew around it. When given a second breathalyser he didn't blow properly into that one either. He was brought to Blackrock garda station.

There, before agreeing to give a blood or urine sample, he asked for a meal. It was refused. He was requested to give a sample of urine. Foley said he wasn't able to. He was asked to give a blood sample. He refused, saying he had a fear of disease. He was charged with crashing a red light and refusing to give a sample.

Now, on 19 December 1991, a point once scheduled as the climax of the Greencore investigation, Foley was again in trouble with the police, again refusing to give a blood or urine sample. He was charged accordingly and was at his office the following morning at 9am and worked a thirteen-hour day.

The final report of the Foley/Barry inquiry was delivered to the High Court on 25 February 1992. The twenty-eight days originally allotted for the investigation had grown to eighty-four days, at £1,750 a day for Foley, the same for Barry, and £10,000 each on top as retainers. Between them, Foley and Barry's fees amounted to £678,507, and there were other costs of £562,929. A total of £1.24m. The granting of the extension beyond 18 December, the 'halfpenny worth of time' mentioned by Mr Justice Kevin Lynch, added fifty-nine days to the inquiry, at a cost in inspectors' fees alone of £206,500.

The report was published on 3 March 1992. This was about two weeks before Foley appeared in Dun Laoghaire District Court, where he was found guilty of crashing a red light and refusing to give a sample of blood or urine back in December 1990. Judge Hubert Wine fined Foley £250 and disqualified him from driving for a year. By now, the saga that started with the financial ambitions of the Gladebrook Four was about to take another turn, as word spread of the scale of the fees charged to investigate the Greencore scandal. Some harsh things were said.

· · · · ·

In the days following the release of the report the matter of the inspectors' fees was raised in the Dáil. As a result of the controversy, Jim Tunney, then Chairman of the Fianna Fáil parliamentary party, was interviewed on the Pat Kenny radio show. The next day, the *Irish Independent* carried a report of Tunney's comments. Two days later the *Sunday Independent* carried a commentary by Senator Shane Ross, who was scathing about the fees.

There was a blizzard of libel writs. Ciaran Foley sued Independent Newspapers, as publishers of the *Irish Independent* and *Sunday Independent*. He sued Jim Tunney, who spoke on the Pat Kenny radio show. He sued RTE for broadcasting Tunney. He sued the *Irish Press* for reporting Tunney's comments. He sued Geraldine Collins of the *Irish Independent*, who wrote the story about Tunney's comments on the radio show. He sued Máirtín McCormaic, who wrote a story on the same page as Geraldine Collins's story, but who didn't write about Foley. He sued Senator Shane Ross.

Aidan Barry issued similar writs. A litigant can chose to go to the High Court, where the case is decided by a jury, and where damages are unlimited, or to the Circuit Court, where there is no jury and maximum damages are £30,000. Foley and Barry chose the Circuit Court. Foley's case came to court a year later, in March 1993. Six months before that, Ciaran Foley had another date in court. In September 1992 he went before Judge Donnchadh Ó Buachalláin at Dun Laoghaire District Court on a charge of refusing a urine or blood sample back on 19 December 1991. He was found guilty. When the judge heard that Foley had a previous conviction for the same offence, he fined him £400 and banned him from driving for three years.

· · · · ·

When the libel case opened in the Circuit Court in March 1993 Ciaran Foley took the witness stand and told Judge Frank Spain how he felt when he read Shane Ross's article. He was 'very distressed', he said. He was 'quite in bits over it'. He said he suffered 'general disdain from large sections of the public' because of what was written about him. He said that what was most important was what judges would think of him. 'I was concerned as to what a judge in the Supreme Court would think of my character when I come in to plead a case.'

The proceedings would focus largely on an opinion piece written by Shane Ross in the *Sunday Independent*. Ross, a Fine Gael supporter, stockbroker and card-carrying right-winger, was outraged by the costs of the inquiry. 'The inspectors were ripping off the state,' he wrote. Ross was careful not to accuse the inspectors of illegality: 'They appear to have done an efficient job,' he wrote, 'but in the process they have decided to charge fees of an immoral, not illegal, magnitude. £250,000 per inspector for six months' work is a public scandal in itself.'

In fact, Ross underestimated the amount the inspectors received. It was in excess of £300,000 each. 'The inspectors were appointed to counter the culture of greed; they have turned out to be a part of it. Their brief was to protect the taxpayer; they're milking him.' Ross added, 'The government turns out to be a good mark, an easy target for predators.' One six-word sentence he used was to have consequences: 'No fees were agreed in advance.'

It quickly became clear that Máirtín McCormaic shouldn't have been sued. He hadn't written anything about which Ciaran Foley was complaining. Geraldine Collins had merely reported what Jim Tunney said. Jim Tunney, now a former TD, a careful speaker who took pride in his enunciation, said that abomination was the 'most gentle word I could abstract from my vocabulary' to describe the inspectors' fees. He also called the fees 'a professional obscenity'. People had complained to him about the fees 'almost hourly'. In his constituency there were countless thousands of people whose income was £35 to £100 a week. At that remark, Colm Condon SC, for Ciaran Foley, objected: 'This is not a political meeting.' Judge Spain asked Tunney to confine himself to answering the questions.

Shane Ross gave evidence that as a senator he had been the recipient of public outrage at the level of fees, when people were being asked to tighten their belts because of serious recession and with such high unemployment. Colm Condon asked what Senator Ross meant by writing that Mr Foley was 'ripping off the state'.

Ross said that he meant that Foley was charging excessive fees. Condon said that the words meant that his client was stealing from the state. Ross said that if he had been saying Foley was stealing he would not have said in the article that Foley had done nothing illegal.

'Tell us what the culture of greed is, in your opinion,' said Condon.

'I suppose . . .' said Ross.

'Stealing!' said Condon, loudly.

Ross said something about making a clear analogy.

'Stealing!' said Condon, more loudly than before.

Ross said something about the unacceptable face of capital.

'Stealing!' said Condon, even more loudly.

Mr Condon now asked a question that would have consequences. He asked if Ross still considered Mr Foley to be a predator.

Ross thought for several seconds and then said, 'Yes.'

Judge Spain gave his verdict. It was not libellous for Jim Tunney to use the words 'abomination' and 'professional obscenity', or for the *Irish Independent* to report that he used those words. Foley's case against Tunney, McCormaic, Collins and the *Irish Independent* failed.

Judge Spain said that although Shane Ross had written that the inspectors had done an efficient job and that their fees were 'immoral but not illegal', that was not good enough. Senator Ross's descriptions of the inspectors as 'ripping off the state', 'milking' the taxpayers and being 'predators' on the taxpayers meant that the inspectors were dishonest and venal. Mr Foley would succeed against Senator Ross and against the *Sunday Independent* for publishing that article.

He awarded Mr Foley £30,000 in damages, the maximum allowable in the Circuit Court. Judge Spain said his decision to award the maximum damages was influenced by the fact that in the witness box Senator Ross maintained a 'stubborn adherence' to the words he had used in the article. 'Predator' was a word which Ross held to as a description of Ciaran Foley. It was Senator Ross's view, sincerely held, whatever its accuracy, that Ciaran Foley was a financial predator. Foley's lawyer, Colm Condon, very deliberately asked Ross, who was under oath, if he still considered Foley to be a predator. Ross had three choices in the seconds during which he considered his reply: he could commit perjury and claim that was no longer his view; he could refuse to answer the question, and face a charge of contempt of court; or he could answer it truthfully. By refusing to commit perjury, refusing to show contempt for the court, by answering truthfully, Ross inspired the judge to award maximum damages.

In July 1993, confirming the fears of the civil servants who negotiated the fees, the Dáil Public Accounts Committee discussed the Greencore inquiry costs and outrage was expressed. Tim Dalton, secretary of the Department of Justice, said his department had been presented with a *fait accompli*, because the fees had been agreed with the inspectors after they were appointed.

Deputy Pat Rabbitte suggested that the indication by the inspectors that they would go to the High Court if the costs of the inquiry were challenged was tantamount to 'polite blackmail'. He said that more effective ways of carrying out such inquiries should be looked at.

Mr Dalton replied: 'As a taxpayer, I could not disagree with that sentiment.'

Another member of the committee, Deputy Padraic McCormick of Fine Gael, saw something to complain about in the fact that the inspectors claimed payment for a seven-day week. 'Not alone were they paid exorbitant fees,' he said, 'but they have no respect for the Sabbath.'

Shane Ross and the *Sunday Independent* appealed to the High Court, where the case was heard by Mr Justice Geoghegan. It was a re-run of the original trial, with Foley saying how hurt he was by the article and Ross claiming fair comment. Foley said he was shattered by being accused of 'ripping off the state'. He said he believed the words to mean he stole money from the state. His lawyer produced a dictionary definition that said 'ripping off' means stealing. The lawyer for the *Sunday Independent* produced a dictionary definition that said 'ripping off' means overcharging.

Justice Geoghegan said that the appeal failed on two separate grounds. One necessary ground for a defence of fair comment, he said, was that the facts must be truly stated. He said that the facts were not truly stated in Shane Ross's article. It was the sentence, 'No fees were agreed in advance', that mattered. This sentence was true and accurate. No fees were agreed in advance between the two inspectors and the state. The sentence was libellous not because of what Ross wrote but because of what he didn't write.

Mr Justice Geoghegan said that Senator Ross had erred by not mentioning that the fees were eventually agreed. 'Any ordinary reader' of the article, he said, would have understood that the inspectors sent in their bills without any agreement having been reached. Therefore, the article was libellous. If instead of, 'No fees were agreed in advance', Ross had written, 'The fees were agreed only after the inspectors had been at work for a month', the sentence would not have been libellous.

Ross believed that it was implicit in the use of the term 'in advance' that fees were agreed subsequently. That was not the judge's view.

Judge Geoghegan said that a second ground on which the appeal failed was that the offending article 'imputed dishonourable and immoral conduct' on Mr Foley's part. The judge said that the article clearly alleged that Mr Foley 'deliberately took advantage of the state and the taxpayer' to receive excessive remuneration.

The term 'ripping off' could not be used. The judge said that he accepted that one might complain that a restaurant or shop was charging prices which were 'a rip off', and that that would not constitute an allegation of immoral conduct. But to say that 'the inspectors were ripping off the state' implies that the inspectors were stealing in the moral sense. From this judgment, it appears that if Ross had written that Foley and Barry's fees were 'a rip off' it would not be libellous. To say they were 'ripping off the state' was libellous.

The use of the word 'predators' also imputed immoral conduct, said the judge. He confirmed the Circuit Court verdict and awarded Mr Foley £30,000, plus costs.

In awarding the damages, Judge Geoghegan said, 'One can only speculate as to why the action was not instituted in the High Court.' Higher damages would have been possible in the High Court. In the High Court the case would have been decided by a jury, not a judge.

There remained the writs issued by the other inspector, Aidan Barry. In the wake of the Foley case the *Sunday Independent* sought to have Aidan Barry's action moved to the High Court. This was opposed by Mr Barry. In April 1996 the *Sunday Independent* settled out of court with Mr Barry. The newspaper agreed to maintain confidentiality on the amount of money it paid to Mr Barry.

No one seemed to notice the irony, that it was the *Sunday Independent* that three years earlier delicately eased its way through the libel laws to blow open the Greencore scandal, that created the demand for an inquiry, that led to Mr Foley and Mr Barry's lucrative employment, that led to widespread complaints about their fees, that were articulated within the *Sunday Independent*, and that landed the *Sunday Independent* in the libel courts.

· · · · ·

The final twist in the saga occurred at the end of 1995, as the various pieces of litigation between the ex-Gladebrook and ex-Greencore people came to fruition. Chris Comerford was suing Greencore, to get his severance package which had been frozen. Greencore was in turn suing Comerford for breach of fiduciary duty. Comerford was suing three of his ex-associates, Keleghan, Lyons and Murphy, claiming that the Talmino loan note was the property of his adult children. They were claiming it was theirs. Greencore had, in its accounts for 1991, put aside £4,000,000 to cope with the aftermath of the scandal, including the legal rows and possible payment of the Talmino loan note.

The Curran Report into the scandal came to the conclusion that Comerford owned the Talmino shares. The Foley-Barry report came to the conclusion that he didn't.

Meanwhile, one of the Gladebrook Four, Michael Tully, who had taken Comerford's side in the dispute, was also suing Greencore in order to get his frozen severance package, and for damages for personal injuries and distress. And he was in turn being sued by Greencore for failing in his duties as company secretary.

All of this was complicated by Greencore's uneasiness about an EU interest in the company, relating to alleged breaches of European competition law during the 1980s. There were efforts under the discovery process to bring into court a number of documents which Greencore might have found embarrassing to have put on the public record.

When the Comerford action reached the High Court in November 1995 there were a number of postponements, as out-of-court settlement negotiations were carried out, covering all the actions involving Comerford, his former Gladebrook associates and Greencore, and by 7 November the shape of a settlement had been agreed.

The Talmino loan note, with accumulated interest, now worth a total of £2.4 million, would be torn up. Comerford would receive a pension from Greencore. This was estimated to be a payment totalling around £70,000, about half his £135,000 salary, annually for the rest of his life. Greencore would also pay a substantial proportion of Comerford's legal costs, and those of his old Gladebrook associates.

Comerford would not receive the severance payment, a company car or share options. Comerford was well off, however, now being employed by Fyffes, the fruit company, as a consultant.

The following month, Michael Tully, former Greencore company secretary, went to court with his claim. He told a sad tale of losing his £93,000 a year job, ending up with £120 a week on the dole. His health suffered, he claimed, and for a time it was touch and go as to whether he would live.

After a few days of this a settlement was announced. Tully, who had received £500,000 at the time of the Gladebrook sale, would receive another £425,000 for the sale of his shares, plus interest of £170,000, and Greencore would pay over £250,000 of Tully's legal fees. Tully will, on reaching the age of sixty-five, receive a substantial pension from Greencore, based on his £93,000 salary. And that was the end of the Greencore saga.

No charges were ever laid against anyone, there was no proof of any laws broken. People got rich, the world moved on. Politicians were occasionally heard to complain about a rising level of scepticism among the citizens.

⑫ The Small Legend of Karl Crawley

The three screws didn't know much about guns. One of them thought the big, dark automatic that Karl Crawley was pulling out was a Luger. But Karl didn't care whether the screws could recognise a Colt .45 when they saw one. Just so long as they had enough cop to do what they were told.

'Freeze, you bastards!'

If you're a screw in Mountjoy prison and Karl Crawley points a gun at you — you freeze. Because you know this guy is no cream puff. This is the guy whose belly has been cut open so many times that it's scarred and mauled like it's been run over by a tank track. He's been in and out of prison so often they've got a special cell for him. He's been declared insane maybe a dozen times and he's got forearms as thick as beer barrels and fists like hammers and he's used them since God knows when to knock lumps out of anything in a uniform. So, watch it, take it easy.

But what the hell kind of gun is that, and where did he get it?

Karl was telling them to open the hard case's cell. First get the hard case out, that's the plan. Then he'd get the others out. The Littlejohns and the UDA blokes. It was going to be dicey, getting up out of the high security basement and then out of the prison itself. And then his troubles would be only starting.

Already that young screw was beginning to fidget, like maybe he was thinking about taking a chance with the Colt .45.

Fuck him, if he wanted to have a go. Karl Crawley was ready. He'd been breaking out of places since he was nine, which was all of fourteen years ago.

. . . . .

The buses went this way and that way — but which one went into town? The reason Karl Crawley didn't know much about buses was that he had spent all but four or five months of his first nine years in orphanages, and he didn't get out much.

It was just after six in the evening when Karl went over the wall and legged it away from St Philomena's. The first thing he'd done was buy some sweets with the money he'd stolen in the orphanage before escaping. Now he had enough money left for the bus fare. But this was Stillorgan and Karl's family home was in Harmonstown, somewhere over on the other side of the river. That meant getting a bus into town and Karl didn't know how to do that.

He wandered down to Stillorgan village and found an old man standing at a bus stop. Karl, in the neat corduroy jacket and short pants that was orphanage uniform, asked the old man if this was where you got the bus into town. The old man was nice. He invited Karl back to his nearby home for tea.

Back at St Philomena's, Karl Crawley's brother, Mick, was getting the business.

'Where's Karl?' The enquiry was made with some ferocity. There was no way Mick was going to squeal on Karl. Anyway, before Karl did a runner Mick too had outlined how he was going over the wall himself next day and he and Karl had arranged to meet in town.

'Where's Karl?' *Clatter, thump, clatter.* The cops, alerted by the nice old man, arrived at the old man's house while Karl was having tea. The cops were nice. They gave Karl a ride in the back of their big blue Consul squad car. They chatted to him. One of the cops gave him a few pence. Karl was fascinated by the big torch in the back of the car. When the kids from St Philomena's went on an outing to town each

Christmas the most coveted present to come back with was a torch. You could have great crack shining the torch around the dormitory at night, and you could use it to read under the bedclothes.

But this cop torch was a powerful square thing with a handle. A thing like that would light up the dorm like a searchlight.

By the time the squad car arrived back at St Philomena's Karl had nicked the torch.

That was 1961.

·····

Karl had been handed over to St Philomena's in 1958, when he was six. It was run by the nuns and discipline was strict, ten times worse than the Bird's Nest Home in Dun Laoghaire, where Karl had been left when he was three months old.

Bernadette O'Boyle, from Donegal, was still a teenager when she married Larry Crawley in Dublin in the 1940s. Her first child, Paddy, died of tuberculosis at the age of two. Her next child, a daughter, was born in 1945. She had three more daughters, in 1946, 1947 and 1948. In 1950 she had a son. She had six more sons, in 1951, 1952, 1953, 1954, 1956 and 1958. By then her husband's haulage business was gone — and so was he, to England.

Karl Crawley was the eighth of the twelve children, born on 21 April 1952.

Alone, the woman simply couldn't cope, no matter how she loved her children. Most of the sons served time in orphanages. The Bird's Nest Home was the first, and for Karl that lasted six years. He left the orphanage via Harcourt Street Hospital, where he had a protracted stay. The reason for the stay was severe bruising. In the child's mind, memories of beatings mixed with the memory of a fall, talk of blood poisoning and suggestions that he might be sent to Cherry Orchard Fever Hospital. Instead, he was sent home. After about a month at home in Harmonstown he was handed over to St Philomena's in Stillorgan.

Mick Crawley was sent there too. And Philip and David and Tommy and Paul Crawley. Philip was taken home by Mrs Crawley the same day she handed in Tommy and Paul. Karl was about eight and Tommy and Paul were about six years younger. Until then Karl hadn't known they existed.

'Hey, Karl, these are your brothers, look after them.' Maybe not those exact words, but that's what it sounded like to Karl.

Sometimes there were a couple of dozen kids in the orphanage, sometimes a lot more than that, maybe eighty. Kids came and went but the Crawleys stayed on month after month, year after year. Them and the kids known as the mongolies — the children afflicted with Down's Syndrome.

Like any place where kids gather in numbers there was toughness, violence, antics that were careless, ruthless or cruel. You looked out for yourself and your own kind. Although Karl was younger than Philip and Mick he had early on assumed the responsibility of leadership, which meant making himself someone to be reckoned with. Top cat.

As well as the usual play-acting, kicking up a row, dashing through dorms and wrecking the beds, there were acts of violence aimed at asserting strength, punishing opponents or knocking the wind out of potential rivals. Outside, getting your eye dyed meant catching a thump that left you with a black eye. In here it meant a guy coming up to you with a big smile on his face and his hand jerks up and *flick!*, he's painting your eye with the little brush from a bottle of nail varnish.

Or it's the small hours of the morning and the Crawleys lie awake until everyone else is asleep. Even the woman in the curtained-off area at the end of the dorm who's job it is to supervise the kids and report any misdeeds to the nuns (and who was the unwitting source of supply of nail varnish). Then Karl and his brothers would slide out of bed, lie on the floor, creep along under the next bed and the next. The whole dorm apparently at rest, and below the beds the Crawleys moving inexorably towards the victim. Put a pillow over his face, and for twenty seconds or so the waking, gasping kid is subjected to a storm of punches to the body.

Then, scatter and creep and slide back to bed before the victim's howls bring the nail varnish woman and the nuns. But the kids know the who and the why, and the lesson is clear: nobody messes with the Crawley brothers.

Violence is how things work. Sometimes you get caught doing something you shouldn't and the nuns give you a thumping. Other times you get away with it. Sometimes you get done over for something you didn't do. Back in the Bird's Nest, all the kids sitting on benches lined along the wall: 'You, come out here.' And in front of everyone you got walloped. The same in Philomena's, except it was the nuns coming into the dorm at night. 'I want you and you and you.'

And, *clatter*. You got out of Philomena's sometimes. Sunday morning, everyone lining up in their black berets and gabardine overcoats and getting a penny to put on the plate in church. Or an outing, where the nuns would break the kids into groups and put an older boy in charge of each group. And you could keep them all in line through fear. Because now you had her on your side.

Paddy Andrews died on a Monday. He'd got a hammering. Karl had got one too, for something or for nothing much. Just a routine hammering. And the kids came up the stairs and walked into the room, same as always, and Paddy Andrews was lying there and the nuns were fussing over him and one had a mirror near his mouth to see if he was still breathing. Then a woman doctor came up and looked at him and told them they were kidding themselves, Paddy Andrews was a goner.

Which was when Karl went over the wall and had to be brought back by the nice coppers in the big blue Consul. Because they'd killed his pal Paddy Andrews and if Paddy was a bit wild Karl was a bit wilder and odds on they'd kill him too.

And even years later, long after he knew that Paddy Andrews died not from a beating but from a burst appendix, Karl would talk about how they had killed his pal Paddy Andrews, they beat him up and he died from it.

Lesson: this isn't kid stuff, it can kill you. You could handle that if the rules were straight. But the rules changed. 'I want you', and a nun was taking Karl down the steps to the basement with the big furnace and the coke all around. He'd stolen £1 from the tailor's room, 10 two shilling pieces. It was the nun with the hurley stick that she used on the back of your legs and the big teeth sticking out on her face like a

301

vampire's, and before she could do a thing Karl had the poker that they used for the furnace and was smacking it off her head.

The nun went down on the ground and lay there, groaning. Karl stood there, and for a second thought of finishing her off. He turned and ran up the stairs, went to bed, told no one, shocked by what he'd done and the fear of what would come of it.

All that came of it was a couple of clatters next day. Lesson: sometimes you hit back, hard, and they back off a little.

Not long afterwards Karl was pushing a merry-go-round, giving some smaller kids a ride. He swung the seat, causing it to jerk against the centre pole, and in retaliation one of the kids threw a bobbin from a reel of thread. Karl ducked, a window cracked. You don't squeal on others, so when Karl was accused he simply denied breaking the window, but didn't squeal on the other kid. He was expelled from St Philomena's.

Lesson: the rules mean nothing, there is no justice. That was 1962. Karl was ten. Karl didn't know it then but he had only another eighteen months to do of the twelve year stretch he would serve in orphanages. After three weeks at home his mother brought him back to St Philomena's. The nuns weren't having any of that. They gave him six shillings and sent him off to St Vincent's, Glasnevin, run by the Christian Brothers. There, Karl got most of his formal schooling. And more of his informal education of what the world is about. He learned about sex, about women, and about men who like boys.

But Karl was getting on a bit now. After eighteen months in St Vincent's he walked out and didn't come back. Philip had been taken out, and besides, Karl was growing up and had spent twelve years in a narrow world and he wanted something more.

Karl's mother couldn't take him in. So he slept rough. But that was all right. There was a big world waiting and Karl Crawley was heading out into it.

That was 1964. Karl was twelve.

· · · · ·

Bernadette Crawley had a tough life. Poverty more often than not, and eleven kids to bring up on her own. At one time, she told friends, she lived with some of the kids in a shed. The result, with the kids being left in orphanages whenever Ma couldn't cope, did not make for a stable home life, yet remarkable bonds of family affection existed between Ma and the kids. The relationship between Karl and his mother swung erratically, erupting at times into violent rows. In November 1977 Karl would be charged at the Dublin District Court with assaulting his mother. There would be times when she would call the police to the house and have him taken away.

Yet one of the biggest causes of anxiety for Karl in the prison years to come would be if his mother didn't visit him. On one occasion, having been refused permission to visit, Bernadette Crawley threatened to sit-in in Mountjoy until she got to see Karl. On another occasion a friend called to the house in Ballybough (to which the family moved from Harmonstown) and found it stripped of furniture. Karl, in prison at the time, had wanted a leather coat and his mother had sold furniture to buy one.

Ma had been dealt a tough hand — and she played it. It had been put up to her and she handled it. Playing the hand you're dealt, handling the things that are put up to you, in Karl's world these are matters of pride, honour and self-respect.

Bernadette Crawley emigrated to Australia in 1977, with one of her daughters. She died there in 1981.

· · · · ·

At first, Karl was a bit wary of the world. It never occurs to you that you're good at what you do until you get out there and see how those guys you thought were hot ain't really that hot. Like, you walk down the street and you see guys in leather jackets and tight blue jeans and you figure that every guy in a leather jacket and tight blue jeans is as tough as he looks, maybe even carrying a blade, and you give him a lot of space.

But then you get to know these guys and know what they can do — and you know that up against you they're not worth a toss. You know that you can do it, whatever it is, whatever it takes, if it's put up to you. You start to feel different, special.

In his age group, in his tiny patch of Dublin turf, Karl was a small legend, a tough guy, a guy to be walked around, to be careful of, a guy who could take care of himself, or throw his weight around if he felt like it.

What Karl was good at was the physical things. He wasn't a big guy, but he was strong, a natural athlete. Even way back in the Bird's Nest where there was a fire escape that was a thrill to climb. And in St Philomena's there was a trick bar, a gymnastic device — and by and by there wasn't anything Karl couldn't do on the bar. A great way to show off, and he enjoyed it too. Spend half a day swinging by his legs if he felt like it.

Karl could go up a wall or a drainpipe quicker than most people could fall off one. First — let's say it's a shop — you go in and buy something. Take your time, make sure you're not served first. Gives you a chance to listen out the place. You can usually tell if there are people upstairs.

Go out, up the pipe, in the window, your mate down below to catch the proceeds when you toss them out. Worst that ever happened was finding a dog upstairs. Karl stuck it in a wardrobe.

Sometimes Karl stayed at home with Ma, at other times he looked after himself. There was work sometimes, dead end jobs. Karl usually screwed up, though, after a few weeks. Someone, some boss, says or does the wrong thing, treats Karl like he was dirt — 'Up yours!', Karl was off. He was always awkward with strangers, preferred to stick with the kind of people he knew, the kind he could respect. The kind who would show respect in return.

Which is not to say that failing to hold down a job was always Karl's fault. One job was in a factory, sweeping the floor. The boss points to his Jaguar out in the yard. 'Clean that, Karl.' Fair enough. Karl wanted to do a good job. He used Vim scouring powder. The Jag's lovely paint job went ragged, Karl lost the job.

When he was thirteen Karl lied about his age and got a job as a helper on an Esso truck. He liked the job, travelling up and down the country. It lasted nine months, then the firm did a productivity deal with the union and one of the consequences was Karl being made redundant. He never again held a job for that length of time.

Between 1964 and 1969, between the ages of twelve and seventeen, Karl enjoyed his longest stretch of freedom. A mixture of work, crime, drugs and travel. The crime was a natural. It was easy, it was a challenge, it was exciting, it provided money. There was nothing else in Karl's world that provided those things. Smash and grab was a favourite and Karl's speciality, given his physical abilities, was vaulting over shop counters for a snatch at a handful of cash.

Karl was one of the best dressed dudes in town. Nicked the clothes. Powder blue jeans, stuff like that. He was particular about the people he hung around with. Hughie, John-Joe, Jimmy, a good team. Heading off down to stroke something — 'Hey, come on, change your clothes! You're not walking up the road with me, dressed like that!'

It might be doing an orchard, or maybe smashing the window of an off-licence and making off with a few bottles. One's as good as the other. Sheep as a lamb.

The drugs came easy. Later on they were always around. Everybody was heavy into cider parties and one sleeping tablet properly used was the equivalent of half a bottle of cider. Better, even. And amphetamines had you buzzing all over. It was about 1967 when Karl spent a week in Steevens's Hospital after doing too much Mandrax.

In the summer Karl and some of the guys would travel. Head for the Isle of Man, work the restaurants for the season. One summer, when Karl was sixteen, he and Mick and a guy named Blackie were doing the season and went to eat in a café. They were told the place was closed, though there were lots of people in there. A nice way of saying you're not being served, scram. Pride was injured. One thing led to another and the owner got a thumping. That brought Karl's first taste of prison. The cop-shop was on the ground floor, the court above that, the nick on the next floor up. Handy set-up, that.

The deal was a £16 fine or a month the hard way. Blackie had got away. Mick used his wages to buy out. Karl had no money. He did the month in the nick.

That wasn't Karl's first conviction, though. That happened when he was working in a hardware shop on Capel Street. The shop was easygoing, let you bring your mate in to help. Karl brought in a mate and one day they left with a load of stuff. Fancy cutlery, picnic knives, combs.

Karl knew parts of the city, Roches Stores, Bolgers, places like that, from shop-lifting. But he didn't know any better than to walk down Store Street, Karl and his mate sharing out the combs and the picnic knives and they walking right past the cop-shop in broad daylight.

'Hold it there a minute, you two!'

The way Karl told it, the two of them got a going over in the cop shop. Ma kicked up murder with the cops. They got probation, so that worked out not too bad.

．．．．．

By 1969 Karl had got all the warning shots he was going to get. The next one would be for real. Karl wasn't a kid any more, he was pushing seventeen and the adult world was about to take him seriously at last. It must have been a bit like running down a steep hill with a huge boulder gathering speed behind you. You could run faster, but you knew that in the end the boulder was going to catch up and flatten you.

Karl was going to get smacked, hard. And the nature of the boy and of his experiences were such that he was going to smack right back. Even had he foreknowledge of the horrific things that the next ten years would bring it is doubtful if Karl could have done anything other than keep running down that hill, waiting for the boulder to catch up.

Anyway, when it's put up to you, whatever it is, you don't back off from it, you go right at it.

In January 1969 Karl was nicked and sentenced to six months in St Patrick's Institution for Young Offenders, found guilty on fourteen counts of house-breaking. It was just three months before his seventeenth birthday.

．．．．．

When you're Karl Crawley and you go into the nick it goes something like this. (Except you don't see it all at first. It takes a while before you work it out, figure all the angles. At first you're just doing your stretch and what happens comes naturally, you don't even think of it as a big manipulation.)

When you look at the screws what you see are dummies, culchies from one-horse towns. Coppers aren't so bad, but there's nothing lower than a screw. Hard men, they think. But they don't know what hard is. And they expect you to do what they say.

And where are they going to learn their job? They learn it from pulling strokes and watching your reactions. They play their games, try to figure what works, how they can manipulate you. Doing this, sometimes they lean on you, provoke you.

When you're a warder and you get Karl Crawley to lock up it goes something like this. You have a guy who has come to despise authority and who will lash out if he feels the need. He doesn't respect you, yet you are responsible for getting him through the day, from breakfast to lock-up, with the least possible trouble. He shows no fear and will do what he wants regardless of the consequences to others or to himself. If you just lock him away they'll call you vicious — if you give him enough freedom to create trouble they'll call you negligent.

And the screws are doing this for a living. Their careers are affected by the way they handle you. Take Soldier. This was much later on, in Mountjoy, when Karl was someone to be reckoned with, a con with a fierce reputation. Soldier was a big thick who used to be in the British Army. One day he says to Karl that the Bigshot will be coming down later.

'Right, Karl. When he comes along you come over to me and ask me for something. Any stupid thing. And I'll say no, and you be polite, right?'

There's an ounce of tobacco in this for Karl, so he plays it cute. The Bigshot comes down through the wing and Karl toddles over and asks Soldier if, sir, I could please have a brush, sir, to sweep the cell, sir, a bit of dirt, sir, if it's not too much trouble, sir.

And Soldier squares his shoulders and says, 'Fuck off, I'm busy!'

And Karl keeps a straight face and does his thank you, sir, and shuffles off. And Soldier makes points with the Bigshot for having this tough guy well under control.

And Karl gets his ounce. Sometimes it's just a little gift, maybe a porn magazine, from a screw. A little gesture of humanity. You take it, but you know that he's just trying to make points with you. Manipulation.

Other times it's a bit of the heavy. And that's how you manipulate right back. Pick someone, as high up in the pecking order as possible, hold him responsible. 'If I get it, you get it.' Usually the reaction is that it's best to leave that head case alone. Sometimes you have to make good on the threat. Nothing personal, but they have to know that you mean what you say. Maybe wait a week, pick your time, then do it.

Maybe you do the screw. Maybe you damage something. Like the lights. That would become a regular. The light fitting up in the ceiling. Jump, smack, bang! And one day a senior warder gets frantic and shouts at you that every time you break one of those light fittings it costs him £38 to fix it.

'Thank you, sir!' drawls Karl. Now Karl knows precisely how much bother he can promise, at thirty-eight quid a go, to the penny.

You can't let them run your life for you. Sure, they'll thump you, you'll thump back, you'll get hurt, but what's new? It's fifty-fifty. The screws have a job to do but you have a life to live. So it's all a big manipulation. A fucking man-ip-you-lay-shun, right?

. . . . .

Karl Crawley's transition from ordinary decent criminal to some kind of small legend within the community of crime and punishment was a seamless one. His legend would derive not from any feats of major lawlessness but from the relentless toughness that such a small-time criminal showed in dealing with the hand dealt to him. He would spend three-quarters of the next decade in prison, in a series of short sentences, always for crimes of a relatively minor nature — house-breaking, stealing a car, stealing drugs from chemist shops. His violence would be confined within the community of crime and punishment — mostly against police and warders, a couple of times lashing out at civilians in an attempt to prevent capture.

He would be declared insane twelve times and declared sane twelve times — probably the only person on the island who could point to twelve official testimonials to his sanity. He would make thirteen escape attempts. His stomach would be opened a dozen times as a consequence of his actions, until surgeons said they could operate no more without killing him. A special cell would be set aside for him in the basement of Mountjoy prison — the Crawley cell.

The thing was, they thought they could tell Karl what to do, which is what jailers are paid to think. Karl didn't like being told what to do. He was impudent, scornful. It didn't have to be a big issue. Just a routine instruction from a warder could bring a cold, contemptuous response from Karl, the words spaced out and delivered with equal emphasis: 'Fuck . . . you.'

It wasn't long before he was put on report for insubordination and the Governor of St Patrick's looked Karl up and down and told him he was here to learn a lesson. 'I bet you never thought there was a place like this.'

A place like this? Karl was looking at the Governor and thinking, I can take a thousand times whatever you can dish out. You're looking at a throw-back from a kinky fucking nun factory, you are.

Three days number one, four days number two, something else number three. Number one was bread and water. Number two was bread and water with a bowl of porridge in the morning. And for number three they put margarine on the bread, or something like that. So what? Karl could take their mickey mouse punishments, or anything else they threw at him, and the joy of seeing the look on the guy's face when you told him to fuck off, that made it worth it.

Karl was released in July 1969 and was back in St Patrick's in September, for house-breaking. This time he got depressed as well as rebellious. He put his athletic talents to use and climbed on to the roof of the prison. When they got him down they declared him insane and sent him to The Drum for three months. The Drum is Dundrum Mental Hospital.

In April 1976, in the course of a *habeas corpus* hearing in the High Court, the Clinical Director of Psychiatry of the Eastern Health Board, Dr Brian McCaffrey, would be asked if Dundrum was suitable for Karl Crawley.

'No, my lord. The patients in Dundrum Mental Hospital are different from Karl Crawley's type. Most of them are psychotic individuals who have had schizophrenic illnesses, psychoses of different types — he is different from them.'

The then Chief Psychiatrist of Dundrum, Dr John J. Smith, would be asked if he considered 'that from Karl's point of view Dundrum is an appropriate place to have him'.

'Well, no, I would not regard it — I would agree with Dr McCaffrey that it is not the ideal situation to treat his type of case.'

'Well, is it an *appropriate* place to treat his type of case?'

'No, I do not think it is appropriate to treat his type of case.'

'Do you consider that the presence of Karl in Dundrum has any effect on the institution as a therapeutic institution?'

'Oh, I do, yes, it is quite disruptive.'

The prison authorities would, between October 1969 and September 1975, send Karl Crawley to The Drum twelve times. When things got too rough The Drum would be used to hold Karl down, sedate him with drugs. Dundrum Mental Hospital would be used as what Dr Brian McCaffrey would describe in the High Court as 'a chemical strait-jacket'.

· · · · ·

At first The Drum was just another challenge. Karl and another patient got up on the roof and stayed there for four hours. It even had compensations of a kind. Karl first mainlined — injected drugs intra-venously — in Dundrum. A patient who was in the hospital for treatment of drug addiction provided an injection of Diconal. After two or three minutes the great feeling started, Karl lying sweating in his cell, and it lasted for about five hours, thinning off at the end.

In January 1970 Karl carried out a dangerous escape involving a long jump from a house on to the outside wall of The Drum. He got down from the wall, chased by the screws, ran through a number of back gardens, fell through a glasshouse, gashing his hand, and was finally caught in a football field. It may be that this attempt went some way to prove Karl's sanity, as he was transferred back to St Patrick's.

Further rows with the screws. The cell was damp, he refused to clean it. He was put in the cellar, which comprised four cells in the basement. And it was here that Karl began the practice that would become an important part of his legend.

A screw comes in. 'What happened to this spoon, where's the handle?' Only the bowl of the spoon remained.

Karl had swallowed the handle. They X-rayed him in the Mater Hospital, found nothing, declared him insane and sent him back to The Drum on 6 February. Karl swallowed another spoon on 20 February. He was taken to hospital and passed the spoon after three days. They took him back to Dundrum. He swallowed another spoon.

Having taken his defiance as far as he could by impudence and violence, Karl had stumbled on a bizarre way of manipulating the authorities. They could lock him up, punish him with bread and water, put him in solitary, push him around — but they were obliged to look after his health. Anytime they thought they had him snookered he could pop something in his mouth and they would have to take him to hospital.

They began X-raying him daily. Karl was put in an isolation cell. No spoons. He swallowed part of a ventilator grill. In a fight with a patient he got a punch which caused the metal inside to perforate his stomach. On 20 March 1970 three pieces of metal were removed from his stomach in St Kevin's Hospital. He contracted pneumonia and spent four months in the hospital. When he left the hospital, with three months of his sentence left to serve, he weighed five and a half stone.

· · · · ·

Three months after his release from St Patrick's Karl was back in prison, this time Mountjoy, after stealing and crashing a car. He was certified insane and dispatched to The Drum three days before Christmas 1970. On Christmas Day he and another prisoner used a rope made of bed sheets to climb out of the ball alley to freedom. The authorities left the bedsheets hanging from the ball alley. Two weeks later another pair used them to escape.

Karl went home to Ma in Harmonstown, and went to bed. Freedom on Christmas Day. His sister Geraldine woke him with the news that there were cops downstairs. Geraldine went down to see what the cops were after, while Karl got dressed. Geraldine came back and told Karl that they were here to ask Ma to let them know if Karl came home.

Karl went down to the parlour and walked in on the cops. The two shades got a bit anxious. Karl was told to take it easy, there were two of them and they could handle him.

'Yeah, I know.'

One of the shades stuck his chin out and said, 'I know karate.'

Karl was amused. 'Yeah, I know.'

'Would you not give yourself up?'

Karl agreed, but said he wanted a couple of hours. He would come down to the cop-shop then. The cops left. Karl went into town and met a relative. She fixed him up with clothes and money and he did a fade to England. After six weeks he was arrested. The night before they sent him back he swallowed a spoon.

That was February 1971. Karl was nineteen.

· · · · ·

The following months were a chaotic mixture of violence, isolation, smashing cells, swallowing spoons, undergoing operations and attempting to escape. Karl wore irons whenever he was released from his cell. On one occasion, while being chased on the roof, he fell thirty feet and broke his left elbow. According to an internal prison document, 'He is usually involved in any fracas and is quick with his fists if annoyed by any other person . . . he is adept at climbing and has already scaled the roof of this institution on three occasions.'

While being held in The Drum in July 1971 Karl climbed on to the roof of the hospital, protesting against being sent to The Drum and demanding that he be taken back to Mountjoy. They wouldn't, of course, give in, and Karl came down eventually. The next month he set fire to his cell in the hospital.

His sentence over, he was released in September and was back in Mountjoy on another twelve month sentence less than ten weeks later. Had he sat back and accepted his sentences, life would have been a lot easier for everyone concerned. But the rationale for his insistence on some kind of independence and control of himself was articulated as, 'I won't let them break me.' Later on he would refine this, using the old radical slogan, 'I'd rather die on my feet than live on my knees.'

Over the period of this latest sentence the prison authorities would test that resolve.

· · · · ·

On Christmas Day 1971 Karl and two other prisoners climbed on to the roof of Mountjoy in another protest. This one was over Christmas food. The protest lasted for twenty-eight hours, with the prisoners throwing slates into the prison yard below. Karl finally came down after insisting that police and the prison doctor be present to ensure that he wouldn't be beaten by the warders.

The punishment given for this was fifty-seven days on bread and water.

However, they couldn't immediately go ahead with the punishment. He had to be first declared insane and sent to The Drum. With spoons being kept out of his reach, Karl swallowed a small battery from a radio and a piece of a bed spring. He was brought to the Mater Hospital and operated on. Then he was declared insane and sent to the Drum. (Another prisoner who had copped on to the swallowing trick had been taken to the Mater at the same time and escaped from the hospital.)

During the next three months Karl was to go through his toughest experience yet. He was confined in solitary for the whole three months, twenty-four hours a day, released from his cell only for visits.

The staff of Dundrum, charged with running a mental hospital for a variety of patients suffering from psychoses, hallucinations and major mental disturbances, could do little but incarcerate Karl. Karl wasn't suffering from a treatable psychiatric disease. All they could do was keep him locked up, and give him drugs.

In the 1976 *habeas corpus* case the Eastern Health Board's Clinical Director of Psychiatry, Dr Brian McCaffrey, was asked, 'When Karl Crawley is present in Dundrum during any of the eleven or twelve occasions is anything more than simple maintenance being achieved?'

'I would say that I would think that most of the treatment there would be just custodial care.'

'Keeping him drugged for a period of time?'

'Well, that was done in '72, yes my lord, I think as a preventive measure to keep him from escaping and hoping that it might stabilise him. I think the drug treatment would just keep him in a chemical strait-jacket for months or whatever time it was, and once it was taken away he comes back as the same Karl Crawley.'

Karl, drugged to the gills, began talking aloud and answering himself. The side effects of the drugs — stiffened muscles, feelings of apprehension, biting his tongue, a feeling that his legs were up in the air — left him with a terror of Serenace, a drug sometimes administered in food or tea. Later, he refused for a time to eat the food, for fear that it was doctored. The experience also left him with a deep fear and hatred of Dundrum.

Medical records show that Serenace drops were administered to Karl Crawley at various periods both in Mountjoy and in Dundrum, on at least two occasions as much as thirty drops per day. Serenace is a colourless, tasteless, odourless drug which has a calming effect, which slows down the recipient's perceptions and actions, but which does not render him or her unconscious. It produces excellent results in the sedation and treatment of psychotics.

Karl Crawley was not a psychotic. The physical effects can be frightening, producing symptoms akin to those associated with Parkinson's Disease. The recipient of the drug experiences muscle stiffness, tremor, drooling, and when walking shuffles like an aged person, with head down and arms hanging by the sides.

The medical records show that Karl also received regular doses of such tranquillisers as Artane, Nydrane, Valium and Largactil, as well as such anti-depressants as Librium and Valamin. He also received sleeping tablets such as Mogadon and Lentizol, as well as vitamins and painkillers to help reduce the pains in his abdomen resulting from successive operations.

In a psychiatric report on Karl, conducted for the 1976 court case, Dr Brian McCaffrey concluded that 'for Karl, the essential part of being a human being is to be . . . able to consciously assess what is going on around him and to use his brain.' The barrage of drugs took away that ability for those three months and Karl lived inside his head, in some bizarre dream world.

When they released him from solitary Karl had lost control of his motor function and had to be taught how to walk.

· · · · ·

It wasn't over yet. Karl was declared sane and sent back to Mountjoy on 17 March 1972. Three days later, a month before his twentieth birthday, he was sent to Portlaoise prison to serve the fifty-seven day bread and water punishment imposed after he climbed on to the Mountjoy roof on Christmas Day. Having just spent three months incarceration as an insane person, drugged from head to toe, Karl was now to receive a stiff punishment for the act committed only days before he was declared insane.

Much of his time in Portlaoise was spent in solitary confinement, several weeks of it in total silence. The method of inflicting the punishment was two or three days on bread and water, then two or three days on normal rations.

He was given a scruffy prison suit to wear, shoes the length of the table. He was put in The Digger, a punishment area. He was instructed to paint his cell. Lilac, he was told, would be a nice colour. Karl painted the cell lilac. The next day, 9 July, he pushed his bed across the cell, jamming the door. He took a page from the *News of the World* and rolled it up to form a tube. He inserted the tube into a ventilator panel. Then he sliced the mattress and set fire to it. He had prepared the paper tube as a breathing apparatus as he didn't believe the screws would be in too much of a hurry to break down the door.

'OK, Crawley, you can have another twenty-one days' bread and water for your Guy Fawkes effort in there.'

Him and his bleeding lilac.

When Karl was released from Portlaoise in September there were four cops leaning on a squad car outside the prison. The shades were doing a John Wayne number. 'There's a bus leaving for Dublin in twenty minutes. If you're not on it we'll talk to you later.'

· · · · ·

District Justice Herman Good looked down from his bench and saw handcuffs around Karl Crawley's wrists. He asked why this was and was told of Karl's history of violence and defiance. Good suggested that if he had to be chained in court he should not be there but in a mental institution. He put the case back for a week to hear medical evidence.

By now, March 1973, Karl was becoming something of a permanent fixture in Mountjoy. In for a month, out for a month. Good would subsequently say merely that the case was 'sad' and hope that psychiatric help would be provided. It wasn't.

The violence, swallowing, climbing on the roof and drugging in The Drum continued. On 17 July Karl was segregated in The Base of Mountjoy, where he would be locked up for twenty-three hours a day.

The Base was 'B' Basement, a segregated unit used primarily for prisoners who had to be kept apart from other prisoners for their own safety. They included sex offenders, UDA members, two English men convicted of a particularly horrible murder, and the Littlejohns, two English brothers jailed for a Dublin bank robbery carried out when the two were allegedly working for British intelligence.

The Base was also used as a punishment area, where unruly prisoners could be put in solitary confinement.

Confinement in The Base became a regular feature of Karl's imprisonment. In May 1974 the prison Medical Officer, with the approval of the Governor of Mountjoy, ordered that Karl's removal from The Base was 'not to be considered'. After that, whenever Karl was sent to Mountjoy, even on a short sentence of months or weeks, or on remand, he was put into the isolation unit. Karl's regular accommodation became known to the inmates and staff as 'the Crawley cell'.

Karl's athletic abilities were by now so well honed by his continued defiance of prison restraints that he could escape with ease from normal handcuffs, or even a strait-jacket. As a result, whenever he was taken out of his cell he was fitted with Figure Eight irons. Figure Eights are metal bands linked together without any length of connecting chain. Placed around the wrists, they leave the prisoner's forearms clamped together, with the hands facing away from each other so they cannot touch.

The prison authorities denied that such instruments were used. In a document, under the signature of the Chief State Solicitor, drawn up in reply to an abortive attempt to take Karl's case to the Court of Human Rights in Strasbourg, the authorities denied that Figure Eights were used on Karl, 'nor have they been used in living memory on any prisoner'.

A person who regularly visited Karl in prison witnessed the use of Figure Eights and recalls having to roll and light Karl's cigarettes during the visits.

· · · · ·

In The Base the swallowing tactic took on a new significance for Karl. He continued the tactic even though surgeons in the Mater Hospital had warned a year earlier that any further operations to remove objects from his stomach could be fatal. Escape from The Base would be extremely difficult. The Mater Hospital would be easier. Besides, there were nurses over there. Nicer to be with than screws. Pop something into your mouth and they have to take you to hospital. Karl called it 'working my ticket to the Mater'.

In October 1974 Karl began arranging an escape attempt. He would work his ticket to the hospital, friends would spring him. A smuggled letter, explaining the details of the plan, was intercepted by the authorities in early November. Karl had been explicit in the letter and was unaware that the plan had been rumbled. On 14 November he swallowed a couple of pieces of bedspring and some broken glass. He was taken to the Mater under heavy guard. The plan was bust, but Karl wasn't giving up.

Still in the Mater on 25 November, Karl crawled through a toilet window and escaped. He made it only as far as Berkeley Road, yards from the hospital, before he was caught.

· · · · ·

It was around nine o'clock one evening in July 1975 that twenty-three-year-old Karl Crawley asked to be taken to the toilet. Two officers must be called when a prisoner is taken out of his cell in The Base. So, counting the duty officer, there were three warders present when Karl returned from the toilet.

Karl produced a Colt .45 and ordered the screws to get their fucking hands up, quick.

The three screws didn't know much about guns. One of them thought the big, dark automatic that Karl Crawley was pulling out was a Luger. But Karl didn't care whether the screws could recognise a Colt .45 when they saw one. Just so long as they had enough cop to do what they were told.

'Freeze, you bastards!' Karl ordered a screw to open the cell of another inmate, a hard case, a guy with a history of violence and armed robbery. That was the plan. Get the hard case out, he'd lead the escape from there. Then get the UDA blokes and the Littlejohns out (nothing political, just that you couldn't very well break out from The Base and not give your fellow cons a chance to do the same).

When the hard case emerged from his cell and saw Karl with the gun and the three screws grabbing air he began laughing. Karl was standing there, muttering under his breath, 'Shurrup for Christ's sake!'

The three screws were looking at one another, trying to figure what's going down.

Karl gave the hard case the gun. The giggling continued, a screw saw his chance and jumped. The great escape was over.

Karl had taken a book called *Yoga and Religion* and cut it into the shape of a gun, carving away all the bits that didn't look like a Colt .45.

After the escape attempt Karl held on to the blades he had used to cut the book, keeping them in his mouth. The screws knew he had them but could do little about it. He let them know that if they tried jumping him he would swallow the blades. He being Karl Crawley, the mad fucker with the history of swallowing anything not nailed down, they knew he wasn't kidding. They finally jumped him in the shower, where he had hidden the blades in his clothes.

· · · · ·

Until 1975 the Karl Crawley saga was known only within the community of prisoners, warders, prison officials, doctors and lawyers. Justice Herman Good's brief intervention in 1973 was the only hint that there was a world outside all of this. In 1975 Karl's mother, Bernadette Crawley, talked to political activist Máirín de Búrca, then operating an Official Sinn Féin Citizen's Advice centre.

De Búrca tried all the official channels. She wrote to the President of the High Court. No reply. She wrote to her local TD, Garret FitzGerald. No reply.

Mr Justice Hugh Kingsmill-Moore, a retired member of the Supreme Court, had been instrumental in closing down Marlborough House, a notorious reform school for boys. Having met him on a couple of occasions, de Búrca rang him, went to his house and explained the background to the Crawley case. Kingsmill-Moore, disturbed by what he heard, wrote to the then Minister for Justice, Paddy Cooney. Cooney wrote back that the matter was 'receiving attention'.

The Prisoners' Rights Organisation took up the case. Their view was that Karl had become entrapped in a cycle of prison, sedation, defiance, release, crime and return to prison and that eventually he would do serious harm either to himself or someone else, and that the willingness of the prison authorities to simply facilitate this cycle, without making any attempt to break it, was neither helping Karl nor protecting society.

That point would later be made by Consultant Psychiatrist Gabriel Nolan in a psychiatric assessment of Karl prepared for a court report. After stating unequivocally that 'Karl Crawley is not insane,' Dr Nolan wrote, 'The question arises, what happens when he has finished his current sentence in ten months time? The most likely outcome is that after a very short period of freedom he will again find himself in trouble and in prison.'

On 18 June and 8 July 1975 eight members of the Prisoners' Rights Organisation picketed the Circuit Court in Chancery Place when Karl appeared there on a charge of assaulting a garda (he was later acquitted). On the second occasion the picketers became the first people to be arrested under Section 4 of the Offences Against The State (Amendment) Act, 1972. Six of them were sentenced to a year each in prison.

The Act had been brought in to deal with emergencies and had been opposed by Fine Gael's Paddy Cooney on the grounds that there would be a 'temptation to use the Act for purposes other than those intended and that the temptation would be yielded to'. Paddy Cooney was Minister for Justice when the temptation to use the Act against the PRO picketers was yielded to.

The picketers did not, eventually, go to prison. The PRO continued agitating on the Crawley case and Bernadette Crawley appeared at press conferences arranged by them to plead on her son's behalf. The ear of officialdom remained deaf.

· · · · ·

On 24 August 1975 Karl Crawley's cell was found bloodstained. He said that he had swallowed bed springs and parts of plastic cutlery. He was X-rayed in the Mater Hospital that day and the two following days but nothing showed up. (Later on, some of the plastic utensils were passed naturally.)

On his return to Mountjoy from the Mater on 26 August Karl was convinced that he would be declared insane again and sent to The Drum. He began to prepare for his move to the mental hospital. He had two pieces of wire from a bed spring and a plastic refill from a Biro pen. He opened an old wound in his left side, just above the hip, and inserted the wire and the refill. He hoped to use the wire to pick the window-lock in The Drum and the refill was to write letters that could be smuggled out. Concealing the wire and pen inside the wound was the safest way of getting them past the screws.

The following day Karl was assured by the Medical Officer that he would not be sent to Dundrum. He tried but failed to retrieve the wire and refill from inside his body. He was in pain and suffering a discharge. On 28 August, deciding that the only way of dealing with the problem was to own up to the authorities and have the items removed medically, he wrote a letter to the Medical Officer, explaining his fear of Dundrum and what he had done with the wound.

The next day, not having received any reply, Karl was exercising in the yard during the one hour a day he was released from the Base. He escaped from his handcuffs and climbed the wall of the main prison building, being chased by two warders. One of the warders fell and was injured, the other brought Karl back down.

Meanwhile, the Medical Officer had opened Karl's letter and arranged to have him brought to the Mater Hospital to have the items removed and Karl's wound treated.

· · · · ·

One day in 1974 a judge of the High Court got an unusual letter.

> Sir, I had a copy of this filled out proper but it was taken bacuse I got help with it. This happened months ago and I felt like givin in but thats what they want so Im sorrey if this one isent grate but its the best I can do. Karl Crawley.

From March 1974 Karl had begun tinkering with the legal machinery in an attempt to make it work for him. He sought an order of *habeas corpus* from the High Court on the grounds that his form of imprisonment was a threat to his health.

> I am not serving a penal servatude sentence like the warrant says I was sentenced to serve. I am been confined as a lunatic yet if I were mad or insane or had a character disorder I should not be placed in the hands of people who will dammage me more by there own igonorance. I have been declared insane by the same people in this prison 11 times. . . .

On one occasion Karl got help from the English bank robber Keith Littlejohn in petitioning the courts. The applications were turned down by the High Court on the grounds that the warrants committing Karl to prison were valid and the conditions of his imprisonment 'even if true would not affect the legality of his detention'. Any complaints about the conditions, Karl was told, should go to the Minister for Justice, not the courts.

Karl was trying all the angles. In November he wrote to the Supreme Court, appealing the High Court rejection of the application. He had a stroke of luck. The appeal came into the hands of Mr Justice Henchy, who was then serving on a committee examining psychiatric services and who therefore had some interest in the area. On 27 January 1976 the Supreme Court directed: 'It is ordered and adjudged that the said Appeal be allowed and that the said Order of refusal by the High Court be set aside accordingly and in lieu thereof it is ordered pursuant to Article 40 of the Constitution that the Prison Governor do produce the body of the said Prosecutor [Karl] before the President of the High Court . . . '

Karl, working the angles from his prison cell, had managed to attract the attention of the highest court in the land.

. . . . .

The chief witness on Karl's behalf when the case was heard in the High Court on 8 April 1976 was Dr Brian McCaffrey, Clinical Director of Psychiatry to the Eastern Health Board, who had been called in to provide psychiatric evidence and who had interviewed Karl four times. Karl was by now represented by solicitor Pat McCartan and barrister Paddy MacEntee.

Karl's mental condition had been diagnosed by McCaffrey, and was agreed by other doctors in the case, as sociopathic. McCaffrey was asked by the President of the High Court, 'If you were faced, as an expert in this field, with the problem of a person who was violent and had the diagnosed condition that you have diagnosed as pertinent in this case, is major tranquillisers one of the treatments appropriate to him?'

'Because Karl is not psychotic and therefore in touch with reality,' said McCaffrey, 'one can talk with him and get through and therefore the need to use drugs could be absent in handling Karl's condition.'

'Could the use of drugs, if one were not in the particular institution, be undesirable?'

'Oh, yes, my lord, those drugs have serious long-term side effects on the heart condition from which an individual can die — aplastic anaemia and other conditions — and therefore they should not be used indiscriminately. One should be extremely careful about prescribing these.'

Dr Samuel Davis, then Medical Officer at Mountjoy, was asked what treatment Karl was under.

'What do you give him?'

'The ordinary Valium or something like that.'

'What do you give him?'

'What do I give him? I only give him stuff for pains and aches.'

'Does he get sleeping tablets?'

'He gets sleeping tablets from time to time, yes.'

'The position is that he is generally kept at a low level?'

'Well, we try to sedate him; we keep him at a low level.'

'Is that for his benefit or the institution's benefit or the benefit of both?'

'For the benefit of everybody.'

Prison medical records show that during that period Karl was receiving one Valium V daily, two Valamin anti-depressants nightly and four Ponston painkillers a day. For three months up to the previous January he had been receiving Serenace drops (unknown to himself), ranging from three per day to thirty per day.

Drugs were so free and easy within the prison system, Karl claimed, that any time he felt the need he had just to ask the screws for a couple of Smarties and there you were.

· · · · ·

It was agreed by all the psychiatrists involved in the case that Karl be diagnosed as a sociopath. That his experience of society, combined with his own personality, was such that he reacted aggressively against authority and did so regardless of the consequences to others or to himself. In his judgment, the President of the High Court, Mr Justice Finlay, summarised the medical evidence.

> He is not, on the agreed medical evidence, either now or consis-
> tently a person who is insane, nor does he suffer from a
> psychotic disease. He does not come within the ordinary
> definition of a psychopath. No evidence was adduced before
> me, nor any suggestion made on behalf of the Respondent [the
> Governor of Mountjoy jail], that he was feigning any part of
> this condition. Some minor conflict appears in the medical
> evidence as to whether the Prosecutor [Karl Crawley] has been
> at any relevant time even temporarily insane or of unsound
> mind but I have come to the conclusion on the evidence that
> at some periods at least the disturbance of his personality has
> been so acute that it rendered him for some time legally of
> unsound mind.

From the evidence of Karl's childhood history Justice Finlay concluded:

> The origin of this condition is almost certainly an upbringing largely in institutions after a broken marriage of his parents which, having regard to his innate personality and intelligence, was almost unbelievably cruel. Whatever its origin it manifests itself in an aggressive and continuous hostility to authority and to the features of society which represent authority. To this is added a higher than average intelligence and an unusually athletic physique and capacity. In pursuit of this hostility the Prosecutor is apparently endowed with a physical courage tantamount to recklessness.

The application for *habeas corpus*, the effect of which would have been to release Karl from Mountjoy, was refused. The judge ruled that Karl's medical needs, 'as distinct from his psychiatric needs', had been met by the authorities, that the restraints employed were for the purpose of protecting Karl from himself. While expressing sympathy with Karl's case, the judge added, 'I must construe the entire concept of torture, inhuman and degrading treatment and punishment as being not only evil in its consequences but evil in its purpose as well.'

The psychiatrists involved had agreed on the need for a specialised unit which would cater for Karl and other prisoners, their number estimated at various times as between six and twenty, who respond aggressively to the imposition of authority but who are not insane. This would be a custodial unit with trained staff and special facilities. Karl himself had suggested such a unit when asked by Dr McCaffrey what form of custody and therapy he would consider proper — but Karl had been reluctant to have this mentioned in court as it might seem he was asking for 'four star hotel facilities'. The President of the High Court said in his ruling that such a unit would be 'most desirable', but added, 'It is not the function of the court to recommend to the Executive what is desirable nor to fix the priorities of its health and welfare policy.'

Karl went back to Mountjoy.

· · · · ·

Something had happened which changed Karl Crawley's status within the community of crime and punishment. It may have had something to do with Karl getting older. The psychiatrists had agreed that sociopathic tendencies diminish from the middle to late twenties. It may have had something to do with the growing dissatisfaction among personnel in The Drum at being used to administer a chemical strait-jacket. It may have had something to do with the fact that Karl's case had attracted attention outside the world of prisons and mental hospitals. (Internationally renowned lawyer Cedric Thornberry became involved in the case for a time, until he was called away by the Steve Biko case in South Africa.) The fact that the Prisoners' Rights Organisation was still agitating about the case was an embarrassment to the authorities. It was probably a combination of these things.

Whatever, Karl was not sent to The Drum again. His last incarceration there was in September 1975. In June 1976, Karl swallowed three pieces of wire from a bed spring in order to get sent to the Mater Hospital. Karl feared that he would not be released from Mountjoy the following month, as scheduled, but would be held as punishment for his Colt .45 antics. He figured that the hospital would make a better base for an escape attempt.

The three pieces of wire were removed by surgery. This was Karl's last use of the swallowing tactic. As far back as June 1973 surgeons at the Mater had warned that any further operations would be at the risk of his life.

From now on Karl Crawley would still be subject to separate confinement in The Base, he would still have his special cell, he would still be handcuffed during visits or on any occasion he left The Base. But The Drum was no more. Karl and the prison authorities had reached some sort of understanding. He retained some sense of himself as an independent being; they would have him under some sort of control.

When Karl was released from Mountjoy in July 1976 he had served a sentence of two years and five months, the longest he had served. Apart from that stretch he was averaging nine months in and three months out. That pattern was to change little. Just over a month after his release from Mountjoy, Karl was back in the District Court, charged with 'entering as a trespasser and larceny'.

· · · · ·

On the day he was released from Mountjoy, 7 July 1976, Karl got an intravenous injection from a friend, a drug addict. The drug was Tiunal, a barbiturate. Welcome home. That night he met his old mates in a pub. Most of them were hooked on something. After that, life was a shower of Smarties. Everything from hash to heroin. Tablets, mainlining, smoking, whatever it took.

Go to a pub in the evening and it's nine pints. Nine pints cost a lot of money. Drugs are cheaper, easier, and they pass the evening just as well. Better.

You can't rip off a barrel of Smithwick's from a pub and carry it home on your back, but you can do a chemist shop and go home with a week's high in your pocket. And if you're going to rip off drugs where better than from the Grand High Altar, the Thomas Cook of mental travel agents — Dundrum Mental Hospital? And who in Dublin would know better than Karl the set-up and the ins and outs of the Drum? In October 1976, three months after his release from Mountjoy, Karl went on a little sentimental journey. He broke into The Drum and stole £132 worth of drugs. And fixed up inside, as soon as he got his hands on the stuff. And was caught in the grounds of the hospital, stoned. And got three months for it.

There was an appeal to the Supreme Court against the High Court rejection of *habeas corpus*, but Karl was never in prison long enough to facilitate the process. By the time the appeal was ready to go ahead Karl's latest short sentence would be finished. An appeal was prepared for the Court of Human Rights in Strasbourg, but that court won't deal with cases which haven't gone through every domestic legal process.

So, Karl went in and out of Mountjoy, confined in The Base whenever he was inside. Dr Brian McCaffrey was given permission to see Karl whenever he deemed it necessary. At one point Tommy, Paul, David and Mick Crawley were in Mountjoy, upstairs doing time, while Karl was down in The Base. The authorities would let one brother at a time go down to chat with Karl, maybe play some chess.

'It was just like St Philomena's.'

Into prison, out, drugs, chemist shops, into prison, out.

Doing the odd ambitious stroke, like the 200 pairs of jeans he tried to nick from Roches Stores (caught, three months). The odd fight, like the time Karl bumped into this guy in a pub in Summerhill. They didn't like each other much. Karl refused to shake hands, the two went outside, agreed it should be a clean fight, fought, then went back in together for a drink. Some fights weren't like that. Karl had acquired scars from a number of knife wounds as well as the scars from the surgeons' scalpels.

In 1980 Karl attended Coolmine Rehabilitation Centre to kick the drug habit. He spent time in hospitals, got disability benefit because of his wounds, for which he had to continue taking medication. Because of his wounds, he qualified for a free bus pass. He worked for a while at the roofing business with his brother Philip. Anyone who had climbed up as many buildings as Karl had, made his way across as many rooftops in the dark, took to roofing like a natural.

Then there was the bank job. Being Karl, he didn't bother with all the paraphernalia of the professional heisters — the lookouts, the bagman, the sawn-off shotguns, the car switch, the safe house. Karl jumped over the counter, grabbed a handful of tenners and jumped back again. When he ran outside the guy who was driving the getaway car had got the butterflies and was already a couple of streets away. Karl ran, with the bank clerks running after him. Karl was faster, Karl was always faster.

When you vault over to join the bank cashiers you put your hand flat on the counter — and you leave fingerprints behind. And the cops had taken enough dabs from Karl to paper a room. He was arrested next morning.

· · · · ·

In the early years Karl's willingness to take any risk in order to assert himself against authority carved around him a space within which he could retain a certain independence, a necessary self respect — albeit at a terrible price to himself.

In the mid-1970s his jousts with authority, using the law as his unlikely lance, served the same purpose. As he entered the 1980s and approached his thirtieth birthday Karl became noticeably less aggressive, more articulate. Psychiatrists believe that sociopathic people often mellow as they approach their thirties. Karl began to achieve perspective on his life. Not unaware of a certain facial resemblance to Paul Newman, he promoted a Cool Hand Karl image. He was simultaneously proud of his record of defiance and aware of the waste that the repeated prison sentences represented.

Slowly, there had been changes in the prison system. Bread and water was gone as a punishment. The Base became mostly a holding area for those who could not in safety mix with other prisoners. When used for punishment, to isolate prisoners, it was for periods of days, not weeks. The Drum still waited for troublesome prisoners, but prisoners were not dispatched there as often as before. Such changes occurred not because of any strategic decision by the authorities to forge an overall policy for the penal system which might make of the jails and The Drum anything other than temporary restraints. The changes derived from piecemeal responses to pressure. Some experts in the field of prisons and psychiatry concluded that the psychiatric support given within the overcrowded system sprang from the authorities' desire not to leave themselves open to accusation in the event of tragedy. It is embarrassing when prisoners hang themselves.

The special unit, custodial and therapeutic, which the psychiatrists involved in the 1976 court case (including the Clinical Director of Psychiatry of the Eastern Health Board and the Chief Psychiatrist at Dundrum) agreed was needed and which Judge Finlay thought 'most desirable', has never been built.

Karl decided to write the story of his life. He wrote dozens of pages in longhand and a friend typed it up. Karl had long thought of writing his story and maybe calling it *The Last of the Hard Men*. Sometimes Karl would think of that and he'd laugh. Because, shit, there's no such thing as a hard man. It's what happens to you that makes you what you are, hard or soft. Life puts it up to you and you can't back away from it. If you get dealt the hand that makes you a hard man it makes you do vicious things, it gets vicious things done to you. But there's no glory in that, it's just the way things are. Where's the choice?

The book never got written, but by his early thirties Karl had achieved a new perspective on his life. He stayed out of jail for a year and then another, and another. The cycle of crime and jail and crime and jail was broken. A whole eleven years of freedom went by, not a day behind bars. Good things happened to Karl, very good. And some very bad things. Karl got drunk, pissed, locked, way out of it. Karl used drugs. Old times, here we go again. And in the new times there are new dangers for drug users. 'When you're locked you get careless,' Karl says.

Karl always thought of the wounds on his ravaged stomach as a potential breeding ground for cancers and an early death. Sometimes the wounds opened up and they had to be dressed and Karl wore a bandage on his abdomen and it was there for days without being changed and the discharge built up. It was like something from a battlefield.

Then, Karl would get himself together, good things happened again and Karl enjoyed life. But there would be no happy ending. In 1990, at the end of those eleven years on the outside, Karl was caught stealing and went back to Mountjoy. He was still playing out a hand dealt long ago.

When he got back on the outside again Karl was homeless. He received friendliness, respect and shelter in a Simon hostel. He attends a methadone clinic, keeping his drug habit at bay. In his mid-40s his handsome face has aged more than it should, that face sometimes betraying a sense of weariness with it all. Karl isn't making plans. He lives day to day. He is mentioned occasionally by important people such as politicians and economists, but only as a statistic. There are X number of drug addicts, the criminals number Y, and there's Z amount of homeless people. Karl's criminality couldn't be condoned, but it has hurt him far more than it has hurt anyone else, and the price he has paid far exceeds the gains that criminality has won for him.

The system, though, never beat him. The punishment didn't crush him, he took it and came back. What laid Karl low was the business of living, of putting together a life that made sense and provided comfort and respect. He lacked the skills for that, and the years of facing up to the battering he gave and got from what is quaintly termed the criminal justice system was something of a distraction from the task of accumulating the comforts of life. Those comforts, in the end, had to come from a bottle, or out of a needle.

He's out there, you pass him on a Dublin street. Karl may sit down beside you in a pub or on a bus and if you had the time to talk to him you might notice an intelligence, a sense of humour and self-awareness, a depth and a decency lacking in many who have led far easier lives, more productive lives. You might instead continue reading your newspaper. Perhaps an article about 'the crime problem' and the solutions proposed by experts and ideologues who insist that we all take responsibility for our actions, there is no room for bleeding hearts at the front line in the war against crime.

Karl has always taken responsibility for his actions, never complained. If it's put up to you, you handle it, you deal with it, whatever it is, you take care of it, because that's where you get your necessary self-respect, playing the hand you're dealt. Karl doesn't whinge.

The expert will point out quite properly that we all have choices. Most people from deprived backgrounds don't commit crime. People choose to go this way or that way.

Choices, though, are exercised within a range of possibilities. And when that range of possibilities is extremely limited, as it is for a Karl Crawley, some accept and some don't. And if the possibilities on offer are insulting or incomprehensible to a proud young man verging on adulthood, he may rage against the dying of hope, the dying of choice, and reach out in this direction or that, making choices of another kind, unknowing and uncaring of what his rage does to others, or to himself. And once that initial choice is made, if choice it is, the range of choices subsequently available becomes narrower, until you're sitting in a damp gaff, hardly here at all, looking at the needle someone has passed along to you and making another choice.

One day, back in the early 1980s, Karl tried to sum things up. 'Look,' he said, 'I didn't set out to be Karl Crawley . . . I . . . I could have been . . .'

He looked around for an example.

'. . . a brilliant . . . book-keeper, or something.'

Then he thought about what he'd just said. And he smiled, big and open and bright as the sun going down.

Karl Crawley was forty-seven when he died in the summer of 1999.

Sources

My thanks to the lawyers, gardaí, victims, criminals, witnesses and suspects who gave me transcripts, books of evidence and other documents, and who filled in the blanks. Given the nature of the events described, it is inevitable that most such people cannot be acknowledged by name, so I will not single anyone out.

Attendance at Court Proceedings:
The trial of Richard Flynn.
The inquest into the death of Father Molloy.
The inquest into the death of Michael Lynagh.
The trial and sentencing of Jesse O'Dwyer, Stephen McKeever, Anthony O'Neill and Neil Kelly.
The trial of Sergeant Peter Diviney.
The trial of Detective Garda Tom Jordan.
The Circuit Court libel suit against Shane Ross and Independent Newspapers.
The High Court appeal in the libel suit against Shane Ross and Independent Newspapers.
The trial of Dessie O'Hare, Eddie Hogan, Fergal Toal, Tony McNeill and Gerry Wright.
The trial of Clare O'Hare.
The court hearing in the matter of George Levingstone's will.
The court hearing in the matter of the Elvis Presley fan clubs.

Published Documents:

Dáil Record for 4 June 1984, Ronald Reagan's address.
Dáil Record for 28 June 1984, Adjournment Debate on the det... Phoenix Park women.
Supreme Court judgment in Lynch case.
Kilkenny Incest Investigation Report. Government Publications, May 1993.
Report of the Advisory Group on Prison Deaths. Government Publications, August 1991.
Report of the High Court Inquiry into the Greencore affair.
The Interim Curran Report into the Greencore Affair.
The Final Curran Report into the Greencore Affair.
Greencore statement to shareholders, 23 October 1991.
Arthur Andersen Report on Siúicre Éireann, Certain Share Transactions and Other Related Matters.

Unpublished Documents:

Karl Crawley's prison records.
Karl Crawley's medical records.
Michael Lynagh's statement to the Irish Council for Civil Liberties.
Finbar Lynagh's statement to the Irish Council for Civil Liberties.
Carmel Lynagh's statement to the Irish Council for Civil Liberties.
Transcript of the first trial of Christy Lynch.
Transcript of the Father Niall Molloy inquest.
Statements to gardaí regarding the death of Father Niall Molloy.
Two statements to gardaí by 'Mary' (pseudonym for Kilkenny incest victim).
Two statements to gardaí by 'Ruth' (pseudonym for Mary's mother).
Statements to gardaí regarding the kidnap of John O'Grady.
Regulation drawn up under Section 9 of the Phoenix Park Act 1925, on 1 June 1984, by Garda Commissioner Wren.
High Court documents and statements in Jane Morgan v Laurence Wren and Others.
ICARFP Notes to Stewards and Group Organisers for 'Rally Against Reagan'.

Books:

INLA: Deadly Divisions, by Jack Holland and Henry McDonald. Torc, 1994.
Round Up the Usual Suspects, by Derek Dunne and Gene Kerrigan. Magill Publications, 1984.
At the Cutting Edge, by Gemma Hussey. Gill & Macmillan, 1990.
All in a Life, by Garret FitzGerald. Gill & Macmillan, 1991.
The SAS in Ireland, by Raymond Murray. Mercier Press, 1990.
Big Boys' Rules, by Mark Urban. Faber and Faber, 1992.
Northern Ireland: A Chronology of the Troubles 1968–1993, by Paul Bew and Gordon Gillespie. Gill & Macmillan, 1993.
An Index of Deaths from the Conflict in Ireland 1969–1993, by Malcolm Sutton. Beyond the Pale, 1994.

Publications:

Dublin Tribune
Irish Independent
The Irish Times
Magill
Sunday Business Post
Sunday Independent
The Sunday Tribune